Teaching Is . . .

Experiences and readings to help you become the kind of teacher you want to become.

Merrill Harmin Southern Illinois University

Tom Gregory Indiana University

SRA

SCIENCE RESEARCH ASSOCIATES, INC.
Chicago, Palo Alto, Toronto
Henley-on-Thames, Sydney, Paris
A Subsidiary of IBM

About the Photographs

A special note of acknowledgment is due to Michael Sexton, photographer, and his publisher, The Westminster Press, for granting us permission to reproduce the extraordinary photographs that appear on pages 24 and 94, and in the photo essays on pages 98 to 105 and 140 to 147. These photographs were part of Dr. Sexton's thesis for his doctoral, granted by the University of Iowa. They were subsequently reproduced in the book *Who Is the School?*. The book reveals many dimensions of the school and the people inside it.

Reprinted from *Who Is the School?* by Michael J. Sexton. Copyright © MCMLXXIII, The Westminster Press. Used by permission.

We also wish to thank the American Federation of Teachers for granting us permission to reprint from the *American Teacher* the photograph that appears at the bottom of page 145.

About the Readings

For permission to reprint the readings, we wish to thank the following:

p. 1   From the book THE CONDUCT OF LIFE AND OTHER ESSAYS by R. Waldo Emerson. Intro. by Sherman Paul. Everyman's Library edition. Published by E. P. Dutton & Co., Inc. and used with their permission. Also used by permission of J. M. Dent & Sons Ltd.

p. 10   Reprinted by permission of the publishers from e. e. cummings, *i: Six Nonlectures*, Cambridge, Mass.: Harvard University Press, Copyright, 1953, by E. E. Cummings.

p. 10   "so many selves(so many fiends and gods": Copyright 1950 by E. E. Cummings. Reprinted from his volume, COMPLETE POEMS 1913–1962, by permission of Harcourt Brace Jovanovich, Inc. and Granada Publishing Limited.

p. 11   "A Credo for My Relationship with Another": Copyright 1970 by Thomas Gordon. From the book, PARENT EFFECTIVENESS TRAINING, published by Peter H. Wyden, New York, New York. Reprinted by permission of the publisher.

pp. 11–12   Excerpted from *The Mystery of Being* by Gabriel Marcel. © 1951 by Henry Regnery Company. Used by permission of Henry Regnery Company.

pp. 12 and 52   Abridged with permission of Macmillan Publishing Co., Inc. from BETWEEN MAN AND MAN by Martin Buber. Introduction by Maurice

© 1974, Science Research Associates, Inc. All rights reserved.

Printed in the United States of America.

Library of Congress Catalog Card Number: 73-91283

ISBN 0-574-19112-7

Friedman. Copyright © Macmillan Publishing Co., Inc. 1965. Also used with permission of Routledge & Kegan Paul Ltd.

p. 15 Excerpted from THE LITTLE PRINCE by Antoine de Saint-Exupéry. Translated by Katherine Woods. © 1943 by Harcourt Brace Jovanovich, Inc. Used by permission of Harcourt Brace Jovanovich, Inc. and William Heinemann Ltd.

p. 17 Abridged from *Tough and Tender Learning* by David Nyberg. © 1971 by National Press Books. Used by permission of the publisher.

pp. 19-20 Reprinted from "An Eschatological Laundry List" by Sheldon Kopp in *Voices*, Winter-Spring, 1969-70. © 1969 American Academy of Psychotherapists. Used by permission of the publisher and author.

pp. 22 and 84-85 From *Suffer the Little Children* by Max Rafferty. Copyright © 1962 by the Devin-Adair Company, reprinted by permission.

pp. 25, 36, 57, and 108 Excerpted from "Kari's Handicap" by Robert Samples in *Saturday Review*, July 15, 1967. © 1967 by *Saturday Review World*. Used by permission of the author and the publisher.

p. 26 From FREEDOM—NOT LICENSE! by A. S. Neill, Copyright 1966, Hart Publishing Company, Inc., New York. Also used by permission of A. P. Watt & Son.

pp. 27, 28, and 51 From CULTURE AGAINST MAN, by Jules Henry. Copyright © 1963 by Random House, Inc. Reprinted by permission of Random House, Inc.

pp. 29-32 "Dewey Outlines Utopian Schools" by John Dewey. © 1933 by The New York Times Company. Reprinted by permission.

pp. 36, 56-57, and 179 From HUMAN TEACHING FOR HUMAN LEARNING: AN INTRODUCTION TO CONFLUENT EDUCATION by George Isaac Brown. Copyright © 1971 by George Brown. Reprinted by permission of The Viking Press, Inc.

p. 36 Abridged from "Some Basic Propositions of a Growth and Self-Actualization Psychology" by Abraham H. Maslow in the *Association for Supervision and Curriculum Development 1962 Yearbook*. Copyright © 1962 by ASCD. Used by permission of the publisher.

p. 38 Adapted from *The Structure of Morality* by Hector-Neri Castaneda. © 1973 by Hector-Neri Castaneda. Used by permission of the author.

pp. 39, 130, 132, 135, 174, and 187 "A Talk with Robert Coles": Reprinted by special permission from LEARNING, The Magazine for Creative Teaching, November 1972. © 1972 by Education Today Company, Inc., 530 University Avenue, Palo Alto, California 94301.

p. 43 Excerpted from "PLAYBOY Interview: Dick Cavett" in PLAYBOY Magazine, March, 1971. Copyright © 1971 by Playboy. Used by permission of the publisher.

pp. 47-48 Excerpted from *The Social Studies: Myths and Realities* by David Kellum. Copyright, 1969. Published by Sheed and Ward, Inc. and used with their permission.

Acknowledgments continued on p. 261.

Contents

To make our word or act sublime, we must make it real. It is our system that counts, not the single word or unsupported action. Use what language you will, you can never say anything but what you are. What I am, and what I think, is conveyed to you, in spite of my efforts to hold it back. What I am has been secretly conveyed from me to another, whilst I was vainly making up my mind to tell him it. He has heard from me what I never spoke.

Ralph Waldo Emerson

1

Beginnings

Do authors ever have anything to say to you?
How much do you say to others?
Can you use yourself, this setting, this book, and others in some productive way?

" Jacqueline Murphy is a woman you should meet sometime. She was the person who told us, "Sure, you should do this book. The education books I've seen are too often dull and too seldom useful. Your style and ideas are different."

How's that for encouragement? Well, we needed it, and we started, and this is the result. The result,

for whatever it may be worth, is as much a product of our good Jacqueline as it is a product of our work. For it was Jacqueline who continually kept this multiple-track book on its tracks and who provided the most sensitive insights along the way. And it was Jacqueline who brightened our work days with her rare intelligence and the very beauty of her person. There was never an editor-advisor-critic more deserving to be listed as coauthor. But she is too modest.

And Jude Kasper. Whenever we needed a reading to fill a gap, it was Jude who went scurrying and scrambling to find it. And her comments on and contributions to parts of the manuscript greatly influenced the shape of what you'll find within.

Finally, we must say a word about Karl Schmidt, our SRA editor, a gentle man who has given us a new concept of what an editor can be. Without Karl we never would have gotten together. And we never would have emerged from the confusions and blocks that too often immobilized us. You've never met a harder-working, more generous editor.

So for what they've given us, we most humbly express our thanks to Karl and Jude and Jacqueline. They were able to remove defects from our writing so gently that it didn't hurt at all. The defects that remain are all their fault, by the way. So don't blame us. "

Is This Book for You? Are You for This Book?

❚❚ We've tried to write this book for the person attempting to orient himself to teaching. Such a person might be in his first education course. Or he might be several years into a teaching career and still be confused about his role. Or he may be set on teaching, someone who has always wanted to be a teacher, ever since second grade. Unfortunately, second graders are not very well equipped to make decisions about the course of their lives.

Making sense out of the complications involved in teaching and trying to find one's way as a teacher is a tough task, damn tough. Tougher than it seems at first.

Some teachers believe they can copy their model teachers, the best teachers they've had. Too often, though, they are likely to find that they and their models are somehow different. They can't adopt the others' style or, if they do, the impact of that style is different. So much for models.

Other teachers fantasize that just because they deeply loved Serbo-Croatian or trigonometric functions or whatever, so will their students. A dream that is likely to vanish. So much for dreams.

Nor are our noblest motivations usually sufficient to point us on our way to become a teacher. Do you

want to be a teacher because you love kids? To save one small part of the world? Or to survive until you make it through law school or write the great American novel? No matter. When you encounter a teacher's daily problems, it is unlikely that these motivations will tell you what to do. So much for motivations.

Neither is tradition likely to orient you to the realities of teaching. At one time a new teacher could lean on existing structures and traditions for support and guidance. But these structures and traditions are shaking and shifting. Teachers are being changed by new realities. And students are not sitting still either. They're not accepting the old ways as they used to. Increasingly they're learning to respect people, not roles or positions. So much for traditions.

That, in a nutshell, is the problem. Traditions, motivations, dreams, and models are not enough to help you become a teacher. If teaching were a simpler task, trial and error might suffice. But the pressures on a modern teacher can be bewildering.

What will you do when you are simultaneously pressured by your students and by your colleagues, many of whom will have contradictory standards and expectations? What will you do when you are pressured by anxious and caring parents, or by a society that wants its

Teaching Is.....

4

schools to help solve social ills (and simultaneously maintain the status quo)? How will you cope with the demands and still keep yourself together? Facing these and other pressures without some basic convictions about yourself and teaching can quickly transform you into a rudderless boat in a swirl of crosscurrents.

That's where this book comes in.

We want to try to help you find yourself as a teacher—to establish a self-image that is comfortable, workable, and defensible—and to help you begin to develop those skills that will allow you to improve that image as you and your profession mature.

Finding yourself is, of course, a very personal process. We're not pretending to offer you a road to absolute or ultimate wisdom. Perhaps we can help you gain some personal wisdom. Mainly, however, we'd like to try to help you become the kind of teacher you want to become. We don't know how to say it any more simply than that.

Our Biases

❚❚ We could write this book from a very objective stance, in the manner of someone looking down on the battle from some remote vantage point, interjecting occasional tisk tisks as we move along. Many textbooks are that way. But we decided not to engage in that kind of game. You see, we have biases. We think they're strongly enough engrained in us that we couldn't hide them very well if we tried—or if we wanted to. So we decided to state our position here.

First of all, it's your life. Only you can decide what to do with it, including whether or not you should teach. We see our job as helping you decide. Some might want to go further. Some professionals see themselves as "gatekeepers to the profession," passing judgment on who may enter and who will be turned away. We don't think they should. We think that if you're stripped of all coercion, given freedom and adequate valid information about yourself and teaching, you'll make a sounder decision than ten gatekeepers could.

Second, we think, to expedite that decision process you need to develop a tentative image of yourself as a teacher. You can call that a philosophy if you want to. Or maybe a dream. But we think an image of where you want to go will help you to push yourself toward your potential.

Third, we'd like to see you build your image of yourself as a teacher (if you do choose teaching) around the single main idea that people are most important. "Ha," you may say. "How trite!" Yes. Everyone says those words easily. Teachers can look you straight in the eye, raise their right hand, and say people, and most especially our students, come first. A recommendation to have the words chiseled into stone above the schoolhouse door would be unanimously applauded. But what do many teachers do? How do they function, operate in their day-to-day, minute-to-minute dealings with those "most important" people? Not as if they always believe people are as important as, say, grades, property, quiet, rules, you-name-it.

Although we really do believe people are most important, we do try to present a variety of views in the book, mostly through the prose, poetry, drawings, photographs, and cartoons of others that we've reprinted. Some will support our general position. Others will batter ours quite a bit. We are not inclined to create an orthodoxy around our ideas because, in addition to our beliefs in the importance of persons, we uphold with equal vigor a fourth belief: process is the key. Searching, feeling, reconsidering our views and ideas in relation to many other views and ideas. We believe it is at least as important for you to learn a process of professional growing as it is to learn the profession's best current wisdom.

In brief, in this book we want to make this point: what's most important is you and your image of yourself as a person and as a teacher, and the ideas you have about your abilities to function effectively within the myriad of constraints and mores, both real and imagined, that enshroud a teacher's life. Moreover, we hope your ideas and images will be responsive to your experiences and your growing maturity. We hope you will learn how to learn, and to become a better person, a more clearly oriented teacher, a more effective professional.

These are our biases. Perhaps the words make some sense to you. Now let's see how you feel about the actions that we see as being consistent with these words."

How We'd Like to See You Use These Pages

In How to Survive in Your Native Land, Jim Herndon describes his attempts to free up a bunch of junior high kids in a public school, really free them—Summerhill free. Despite all his efforts, they wouldn't do anything but use the permanent hall passes he'd issued them. They wouldn't touch all the "neat" things that had worked so well with his previous classes. He finally figured out what was going on. All those things weren't really neat at all; they were just better than the crummy things we usually do in classrooms. And just because they weren't "better" they weren't necessarily good enough to excite a group of kids given the freedom to do or not to do them, as they wished.

In this book we've put together a whole bunch of stuff that we're presumptuous enough to think is better than what is often found in teacher-education texts, and because of that we're guessing you'll find your work in the book a palatable experience. But very little of the stuff in here is "neat" in Herndon's sense of the word. If you really had a free choice, we're not sure how much of the book you'd use. We're fairly certain you wouldn't use all of it; we wouldn't use all of it in our free time (the acid test).

But if you're about the task of getting a better orientation to

teaching, we've tried to give you a "better" way to do it, which does not imply that this book will be only fun. Some of it is work, but hopefully not trivial, nonproductive work. You may find the "work" so productive, in fact, that it won't seem hard at all. That may be idealistic, but we never said we weren't idealists.

By the way, we would encourage you to be selective in your use of the book. It's hard for us to envision that person who would find worth in everything we've included. But, then again, there are probably worse things. For instance, you could choose to do nothing with the book, an event which would do untold damage to a couple of authors' egos."

Types of Type

❚❚ Using this book could be confusing simply because it contains three different kinds of material. In order to minimize the confusion, we use three different typefaces. **❚❚**

Author Talk   Whenever we're talking, as we are now, we'll use this typeface.

Readings   Whenever the material is a reading, written by another author, we'll use this typeface.

Experiences   Whenever the material is an experience that we recommend you try, we'll use this typeface.

Please Write in This Book

❚❚ All through the book, we've tried to leave space for you to write down your ideas, your reactions to what we or the bits and chunks of reading we've included are saying. Or your feelings at a particular time. Or how you see your view of yourself as a teacher changing as you progress through these pages.

You can use your commentary as a dear-diary kind of operation—by keeping the book and in a few years looking back through your comments from a more experienced and mature vantage point.

Or you can sell or give your book to another reader, who then will have the advantage of not two authors, but three, or four, or five.

Or you can send your book or parts of it to us. If this enterprise should ever do well enough to merit a second edition, we're already planning to include as many of your comments, drawings, epithets, and the bits and hunks of readings you suggest, as we have room for. We envision this as a way to make the book come alive or, as we put it later on, to make it say things in <u>your</u> language, spring from <u>your</u> values, and speak out of <u>your</u> experiences.

Whatever you have to say about the book, we hope you'll say it in writings or in drawings, in any format that allows you to communicate what you have to say. And we hope you'll do it often. **❚❚**

formed into a group, as we recommend you do with this book, you may be able to take advantage of three key sets of benefits:

- A group can become a support system. It becomes a source of help when you need it. It legitimizes your efforts and allows you your goals. It accepts and understands you and the things you do and say. A group places few conditions on this acceptance and makes few judgments about its members.

- A group can become a rich, diverse resource. Among any group of individuals there is a wide variety of human experiences, expertises, values, and aspirations. A group makes this rich diversity public, enabling its members to tap its human resources and thereby enhance their own potential to learn and improve.

Becoming a Group

// We encourage you to go through the experiences in this book with a friend, preferably a whole bunch of friends. Many of the experiences we've included in these pages have little value when done alone. They seek other human perspectives in addition to your own.

The importance of others to your own learning may already be apparent to you. If it isn't, some of the experiences in this book, and especially in this part, may bring the point home to you. We've included many of these experiences because we believe it is generally useful for a group of people working together to spend time at the outset getting to know each other. When people get to know one another better, they are in a better position to help one another and to use each other's ideas and experiences. A climate of appreciation, trust, and cooperation builds. Learning becomes easier and richer.

We think the richness embodied in a group ought to be allowed to develop. This kind of development is so important to us (and we hope to you) that we don't wish to leave the formation of your group to chance. We believe that most classes taught in most schools miss an enormous resource simply because they don't take the time to build a supportive group out of a collection of individuals. If an assortment of individuals is

• A group can become a source of feedback. Each member functions as a mirror for the other members, reflecting his image of each of them. In our day-to-day lives other people mirror us in a limited way; they're restricted by how much they can trust us to accept their image of us for what it is, just one piece of additional information. They need to trust us before they can risk honestly conveying their perceptions of our ideas and acts. A group builds this kind of trust and encourages this kind of risk.

When people get to know each other within the context of a group, they sometimes re-learn a most valuable lesson: That all humans are to be respected, themselves included. Knowing others affirms each person's sense of humanness. We learn that we are not as peculiar or defective as we feared. We learn that we are ok, too.

Knowing others in this context also helps us keep our acts humane. As we build our empathy for others, we are less likely to act in ways that satisfy our own needs at their expense. The experiences we've included in this part are designed to help you invest time to understand and appreciate others.

You may not have had much experience with a supportive approach in an academic classroom, or in any setting for that matter. If so, we hope you'll give it a try with an open mind. Especially consider the possibility that you will want to use similar experiences with students you may someday teach. We think student groups can be enormously helpful to a teacher if the teacher knows how best to approach group experiences.

We recommend that you spread the experiences in this part over several group meetings. Spacing experiences will build interpersonal understandings and group cohesion gradually.

Because the first three experiences work well as a package, we suggest using them together in the first group meeting. Then consider distributing the other experiences over some of the subsequent meetings. **//**

Who, if I may be so inconsiderate as to ask, isn't egocentric? Half a century of time and several continents of space, in addition to a healthily developed curiosity, haven't yet enabled me to locate a single peripherally situated ego. Perhaps I somehow simply didn't meet the right people, and vice versa. At any rate, my slight acquaintance with senators pickpockets and scientists leads me to conclude that they are far from unselfcentered. So, I believe, are all honest educators. And so (I'm convinced) are streetcleaners deafmutes murderers mothers, mountainclimbers cannibals fairies, strong men beautiful women unborn babes international spies, ghostwriters bums business executives, out and out nuts cranks dopefiends policemen, altruists (above all) ambulance-chasers obstetricians and liontamers. Not forgetting morticians—as undertakers (in this epoch of universal culture) prefer to denominate themselves. Or, as my friend the distinguished biographer M R Werner once subrosafully remarked, over several biscuit duboûchés "when you come right down to it, everybody's the whole boxoftricks to himself; whether she believes it or not." . . .

so never is most lonely man alone
(his briefest breathing lives some
    planet's year,
his longest life's a heartbeat of some sun;
his least unmotion roams the
    youngest star)

—how should a fool that calls him
    "I" presume
to comprehend not numerable whom?

e. e. cummings

so many selves(so many fiends and gods
each greedier than every)is a man
(so easily one in another hides;
yet man can,being all,escape from none)

so huge a tumult is the simplest wish:
so pitiless a massacre the hope
most innocent(so deep's the mind of flesh
and so awake what waking calls asleep)

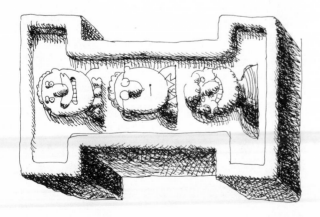

You and I are in a relationship which I value and want to keep. Yet each of us is a separate person with his own unique needs and the right to try to meet those needs . . . I will try to be genuinely accepting of your behavior both when you are trying to meet your needs and when you are having problems meeting your needs.

When you share your problems I will try to listen acceptingly and understandingly in a way that will facilitate your finding your own solutions rather than depending upon mine. When you have a problem because my behavior is interfering with your meeting your needs, I encourage you to tell me openly and honestly how you are feeling. At those times, I will listen and then try to modify my behavior.

However, when your behavior interferes with my meeting my own needs, thus causing me to feel unaccepting of you, I will tell you as openly and honestly as I can exactly how I am feeling, trusting that you respect my needs enough to listen and then try to modify your behavior.

At those times when either of us cannot modify his behavior to meet the needs of the other, thus finding that we have a conflict of needs in our relationship, let us commit ourselves to resolve each such conflict without ever resorting to the use of either my power or yours to win at the expense of the other losing. I respect your needs, but I must also respect my own. Consequently, let us strive always to search for solutions to our inevitable conflicts that will be acceptable to both of us. In this way, your needs will be met, but so will mine—no one will lose, both will win.

As a result, you can continue to develop as a person through meeting your needs, but so can I. Our relationship can always be a healthy one because it will be mutually satisfying. Thus, each of us can become what he is capable of being, and we can continue to relate to each other in mutual respect, friendship, love and peace.

Thomas Gordon

❙❙ Why is anything as simple and straightforward as honesty so terribly difficult to sustain in our day-to-day human experience? ❙❙

We can, for instance, have a very strong feeling that somebody who is sitting in the same room as ourselves, sitting quite near us, someone whom we can look at and listen to and whom we could touch if we wanted to and to make a final test of his reality, is nevertheless far further away from us than some loved one who is perhaps thousands of miles away. . . . We could say that the man sitting beside us was in the same room as ourselves, but that he was not really *present* there, that his *presence* did not make itself felt. But what do I mean by presence, here? It is not that we could not communicate with this man; we are supposing him neither deaf, blind, nor idiotic. Between ourselves and him a kind of physical, but merely physical, communication is possible; the image of the passing of messages between a reception point and an emission point, which we have rejected on several other occasions, is in fact quite applicable here. Yet something essential is lacking. One might say that what we have with this person, who is in the room, but somehow not really present to us, is communication without communion: unreal communication, in a word. He understands what I say to him, but he does not understand *me*: I may even have the extremely disagreeable feeling that my own words, as he repeats them to me, as he reflects them back at me, have become unrecognizable. By a very singular phenomenon, indeed, this stranger interposes himself between me and my own reality, he makes me in some sense also a stranger to myself; I am not really myself while I am with him.

The opposite phenomenon, however, can

...also take place. When somebody's presence does really make itself felt, it can refresh my inner being: it reveals me to myself, it makes me more fully myself than if I were not exposed to its impact.

Gabriel Marcel

We learn about ourselves by being known by others, for that "reveals me to myself." We believe that when a teacher does nothing more than understand a student, and communicates that understanding, and when he helps students have experiences that help them understand each other, he does mountains of teaching.

The difference between [the "I-Thou" relationship and the "I-It" relationship] is not the nature of the object to which one relates, as is often thought. Not every relation between persons is an I-Thou one, nor is every relation with an animal or thing an I-It. The difference, rather, is in the relationship itself. I-Thou is a relationship of openness, directness, mutuality, and presence. It may be between man and man, but it may also take place with a tree, a cat, a fragment of mica, a work of art—and through all of these with God, the "eternal Thou" in whom the parallel lines of relations meet. I-It, in contrast, is the typical subject-object relationship in which one knows and uses other persons or things without allowing them to exist for oneself in their uniqueness: The tree that I meet is not a Thou before I meet it. It harbors no hidden personality that winks at me as I pass by. Yet if I meet it in its uniqueness, letting it have its impact on me without comparing it with other trees or analyzing the type of leaf or wood or calculating the amount of firewood I may get out of it, then I may speak of an I-Thou relationship with it. The person that I meet is, by courtesy of our language and our attitudes, a "person" before I meet him. But he is not yet a Thou for me until I step into elemental relationship with him, and if I do not step into this relationship, even the politest forms of address do not prevent his remaining for me an It. I cannot, of course, produce an I-Thou relationship by my own action and will, for it is really mutual only when the other comes to meet me as I him. But I can prevent such a relationship from coming into being if I am not ready to respond or if I attempt to respond with anything less than my whole being insofar as my resources in this particular situation allow.

Maurice Friedman

A problem for even the best of teachers is that students come to him with the prejudgment that he is an It—a "teacher" rather than a human being. As teachers, we all too often yield to this image by assuming the role of the all-knowing, the all-seeing, the invulnerable.

Displaying our humanity seems so difficult under these circumstances. But it isn't. We can display it in simple ways: by saying "I don't know," by appreciating a good joke even if it's at our expense, by allowing a tear to invade the corner of our eye. All that is needed is the courage to display it.

1

Voting

A quick and convenient way to reveal group members' attitudes and ideas. (Useful for any age group, any context.)

A group experience. Requires five minutes for step one; ten to twenty additional minutes if step two is used. Appoint a leader.

1 One person, perhaps the leader, addresses the group with some "voting" questions such as those below. Group members merely raise their hands to vote. Avoid discussion, although a discussion may be invited after the voting list is completed. No tally is made of the persons voting for each question. The fun is seeing approximately how many in the group—and which ones—vote the same way you do.

- How many are married? Engaged? Otherwise attached?
- How many had no breakfast this morning?
- How many are hungry right now?
- How many are sleepy right now?
- How many usually get along on less than six hours sleep a night? Four hours?
- Who has no parents alive?
- Has anyone ever seriously thought of committing suicide? Anyone ever succeed?
- How many would be willing to die for a

cause that is currently very meaningful to them?

- How many believe in God?
- How many have changed their religious beliefs since childhood?
- How many believe that all abortions should be legal and easily available?
- Who is fairly certain that he or she will make an excellent teacher? Average teacher? Lousy teacher?
- Who questions his potential competence as a teacher?
- How many think this voting experience is dumb?

2 (Optional)
Next, sit with a neighbor. Each pair comes up with a few voting questions. Within the limits of available time, pairs volunteer to ask their voting questions of the group. Questions can deal with any topic. For convenience, begin with the phrase, "How many . . ."

3 (Optional)
The group might then ask if someone (or some pair) would prepare a voting list for the class to be used at some future date. Such a list could focus on one topic, or could deal with several topics (as did the sample list). The volunteer is asked to notify the group when he completes his voting list so that group time can be set aside for another voting experience.

Of course, this voting experience can be repeated as many times as desired. We think it provides a simple, quick way to raise issues and then to survey the positions of members of your group.

2

Name Tags and Milling

An experience to help individual members establish an identity, learn others' names, and begin to relax with the group.

A group experience. Requires about twenty minutes. Appoint a leader.

1 The leader passes out blank 4" X 6" index cards or pieces of paper that can serve as large name tags. He also hands out pins or masking tape, to attach the tags.

2 Each person writes his name in the center of his tag, in large letters so that it can easily be read. Then, the group can do one of two things.

a. As a group, decide what kinds of things will help you get to know each other best, "identifications" that will be most enlightening. For example, one group we've worked with asked each member to write:

- The best book you've read in the last year
- Three things you like to do
- Something about your background and upbringing that has been especially strong in making you the person you are
- An important goal you'd like to accomplish in the next year

b. Or, the leader might ask the group to write four or five things that he's selected. Here are some additional suggestions:

- The key word "school" and then, after that word, three or four words about school that come to mind
- An ending to this sentence: "Life is a cafeteria in which I . . . ."
- The names of three famous people you admire, with a plus sign to identify these people
- The names of some famous people you dislike, with a minus sign to identify them
- The following three goals for schools, written in the order that they seem important to you: preparation for life, wisdom, student self-respect

Consider also: personal strengths, motivations for being in this group, a sketch of a

flower, a sketch of oneself, the letter of the alphabet that one most wants to be, or any words or drawings or symbols that might serve to reveal one person to another comfortably and interestingly.

3 Then, the leader asks each person to put on his name tag and to mill around the room slowly, without speaking, looking at others' tags, trying to get a sense of who else is in the group. The leader might ask persons to shake hands as they mill about, or even to shake elbows. Or he may ask them to smile at each other. He might also ask each person to learn the names of, say, two people he didn't know before.

· · ·

If these name tags are retained and worn for the first few group meetings, participants more quickly lose some of their anonymity and build a basis for constructive relationships.

And if participants are asked to end the milling by forming trios, with three people who do not know each other sitting together, the leader is in a position to begin the next experience, Sharing Trios. Personally, we often move into Sharing Trios immediately after Name Tags and Milling.

Grown-ups love figures. When you tell them that you have made a new friend, they never ask you any questions about essential matters. They never say to you, "What does his voice sound like? What games does he love best? Does he collect butterflies?" Instead, they demand: "How old is he? How many brothers has he? How much does he weigh? How much money does his father make?" Only from these figures do they think they have learned anything about him.

If you were to say to the grown-ups: "I saw a beautiful house made of rosy brick, with geraniums in the windows and doves on the roof," they would not be able to get any idea of that house at all. You would have to say to them: "I saw a house that cost $20,000." Then they would exclaim: "Oh, what a pretty house that is!"

Antoine de Saint-Exupéry

❚❚ Charles Silberman has something to add to this on page 177. ❚❚

3

Sharing Trios

A way to share personal ideas and experiences and to build a supportive group climate.

A small-group experience. Requires from fifteen minutes onward, depending on how many topics are discussed. Appoint a leader.

Divide the group into trios. Each person in the trio then identifies himself as A, B, or C.

The leader calls out a topic, such as "A happy school experience I remember." In each trio person A speaks briefly to that topic. B and C listen. When A is finished, B takes a turn. Finally, C speaks to the topic.

After all three persons have had a turn speaking, and if time remains, the trio might discuss the topic informally or might give members an additional turn to speak. The time for each topic is kept short, however; the experience is designed to help people get to know one another and share ideas, not to settle disagreements or fully explore issues.

The leader judges time and calls out a new topic when he senses that everyone has had at least one turn to speak. Or he could call out two topics and, when it comes his turn to speak, an individual could choose which topic to address.

Sharing trios are often most interesting when many different people are given a chance to interact. To facilitate interaction, the leader might pause before introducing a new topic and ask the A in each group to leave the other two persons in his group and join a new pair. In this way, a different member of each trio can be shifted after each topic.

Safeguard

To remind group members that they should take responsibility for their behavior in a self-revealing experience, we like to make some sort of announcement at the outset:

You may reveal as much or as little of yourself as you choose. Consider how much risk you want to take in disclosing yourself. You might even want to experiment with different stances, looking for the stance that is most comfortable and productive for you.

Feel free at any time to say, "I'd rather pass on that question right now," or simply, "I'd rather not talk about that." Don't allow yourself to be pressured into talking about something you would rather keep to yourself.

Sample Topics

Here are potential topics for sharing trios. Some of these topics are more personal or sensitive than others. A mixture of different kinds of topics most often allows participants to exchange interesting information about themselves.

- My family background
- A good teacher I had
- A terrible teacher I had
- My thoughts on public aid to private schools
- The place of corporal punishment in schools
- A time I felt highly respected by others
- My views on socialism
- My first kiss
- Why I'm interested in becoming a teacher
- As a child I . . . .
- A choice I'm facing
- What schools should do about sex education
- A time I felt rejected
- My views on the rights of a teacher, as a professional person, to join a union
- Something about love in my life of which I'm proud
- My feelings about crying
- My concerns about the future
- A person who drives me up the wall
- When I'm alone, I usually . . . .
- A crazy thought that sometimes occurs to me

P eople desire affection, respect, and security. Most of us are even willing to lie for them. Then we get lies in return. *It is not necessary to lie, to deny conscience, to hide.* Somebody has to stop the lying and hiding in schools, and stop teaching lying and hiding to kids. Somebody has to take the trouble to examine his own self, his own style of life, so he can feel his personal humanity and can meet new situations on the merit of himself as a person rather than on the presumed merit of a credential or a course of training. To be an example of this is the best thing a teacher can do for kids: to make it possible to experience affection, respect, and security, and the exhilarating freedom of not having to lie, is the absolute, rock bottom, best goddamn thing any person can do for another. It opens the world.

David Nyberg

❝ Here we'd just like to ditto what we said back on page 5. **❞**

The leader may achieve closure of the experience by asking these "voting" questions of the entire group:

- How many found this an interesting experience?

- How many would like to repeat this experience with this group?

- How many discovered something about themselves that was interesting to them?

- How many found ideas that might help them use this setting and these people to enhance their own learning?

- Is anyone willing to share with the group what they learned from this experience? You could share your ideas by finishing the statement, "Today, I learned . . . ."

- My thoughts on ways to change schools
- I get rebellious when . . .
- I am a diligent worker when . . .
- The last time I was in prison
- What I see as the purposes of education
- My feelings on interracial marriage
- What I like about this group
- My attitudes on abortion
- My views on religion
- My opinion of snoopers who look in other people's medicine cabinets
- My views on report cards and working for grades
- Something I like (dislike) about myself
- How I handle anger
- How I view busing to achieve school integration

4

Risk Not, Grow Not

An opportunity to experience openness with another person and to build intimacy within the group.

A self-directed experience. Requires at least thirty minutes. Appoint a leader.

Pair off, each of you sitting with someone you do not know well. After introducing yourself, go over the directions below until you both agree to begin. Then continue with the activity for the allotted time, which should be at least twenty minutes.

Listed below are some rather intimate questions. In this experience you ask your partner questions from the list or other questions that occur to you. Even if you use the list, you may want to start with less intimate questions.
Take turns initiating questions. But follow these three rules:

1. You may decline to answer any question simply by saying, "I pass." Your partner should then ask a different question. A pass is much better than an answer you don't think represents your true feelings.

2. Your communication with your partner must be held in strict confidence.

3. Take your time. Do not rush to think of a question or to answer one. Pause as long as you need to.

Questions

- What's your favorite hobby or leisure interest?
- Wouldn't you really like to be something more prestigious than a teacher?
- What do you feel most ashamed of in your past?
- What's the most serious lie you've told?
- How do you feel about couples living together without being married?
- Have you ever had a mystical experience?
- What do you regard as the chief flaw in your personality?
- What turns you on the most?
- What turns you off the fastest?
- With regard to political parties, do you consider yourself a liberal or a conservative?
- What features of your appearance do you consider most attractive?
- What features of your appearance do you consider least attractive?
- How important is money to you?
- What person would you most like to travel with right now?
- How do you feel about swearing?
- Do you smoke pot, or are you into drugs?
- Do you enjoy controlling or directing people?
- Do you believe males are equal, inferior, or superior to females?
- Have you ever felt tempted to kill yourself?
- Have you ever felt tempted to kill another person?
- Under what conditions would you participate in a revolt against a government?
- What emotions do you find most difficult to control?
- Is there a particular person you wish would be attracted to you? Who?
- What foods do you dislike most?
- At this moment what are you most reluctant to discuss?
- What do you think your IQ is? How do you feel about your IQ?
- Is there any feature of your personality that you are proud of? What is it?
- In what way have you disappointed yourself or your family the most?
- What is/are your favorite TV program(s)?
- At present what's your most chronic problem?
- What was the subject of the most serious quarrels you've had with your parents?
- What's the subject of your most frequent daydreams?
- How are you feeling about me right now?
- Why are you interested in teaching?
- With what problem do you feel the greatest need for help?
- When you were a child, for what did you receive the most punishment or criticism?
- In high school, what activities did you participate in?
- How could you improve your current living arrangement?
- Do you have any misgivings about the group so far?
- Do you like your name?
- If you could be anything/anyone—besides yourself—what/who would you be?
- Who in our group don't you like?
- What was your first impression of me?

1. This is it!
2. There are no hidden meanings.
3. You can't get there from here, and besides there's no place else to go.
4. We are all already dying, and we will be dead for a long time.
5. Nothing lasts.
6. There is no way of getting all you want.
7. You can't have anything unless you let go of it.
8. You only get to keep what you give away.
9. There is no particular reason why you lost out on some things.
10. The world is not necessarily just. Being good often does not pay off and there is no compensation for misfortune.
11. You have a responsibility to do your best nonetheless.
12. It is a random universe to which we bring meaning.
13. You don't really control anything.
14. You can't make anyone love you.
15. No one is any stronger or any weaker than anyone else.
16. Everyone is, in his own way, vulnerable.
17. There are no great men.
18. If you have a hero, look again; you have diminished yourself in some way.

The leader may achieve closure on the experience by gathering the pairs and conducting an open discussion of the experience. It might be useful to start the discussion with these voting questions:

- How many of you were pleased with the degree of openness your pair achieved?
- How many found that your self-disclosures brought out feelings of warmth and closeness with your partner?
- How many found the experience generally negative?
- How many regret saying some of the things you said?
- How many wish that you had more time to continue this experience?
- How many feel that this experience has increased your understanding or acceptance of yourself?
- How many think a similar form of exchange between partners would be useful for students in high school? For students in elementary school?
- Does anyone have a question he would like to ask the whole group?

19. Everyone lies, cheats, pretends (yes, you too, and most certainly I myself).

20. All evil is potential vitality in need of transformation.

21. All of you is worth something, if you will only own it.

22. Progress is an illusion.

23. Evil can be displaced but never eradicated, as all solutions breed new problems.

24. Yet it is necessary to keep on struggling toward solution.

25. Childhood is a nightmare.

26. But it is so very hard to be an on-your-own, take-care-of-yourself-cause-there-is-no-one-else-to-do-it-for-you grown-up.

27. Each of us is ultimately alone.

28. The most important things, each man must do for himself.

29. Love is not enough, but it sure helps.

30. We have only ourselves, and one another. That may not be much, but that's all there is.

31. How strange, that so often, it all seems worth it.

32. We must live within the ambiguity of partial freedom, partial power and partial knowledge.

33. All important decisions must be made on the basis of insufficient data.

34. Yet we are responsible for everything we do.

35. No excuses will be accepted.

36. You can run, but you can't hide.

37. It is most important to run out of scapegoats.

38. We must learn the power of living with our helplessness.

39. The only victory, lies in surrender to oneself.

40. All of the significant battles are waged within the self.

41. You are free to do whatever you like. You need only face the consequences.

42. What do you know . . . for sure . . . anyway?

43. Learn to forgive yourself, again and again and again and again.

Sheldon B. Kopp
"An Eschatological Laundry List:
A Partial Register of the 927 (or
was it 928?) Eternal Truths"

5

You Can't Tell a Book

A chance to explore how others see you and to consider problems arising from incorrect or incomplete first impressions.

A group experience. Requires approximately one hour. Appoint a leader.

1 The group divides itself into trios, preferably comprised of people who have not worked together before. Introduce yourselves to each other and identify an A, B, and C in each group.

a. The leader asks participant A to take three minutes to tell the other two persons in his group as much about himself as he feels comfortable doing. He can talk about his hopes, his personality, his hobbies, his fears—whatever he chooses. After three minutes, the leader interrupts and asks B to do the same. In three minutes, the leader gives C a turn.

b. The trios are then given time so that each person can get feedback from the other two in his group. First, B and C together tell A (1) what they remember hearing him say about himself and (2) what they infer or conclude about him from what he said or what he left unsaid. Then, A and C take two minutes

and give feedback to B. And when they are finished, A and B provide feedback for C.

c. When the leader judges sufficient time has been allowed (he might call out a one-minute warning), he introduces the next step.

2 Before step two, the leader reminds the group that first impressions are often incorrect, but that many people make judgments on the basis of first impressions. And often we do not know exactly what first impressions we communicate to others, so that it is difficult for us to correct erroneous impressions. Because our perceptions of another's impressions of us are sometimes inaccurate, these inaccurate perceptions can adversely affect the way we respond to new people. If I think you think I'm a klutz, I may well become a klutz. This next step may help participants to more accurately understand their initial impact on other people.

a. Take a piece of paper and write some notes about your impressions of each of the other two in your trio. Also write which of these impressions, if any, have changed.

b. Then, each participant, starting with A, is given a chance to read or talk about his notes. With as much honesty and openness as he comfortably can muster, A tells what he wrote about B and C. Then, B tells what he wrote about A and C. Finally, C tells what he wrote.

c. After all members have reported, the trio might want to have an informal conversation that takes into consideration questions

and issues like the following:

- How teachers sometimes have had incorrect impressions of me
- How "slow" students and minority group members sometimes suffer from stereotyping and prejudice based on first impressions
- What, in general, might be done to reduce problems growing from incorrect or incomplete first impressions

• • •

The leader might want to conclude the activity with some "voting" questions:

- How many found this experience to be generally worthwhile?
- How many learned something?
- How many found the experience uncomfortable?
- How many feel they need to give more thought to an issue(s) raised here?
- How many enjoyed getting to know the others in their trio through this experience?
- How many might want to use this kind of experience with their students someday?

The box in step 1c refers to feedback the leader gives including:

- What I would still like to find out from the other two members of my group
- What I learned about myself
- What I want to think about more
- What was difficult in this experience for me

At one time, Max Rafferty was Superintendent of Public Instruction for the State of California. That says something about Max Rafferty. Or California. Or Education. You decide.

The children are being ushered along a facile runway, paved ever so smoothly with construction units and field trips, socializations and sharings, assemblies and group dynamics. The priests who prod them forward are hot-eyed, with telltale patches of saliva gathering in the corners of their mouths; they are devotees of the mediocre, which they worship under the sacred alias of Democratic Methods. They have been crammed to the craw with educationism, as long ago the zombie followers of the Old Man of the Mountain were stuffed with hashish. Their temples are the great universities which marble the land, stretching out their thousand campaniles to a Heaven of Demonstrable Utility and turning out swarms of neophytes each year to preach the gospel of Group Adaptation. Their secret crypts and inner sanctums are the graduate schools, which confer upon the masters of the cult certain cabalisms and charms in the guise of critiques and seminars, but which avoid any tinge of concern with literary or cultural refinements as a Moslem would a pork chop.

At the end of the runway lies, as it lay twenty centuries ago, a special kind of hell. We have improved somewhat upon the Carthaginians in the kind of fire which we provide and in the special types of fuel with which we stroke the flames. Just as our idol is no longer of massy bronze, so also is our conflagration one of the spirit rather than the flesh. But it burns deep.

It scorches genius.

It sears creative imagination to the bone.

It withers nonconformity.

Max Rafferty

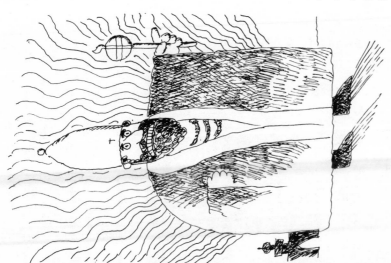

" Now that we've sprinkled a
number of masculine pronouns
through our prose, it seems
important to us to recount one of
the ideas we played with as we
developed the book. We, like so
many men and women, have become
conscious of the limits of our
language, specifically the masculine bias it conveys because of its
lack of neutered pronouns. An early
issue of Ms. suggested such a set
of pronouns. We thought we'd try
using them. It would be very chic to
be in the vanguard of a new linguistic movement, we thought. We
passed around a hunk of the manuscript with lots of ters and tems
and teys (for his/hers, him/her,
and he/she) all through it. Well,
the only problem was that nobody,
man nor woman, could read it in
anything but a halting manner.
Discretion being the better part
of valor, we turned tail and ran.
We tried, and we're sorry it
didn't work. **"**

II
(Re)Becoming a Learner

What kind of learner were you?
What kind of learner are you?
What are your expectations of yourself
and others as learners?

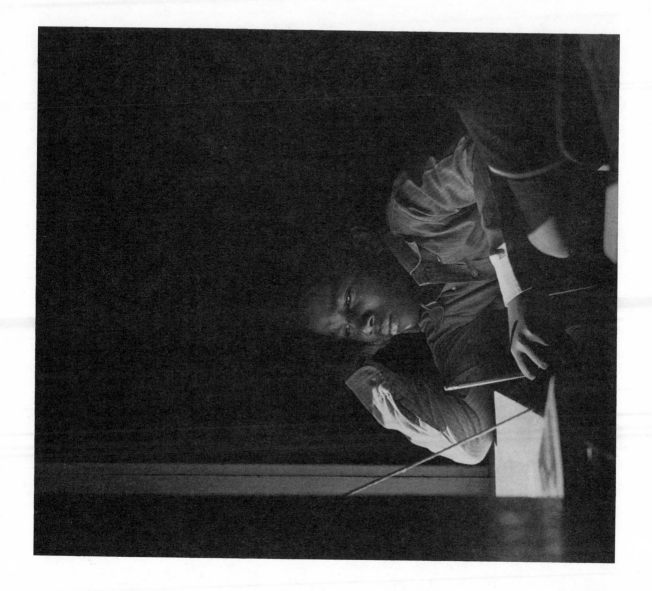

We wish we could take for granted that schools were places where people are allowed, encouraged, and helped to learn. But this is an assumption, one that all too often we see proved false. We think John Holt's on target when he describes little kids—preschoolers—as vibrant, alive learners, asking questions and seeking answers to their important questions. Pre-schoolers think. Moreover, they think about what's important to them. In this way, they learn.

When those same vibrant, alive kids hit school, something happens. They begin to learn that their questions aren't the important ones. The important ones are the teacher's. And the major activity of school becomes finding answers to teachers' questions. How one gets the answers apparently doesn't matter because school seldom deals with that process.

Get them answers, kid! (The name of the school game.) Get them answers by guessing, memorizing, peeking, or even thinking; but get them.

As a result of this kind of schooling, most of us become expert at studenting and forget how to learn. Maybe you were lucky or strong enough and have survived school, including college, with your learning engine relatively intact. Or maybe your school experience wasn't as confining as the one we've described. We hope so, for we think it's an utter disaster for anyone to pretend to teach kids when he, the teacher, doesn't know how to learn.

In this part we're trying to give you an opportunity to check for vital life signs in your own capacity to learn, and to enjoy again the pleasure of learning.

Of course. The only way it could be explained is that snow is a cloud lying down. The ocean breathes a cloud into the air and it becomes tired as it ripples up and down across the desert. When it must rest, it will lie down on a mountain. Maybe it's making love to the mountain. Oh, if it is, I wish I were a mountain. If it stops too long, it can't leave the way it came. The mountains bleed their cloud away and it becomes soiled. But what beautiful punishment . . . it can escape out of the inside of an aspen tree to get back into the air . . . but only a little at a time. That's what it costs to be too tired. Maybe though, it could . . .

"Karl!"

Damn you! It was silent, but she thought it.

Aloud, she said, "Yes, Mr. Clyde?"

"Have you solved the problem yet?"

"Oh, . . . no; I'll need more time."

The teacher's voice rang with bitterness, "You're the only one who needs more time. Have it here by 8 in the morning."

Robert E. Samples

Q. Why should a child do only what he likes to do? How can he face life which demands a thousand unpleasant duties?

A. The answer to this question would require a thick book. Childhood is not adulthood; childhood is playhood and no child ever gets enough play. The Summerhill theory is that when a child has played enough he will start to work and face difficulties, and I claim that this theory has been vindicated in our old pupils' ability to do a good job even when it involves a lot of unpleasant work.

"But pupils new to Summerhill regularly seem to be able to do little more than test the limits of their new-found freedom. How do you think you'd respond to a Summerhill kind of freedom? How are you responding to the kind of freedom we're trying to give you in this book?"

A. S. Neill

6 Learning About Learning

A way to find out under what conditions important kinds of learning occur for you and others.

A self-directed experience. Requires about forty minutes.

Break the group into trios, comprised of members who have not yet worked together.

1 First, spend five to ten minutes alone, writing down the five most potent learning experiences you can recall. Each experience should have had relatively discrete duration. In other words, the experience should be a *time*, lasting for ten minutes or for a year, when you recall that you were really learning something important to you. Do your best to come up with the five that were most significant for you.

2 Next, again alone, analyze your five learning experiences. Try to identify and write down why each was potent for you. What elements made each experience significant? Consider the following:

- In what setting did each experience occur? In a classroom, or elsewhere? Was the setting crucial to the experience?
- Who was involved? Were you alone or with others? Did a "teacher" bring about an experience, or did you, or did it happen spontaneously?
- Was there anything special about what you learned? Did the learning fall under the rubric of "subject matter," or was the learning more unusual and/or personal?
- Was there anything unique about *you* at the time of each experience? For example, did you feel an especially strong need to learn?

3 Next, try to share your experiences and why each was potent for you with the other two members of your trio. Try to draw generalizations about the conditions under which you learn best. Do you find any similarities between what you and your partners experienced? Or are your experiences and your learning processes unique?

4 If you are using this book within a course, try to answer the following sticky but, to us, sensible question. What elements must this course have to equal or possibly replace one of your top five experiences? In other words, describe and prescribe the conditions that must exist for this course to have a significant impact on you? Write down your prescription and give it to your instructor.

7

On Your Own

An experience that tries to exhort you (but not particularly help you) to learn.

An independent experience. Requires no special amount of time—except enough.

We'd like you to learn. On your own. With very little help. We don't care *what* you learn, but we care *that* you learn. The problems you'll have in directing your own learning are probably inversely proportional to the number of independent learning experiences you've had. For some, what we're suggesting will translate into grabbing the freedom you've been fighting for; you want to learn, you know how to learn and what you want to learn, and simply need to be given the time to do it. For others, what we're suggesting may produce the trauma of figuring out whether or not you are intellectually dead, whether you *can* learn on your own. What kind of learner are you?

This experience springs from our concerns about the "education" we all have received. Specifically, we are concerned that our experience in schools often leads us to view "teaching" as the spoon-feeding of information to highly dependent learners. Seldom in our school experiences, at any level, have we had the opportunity to direct our own learning, to learn those things of importance to us—and perhaps only to us.

We think that independent learning is much of what education is about. And we think that anyone who intends to teach—anyone who wants to do more than just go through the motions of teaching—needs to know how to learn independently. So we ask you to learn (or relearn) how to learn.

Another way of posing the experience would be to ask, "If you had the opportunity to learn anything you wanted to in any way you wanted to, what would you do?" Or fill in the statement: "You know, Merrill and Tom, for a long time I've wanted to learn how to (or about) _____

_____

_____

_____

_____

_____

_____,

but I've never gotten around to it."

Once you've figured out what you want to attempt, seek the help you need from others and do it. We ask only two things: that you do something you can get really excited about, and that you let others in on the fun by telling them your plans.

You may be tempted now to ask a lot of "student" questions, questions that have much to do with studenting but little to do with learning: Will this experience fulfill the requirement? Does the learning have to relate to teaching? Do you want a paper of some kind? How do I prove to you that I've completed the assignment? These are quite logical questions and they all have two things in common. First, they all tend to sustain dependence—they require someone else to tell you what's good for you and when it's good for you and how much is good for you and why it's good for you. And, second, they all have nothing to do with learning.

So don't ask them.

...

If not asking student questions immobilizes you, you first may need to try something that requires a little less learning of you and a little more studenting. If so, skip this experience for now. Instead, look at the next one—the educational equivalent of a decompression chamber that can prepare you for the rigors of independence.

But don't let this one go for good. It's too crucial. For us, deciding that you can't learn on your own is very close to deciding that you can't help others to learn on their own.

|| We're asking you to attempt this task because we don't want you to be merely a spoon-feeding teacher. We aren't saying that by having one independent learning experience you'll be magically transformed into a teacher who wants to provide independent learning experiences for his own students. That's unlikely to happen. We can be sure, though, that you'll probably not provide these opportunities for your students if you have never experienced them as a learner. ||

The function of education has never been to free the mind and the spirit of man, but to bind them; and to the end that the mind and spirit of his children should never escape, *Homo sapiens* has employed praise, ridicule, admonition, accusation, mutilation, and even torture to chain them to the culture pattern. Throughout most of his historic course *Homo sapiens* has wanted from his children acquiescence, not originality. It is natural that this should be so, for where every man is unique there is no society, and where there is no society there can be no man. Contemporary American educators think they want creative children, yet it is an open question as to what they expect these children to create. And certainly the classrooms—from kindergarten to graduate school—in which they expect it to happen are not crucibles of creative activity and thought. It stands to reason that were young people truly creative the culture would fall apart, for originality, by definition, is different from what is given, and what is given is the culture itself. From the endless, pathetic, "creative hours" of kindergarten to the most abstruse problems in sociology and anthropology, the function of education is to prevent the truly creative intellect from getting out of hand. Only in the exact and the biological sciences do we permit unlimited freedom, for we have (but only since the Renaissance, since Galileo and Bruno underwent the Inquisition) found a way—or *thought* we had found a way—to bind the explosive powers of science in the containing vessel of the social system. ||

Jules Henry

|| The political structure of the school, with its Board of Education elected by a majority of the adult community, very much reinforces Henry's point. Among the "safeguards" this process insures is that we will always have schools with which the adult community will feel comfortable. Parents have and probably will always want the school to reflect and reinforce the basic values that they covet. As a result, schools invariably support the status quo. Anybody with the idea of walking into a school and trying to change even a small part of it to better fit his own grand design for a new social order is in for a rude awakening. We reinforce this point on page 123. ||

The most Utopian thing in Utopia is that there are no schools at all. Education is carried on without anything of the nature of schools, or, if this idea is so extreme that we cannot conceive of it as educational at all, then we may say: nothing of the sort at present we know as schools. Children, however, are gathered together in association with older and more mature people who direct their activity.

The assembly places all have large grounds, gardens, orchards, greenhouses, and none of the buildings in which children and older people gather will hold much more than 200 people, this having been found to be about the limits of close, intimate personal acquaintance on the part of the people who associate together.

And inside these buildings, which are all of them of the nature of our present open-air schools in their physical structure, there are none of the things we usually associate with our present schools. Of course, there are no mechanical rows of screwed-down desks. There is rather something like a well-furnished home of today, only with a much greater variety of equipment and no messy accumulations of all sorts of miscellaneous furniture; more open spaces than our homes have today.

Then there are the workshops, with their apparatus for carrying on activities with all kinds of material—wood, iron, textiles. There are historic museums and scientific laboratories, and books everywhere as well as a central library.

Parenthood Required

The adults who are most actively concerned with the young have, of course, to meet a certain requirement, and the first thing that struck me as a visitor to Utopia was that they must all be married persons and, except in exceptional cases, must have had children of their own. Unmarried, younger persons occupy places of assistance and serve a kind of initiatory apprenticeship. Moreover, older children, since there are no arbitrary divisions into classes, take part in directing the activities of those still younger.

The activity of these older children may be used to illustrate the method by which those whom we would call teachers are selected. It is almost a method of self-selection. For instance, the children aged say from about 13 to 18 who are especially fond of younger children are given the opportunity to consort with them. They work with the younger children under observation, and then it soon becomes evident who among them have the taste, interest and the kind of skill which is needed for effective dealing with the young.

As their interest in the young develops,

their own further education centers more and more about the study of processes of growth and development, and so there is a very similar process of natural selection by which parents are taken out of the narrower contact with their own children in the homes and are brought forward in the educational nurture of larger numbers of children.

Learning by Association

The work of these educational groups is carried on much as painters were trained in, say Italy, when painting was at its height. The adult leaders, through their previous experience and by the manner of their selection, combine special knowledge of children with special gifts in certain directions.

They associate themselves with the young in carrying on some line of action. Just as in these older studios younger people were apprentices who observed the elders and took part along with them in doing at first some of the simpler things and then, as they got more experience, engaged directly in the more complex forms of activity, so in these directed activities in these centers the older people are first engaged in carrying on some work in which they themselves are competent, whether painting or music or scientific inquiry, observation of nature or industrial cooperation in some line. Then the younger children, watching them, listening to them, begin taking part in the simpler forms of the action—a minor part, until as they develop they accept more and more responsibility for cooperating.

Emphasis on Development

Naturally I inquired what were the purposes, or, as we say now, the objectives, of the activities carried on in these centres. At first nothing puzzled me more than the fact that my inquiry after objectives was not at all understood, for the whole concept of the school, of teachers and pupils and lessons, had so completely disappeared that when I asked after the special objectives of the activity of these centres, my Utopian friends thought that I was asking why children should live at all, and therefore they did not take my questions seriously.

After I made them understand what I meant, my question was dismissed with the remark that since children were alive and growing, "of course, we, as the Utopians, try to make their lives worthwhile to them; of course, we try to see that they really do grow, that they really develop." But as for having any objective beyond the process of a developing life, the idea still seemed to them quite silly. The notion that there was some special end which the young should try to attain was completely foreign to their thoughts.

By observation, however, I was led to the conclusion that what we would regard as the fundamental purposes were thoroughly ingrained in the working of the activities themselves. In our language it might be said to be the discovery of the aptitudes, the tastes, the abilities and the weaknesses of each boy and girl, and then to develop their positive capacities into attitudes and to arrange and reinforce the positive powers so as not to cover up the weak points but to offset them.

The Inevitability of Learning

I inquired, having a background of our own schools in mind, how with their methods they ever made sure that the children and youth really learned anything, how they mastered the subject matter, geography and arithmetic and history, and how they ever were sure that they really learned to read and write the figure. Here, too, at first I came upon a blank wall. For they asked, in return to my question, whether in the period from which I came for a visit to Utopia it was possible for a boy or girl who was normal physiologically to grow up without learning the things which he or she needed to learn—because it was evident to them that it was not possible for any one except a congenital idiot to be born and to grow up without learning.

When they discovered, however, that I was serious, they asked whether it was true that in our day we had to have schools and teachers and examinations to make sure that babies learned to walk and to talk.

It was during these conversations that I learned to appreciate how completely the whole concept of acquiring and storing away things had been displaced by the concept of creating attitudes by shaping desires and developing the needs that are significant in the process of living.

Relation to Economic Ideas

The Utopians believed that the pattern which exists in economic society in our time affected the general habits of thought; that

because personal acquisition and private possession were such dominant ideals in all fields, even if unconsciously so, they had taken possession of the minds of educators to the extent that the idea of personal acquisition and possession controlled the whole educational system.

They pointed not merely to the use in our schools of the competitive methods of appeal to rivalry and the use of rewards and punishments, of set examinations and the system of promotion, but they also said that all these things were merely incidental expressions of the acquisitive system of society and the kind of measure and test of achievement and success which had to prevail in an acquisitive type of society.

So it was that we had come to regard all study as simply a method of acquiring something, even if only useless or remote facts, and thought of learning and scholarship as the private possession of the resulting acquisition. And the social change which had taken place with the abolition of an acquisitive economic society had, in their judgment, made possible the transformation of the centre of emphasis from learning (in our sense) to the creation of attitudes.

They said that the great educational liberation came about when the concept of external attainments was thrown away and when they started to find out what each individual person had in him from the very beginning, and then devoted themselves to finding out the conditions of the environment and the kinds of activity in which the positive capacities of each young person could operate most effectually.

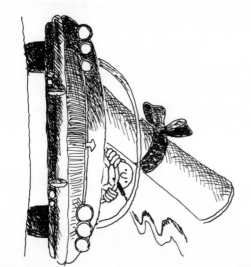

31

in the capacity of the environment to support worthwhile activities, provided the environment was approached and dealt with in the right way.

John Dewey

❚❚ On page 26 Neill echoes the philosophy that Dewey describes in the last paragraph of this reading. **❚❚**

Attainments vs. Capacities

In setting creation, productivity, over against acquiring, they said that there was no genuine production without enjoyment. They imagined that the ethics of education in the older period had been that enjoyment in education always had to be something deferred; that the motto of the schools, at least, was that man never is, but always is to be, blest; while the only education that really could discover and elicit power was one which brought these powers for immediate use and enjoyment.

Naturally, I inquired what attitudes they regarded as most important to create, since the formation of attitudes had taken the place with the young of the acquisition of information. They had some difficulty in ranking attitudes in any order of importance, because they were so occupied with an all-around development of the capacities of the young. But, through observation, I should say that they ranked the attitude which would give a sense of positive power as at least basic and primary as the others, if not more so.

This attitude which resulted in a sense of positive power involved, of course, elimination of fear, of embarrassment, of constraint, of self-consciousness; eliminated the conditions which created the feeling of failure and incapacity. Possibly it included the development of a confidence, of readiness to tackle difficulties, of actual eagerness to seek problems instead of dreading them and running away from them. It included a rather ardent faith in human capacity. It included a faith

8

With a Little Help from . . .

An experience designed to help you move toward independence.

A relatively independent experience that is aided by others. Requires no special amount of time—except enough.

If and when a teacher in a classroom says to students, for example, "The time is your own. What do you want to learn?", the students are as likely to react with frustration and avoidance as they are with delight and enthusiasm. How are young people who have for years been *directed* in school suddenly to know what interests them? Or how to proceed in learning about these interests?

We think that teachers who wish to move students toward self-directed learning should offer some assistance to the students who need it. To practice what we preach, we are offering some assistance to those of you who are tackling independent learning, and want help.

Our assistance is in the form of two lists: a list of possible topics and a list of possible procedures to employ as you approach and deal with a topic. Use this help only as you need it. If the procedures we're suggesting smack too much of studenting and the topics we enumerate are too limiting (mostly they

deal with teachers' problems), consider it a good sign. You're beginning to think about what's not important to you. You may not want to buy our Edsel, but can you design your own Mustang?

Basically, we want you to consider this experience yours. Choose your own issue to study and choose your own methods for going about it.

As you are weighing the various topics listed at the end of this experience, you may want to scale their importance to you. To facilitate this rating, we have duplicated the list of topics (and provided space for you to add your own) on pages 245–46. There, you'll find a rating form in which you can indicate the degree of interest you have in the topics posed.

We also recognize that others in your group may be interested in topics similar to yours and that you may want to work together. This duplicate list can help you find each other. Fill out the rating form, tear it out of the book, and give it to your group leader, instructor, or someone who's volunteered to tabulate the results. Then, set about the task of organizing any group inquiry you would like to undertake.

Be careful not to assume that everyone prefers to work in a group. Many will prefer to go it alone. No reason not to respect that preference.

As we've already said, most of the suggested topics deal with teachers' concerns. You may share some of those concerns now or you may develop them later, either during experiences with this book or at some other time in your professional preparation. Fine. Use this list or the rating form whenever you

feel it's appropriate. You're the learner. You should be in control.

Possible Topics to Consider

1. How can a teacher deal with pressures from parents and/or principals?
2. What are alternatives for dealing with discipline problems?
3. What do you think of tenure, salary schedules, and the teacher job market?
4. Can school make much of a difference in society, or is school just an elaborate ritual to sort out the strong from the weak?
5. Should teachers organize and fight for better working conditions the way other unions do?
6. What are "free schools" and what do they do?
7. What legal responsibilities do teachers have?
8. What's the best way to handle grades and report cards?
9. What philosophies of education can you choose from?
10. What can be done for slow learners?
11. How might new and innovative teachers relate to old and traditional teachers in the same school?
12. What are some ways to begin a school year? What should teachers do the first few days of school?
13. How many teachers outgrow their initial lack of confidence? What helps to gain confidence?
14. How does a teacher get students to like him without losing their respect?

15. How does a teacher get students to like the subject?
16. In what ways can schools or teachers or rooms or students be organized?
17. How does a teacher get certified to teach in various states?
18. How can new teaching styles be introduced in a school operating on traditional assumptions and using traditional procedures?
19. What models of excellent teachers are available to you and what can be learned from observing them?
20. How do students get motivated to learn?
21. Why do students forget so much of what they learn and what, if anything, can be done to improve the situation?
22. How much freedom should a teacher give students?
23. How did schools get where they are—what can be learned from looking at the history of education?
24. How can I tell if I know my subject well enough to teach?
25. Should private and religious schools be supported with public funds?
26. Should teachers ever lie to students?
27. Should teachers expose their personal lives to students?
28. How should controversial issues be handled in the classroom?
29. Does the power that a teacher holds tend to corrupt him?
30. What's the best way to plan lessons?
31. How do you envision schools of the future?
32. To what extent should I sacrifice myself for my students?

33. Is there a theory of teaching?
34. How should I handle racial conflict in the classroom?
35. Am I good enough to be a teacher: strong enough, smart enough, creative enough?
36. Can teachers learn to improve, or are good teachers just born that way?
37. What goes on in a faculty meeting?
38. Can I use this book's approach to learning in my teaching?
39. What do I do when I don't know what to do? How can I, a teacher, get help?
40. Do I have the patience to be a teacher?
41. How can I explain ideas so they will be clear to students?
42. How can I get to know a whole class of students and remember their names?
43. What do I do when I don't like a particular child?
44. Can I relax and be myself when I'm teaching?
45. How can schools get rid of dead-wood tenured teachers?
46. What is more important to my teaching: the goals I achieve or the process I use?
47. What are my real motives for teaching? Should I be a teacher?
48. Why don't people learn more from experience? Why are errors of the past repeated so often?

Possible Procedures to Use

- Give a creative response or write a fictitious response to the topics that interest you.
- Write a paper trying to convince your group that everyone should work on your topic, it is that important. Duplicate and distribute the paper to the group.
- Check the *Education Index* in the library for recent articles written about your topic.
- Design some experiences that relate to the topic.
- Look in the card catalog in the library, checking the available books on your topic.
- Ask the group leader or a visiting expert to give you a lecture on the topic.
- Check the *ERIC Index* (the *Educational Resources Information Center Index*) in the library. See what studies pertain to your topic.
- Decide what specific questions you want to answer as you explore your topic. Questions often provide a convenient focus for study. Anytime you get bogged down or derailed, they can put you back on course.
- If you get stuck, ask a group member or the group leader how you could proceed with your topic.
- Consider conducting a small experiment to test an idea you have. Or conduct a survey to find the information you want.
- Make some time deadlines to guide your work. Perhaps ask someone to remind you of deadlines—to help you keep to your schedule.
- Specify as exactly as you can what you hope to get out of your study of the topic. Are there questions you would like to answer? Skills you would like to demonstrate? Statements you would like to make and defend? If you know exactly where you are going, you will be able to determine when you have arrived.

- Explore your topic in the *Encyclopedia of Educational Research, The Review of Educational Research,* and the *Encyclopedia of Education.*

- Write a report of your thinking and findings and perhaps the procedures you used. Ask one or two people to read it and to give you their reactions. Then, revise your work, if you like, and offer it to interested readers.

- Ask your instructor, if you have one, if he would like to read your report and give a reaction.

- Sit with a few others who are studying different issues. Suggest that members of this group help one another as work progresses. Share problems and triumphs. Finally, evaluate each other's work. If you like, have the most interesting findings reported to the whole group.

...

If you decide to tackle one of these topics, we'd like to point out, to you and those working through this book with you, that you'll become something of an expert-in-residence on that topic and maybe on other topics. Somewhere along the way, your experiences together will probably touch upon your topic(s). If and when they do, we hope you'll share what you've learned with your group.

❚❚ Part I was an attempt to make you feel comfortable in sharing experiences. Did it achieve its goal? ❚❚

For learning to take place at all the learner must open himself to new experience. The nature of the experience may vary from the concrete to the abstract, but before he can learn anything a learner must be willing to expose himself to new experience. Teachers use a variety of methods, from enticement and reward to threat and reproof, to motivate students to take this step. There is unavoidably always some risk when one moves into the unknown, or not-yet-known, worlds of new experience. The most primal risk is that one will change. And the status quo is comfortable. Security, no matter how false or how well sustained by the denial of reality, seems preferable to "what might happen."

The ideal pedagogical condition is where a learner, fully possessed of feelings of personal adequacy as an explorer in the universe of experience, finds the adventure of new experience a prospect of challenge and excitement. Thus he learns. And he thirsts for yet more experience.

George Isaac Brown

❞ Are you thirsty yet? ❞

If you saw her running between classes with too many books in her arms and a little bit late, you would never notice that she was different. When she sat in class engrossed in the patterns the window light made on the floor, she seemed commonly inattentive. But once you got to know her, you fully realized that she was different. She flushed with a kind of awareness. Kari was handicapped. But her handicap wasn't a limp or a distorted speech pattern. Her handicap was creativity.

Robert E. Samples

❞ See what Henry has to say about creativity and schooling on page 28. ❞

In the normal development of the normal child, it is now known that *most* of the time, if he is given a really free choice, he will choose what is good for his growth. This he does because it tastes good, feels good, gives pleasure or *delight*. This implies that *he* "knows" better than anyone else what is good for him....

Capacities clamor to be used and cease their clamor only when they *are* well used. Not only is it fun to use our capacities, but it is also necessary. The unused capacity or organ can become a disease center or else atrophy, thus diminishing the person....

This force is one main aspect of the "will to health," the urge to grow, the pressure to self-actualization, the quest for one's identity. It is this that makes psychotherapy, education and self-improvement possible in principle....

This inner core, or self, grows into adulthood only partly by (objective or subjective) discovery, uncovering and acceptance of what is "there" beforehand. Partly it is also a creation of the person himself.

Abraham H. Maslow

❞ Maslow's ideas here relate to a point we made about gatekeepers on page 5. ❞

Choosing to Choose

11 So far you've had some experiences that have hopefully made you a comfortable part of a close group of friends. You've also had a chance to get your learning engine cranked up and running. Up to this point we've dealt with teaching only tangentially. But now we deal with it directly. We think the place to start is at the beginning, by examining the issue of why you're considering teaching.

You may be considering teaching for some very good reasons. For example, you may have already had enough teaching-like experiences to convince you that you've got what it takes.

You may also be here for many other reasons. Are you, for example:

- The person who would rather be a nurse but is afraid of chemistry?
- The person whose parents won't pay his way through school unless he gets a good practical education, including a teaching certificate?
- The person who wants to avoid the Arts and Sciences' foreign language requirement?
- The person who's already changed majors twice and just can't find anything else but education?
- The person who wasn't gifted enough for pre-med?
- The person who doesn't know what to do with a major like his but teach it?

We could say that these represent poor reasons for coming to teaching. But we won't say that, because they aren't poor reasons for coming to teaching. A lot of excellent teachers came to teaching for reasons just like these. But they are poor reasons for staying in teaching. We believe you need to find sound, satisfying reasons for staying in teaching. Or you should get out.

Not only that, but you need to find a satisfying role in teaching. Here are some examples of persons who have not yet eliminated their role confusion:

- The secondary education major who feels he'll do best with younger kids but hasn't mustered the ego strength to counteract the relatively low status that elementary education has on some campuses.
- The man who would like to work with small kids but is afraid that elementary education is too feminine.
- The student who just loved foreign language as a student but can't come up with strong reasons for teaching it to others.
- The elementary education major who's confusing teaching with mothering (or fathering).

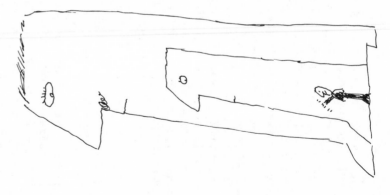

Then there is the matter of teaching style. Will you be a stand-up lecturer? A discussion leader? A non-directive stimulator of student interests? Or what?

As we noted in the first few pages of this book, it isn't likely that you will be able to get your orientation to teaching from traditions, or noble motivations, or love of subject matter, or model teachers. It's not easy, but you will have to find your own way.

All of this is our way of saying that you have a lot of decisions to make if you're to make the most of your potential teaching-self. We hope you'll make these decisions carefully. To reiterate, we'd like to help you with those decisions. **"**

In ultimate analysis each one of us is the primary subject of morality. We want in the end to know what to do in each circumstance of our lives, so as to build a happy life at every step. Happiness is a hard topic, but it certainly includes the realization or the striving for the realization of some most satisfying plan of life. A happy life is woven by actions that issue from profound abilities that intertwine with profound capacities for satisfaction. But what are those abilities? They are not necessarily those abilities that seem to us at a given moment the most pleasurable. No, the most important thing we must learn is to develop the discipline to sacrifice the larger present tempting good, which is superficial or short-lived, for the smaller present untempting good, which is profound and long-lived. To acquire this discipline is not enough: we must be able to exercise it correctly. We must, therefore, know as much as we can about our own profound abilities. This is the point of the eternally valid old precept *know yourself.*

The culmination of learning, understanding, and thinking is the deepening and broadening of your self-knowledge. Theoretical learning is complemented by the acquisition of a better understanding of one's self. Each one of us is a theater of consciousness, the most superb thing in the universe, activated by a marvelous bundle of mental and physical powers. Know their rank, master them, and exercise them.

Hector-Ner Castaneda

38

One of the most hopeful things I have seen in my lifetime is that the younger college students here at Harvard, and some of the students I've met in other parts of the country in the course of my work, think that teaching is an honorable and valuable profession. In the past, these students have wanted to go into medicine, into law or architecture, and now they want to be teachers. It's lovely to see men wanting to be elementary school teachers. And to see women interested in teaching as a real professional goal for their entire lifetime. I think it does reflect some changes.

Robert Coles

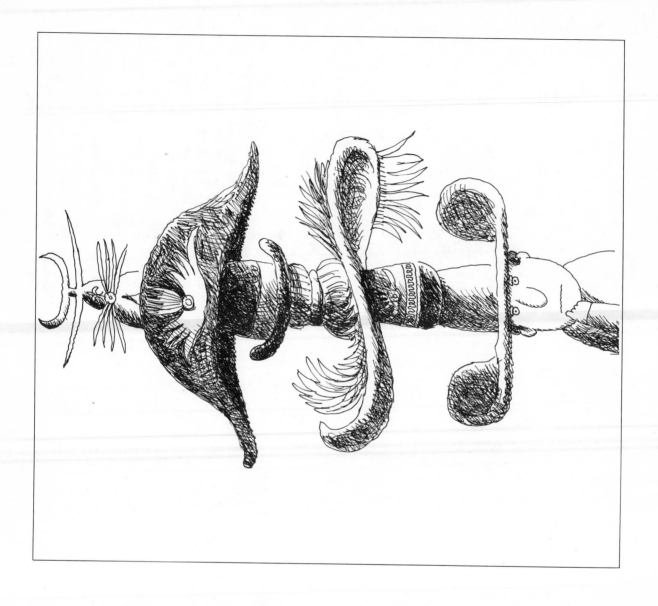

III
Trying on Styles

How do teachers help students learn?
What teaching styles suit you best?
What kind of teacher do you want to become?
What are the limits to your teaching-self? How will you find out?

Somewhere along the way, each of us bumps up against the problem of deciding what he wants to do with his life. Maybe you haven't bumped yet. Maybe you have, and have confronted the problem squarely enough to feel pretty secure in your plans for the next few years.

Maybe you bumped, but backed off because you were unwilling or unable to deal with issues that arose.

Throughout much of this book and in all of this part, we'll be encouraging you to do some productive bumping, at least in relation to teaching. Deciding for or against a career (or checking out a decision already made) is partly a process of comparing ourselves—our capabilities, interests, and values—against an image, perhaps a stereotype, we have of that career. Two factors often confuse that process and make our decisions unsound. One is that we sometimes see ourselves inaccurately in some important way. We may think we can do things we can't. Or we may think we can't do things we can. The second is that our image of a career, in this case teaching, is distorted in some important way. For example, if your image of good teaching is what Ms. Brown, the greatest teacher you've ever had, did, you're partly right. Also you're undoubtedly partly wrong. You're not Ms. Brown. You won't have you for a student. You may not even be teaching what she taught. Nonetheless, you have an image of good teaching right now and we think you'll find it informative, either now or later in the book, to set your present image down on paper. Try the next experience and see if it helps you build a more concrete understanding of your image of teaching.

Draw-A-Teacher

A quick way to become more conscious of your image of teaching.

An individual or group experience. Requires about ten to fifteen minutes.

Draw a picture of a teacher teaching a class. You can use the space provided. Don't let lack of artistic talents impede you. We promise not to ask you to submit your drawing to public scrutiny. Take as much time as you need to draw your picture.

Then, you can learn from this experience in one of two ways. Decide which is best for you.

Way One: Forget about this picture until later. Coming back to what you've drawn after several weeks of working on yourself as a teacher can be useful. And so we will return to this experience in the last part of the book. But don't look back there now. (Shades of Orpheus.)

Way Two: Or learn a little about your view of teaching at this point in time by turning to page 227 and interpreting your picture according to the criteria listed there. (Shades of Pandora.)

42

Playboy: Why is there so much tension involved in doing the show?

Cavett: In actually sitting there and doing it? Your mind is split in about six or more ways at all times. To the viewer, it looks like all the host—that sounds so much folksier than "star," doesn't it—has to do is follow the conversation. But you're not only doing that; you're thinking ahead, wondering whether to change the subject or pursue it, trying to decide whether there's time in this segment to start something new, dying inside when the guest launches into a long story and you know there's less than a minute left before the station break and that the guest will be thrown and the story ruined if you interrupt, thinking his last story may involve the show in a lawsuit and wondering if you should say something that might help or let it pass, knowing that an upcoming guest has said, "if that schmuck is still out there when I come on, I'll leave," wondering what it was he told you not to forget to ask him and trying to decide, of five things you wanted to get to, which two to leave out, and wondering why the audience seems restless and wondering what signal the stage manager just gave you that you missed. Usually these things all come together just about the time you've decided your fly is open and that's what the ladies in row E are whispering about and why the stage manager signaled. It's a wonderful job for people who have never had a nervous breakdown but have always wanted one. . . .

Dick Cavett

being both arbitrary
We talk about five
ng styles, not
e exist, but
o provides us a
convenient way to focus you on
different facets of teaching.
Then we encourage you to try on as
many of these five as you care to
(and dare to), to see if you can
gain insights into the kind of
teacher you want to become.

Good teachers usually intermix
many of our five aspects of teaching, so we don't want to leave you
with the impression that these are
pure types. They aren't. A part of
your later development as a teacher
will be to provide the modulations
for this comparatively gross
partitioning.

The message we want to get
across is that you must be able to
select a teaching-self by choice,
because it's appropriate—rather
than by default, because it's the
only one you know. Therefore,
we'll introduce you to some alternatives.

We have defined our five styles
of teaching as:

Presenting Subject Matter—
Conveying subject matter to
students in palatable ways;
perhaps the most often used
and regularly abused of all
teaching styles.

Helping Students Discuss—
Helping students to share questions and answers, to put
thoughts into words, and to
feel secure in expressing these
thoughts publicly.

Helping Students Discover—
Structuring a situation and
guiding students so that they
stop and think, wonder, explore, and figure out for
themselves; encouraging the
process of learning itself and
the skills involved in
learning.

Dealing with Feelings—
Acknowledging that students'
emotions and impulses sometimes impede their ability to
learn or your ability to teach
and attempting to react constructively (or at least not
destructively) to such disruptions.

Enriching Humanness—
Giving primary allegiance to
the idea of helping students
become more capable, fully-
functioning, self-actualizing
individuals, even when doing
so necessitates a move away
from subject matter.

There are many ways in which
these five styles relate to each
other. For example, we see the
five styles as being spread across
three continua, with presenting
subject matter being near the left
end of each continuum and enriching
humanness being near the right.

Predictable (safe)	Element of teacher risk	Unpredictable (unsafe)
Cognitive (intellectual)	Nature of subject matter	Affective (emotional)
External (objective)	Relationship to students' experience	Internal (subjective)

Many individual lessons won't fit this generalization, but we think enough will, so you can think of the process of trying on successive styles as resulting in a gradual progression from one end of these continua to the other. For example, presenting subject matter is a style in which you are teaching a safe, predictable, highly cogni- tive subject matter that is largely external to what your students are concurrently experiencing. Enrich- ing humanness, on the other hand, is a style in which you are teaching an unpredictable, highly affective subject matter that is very central (internal) to their concurrent experiences.

As a way of beginning to decide what kind of teacher you can be, or want to be, or whether you want to be one at all, we recommend trying at least three of these teaching styles, any three, but at least three. And then, learn whatever you can from the expe- rience.

By "trying on," we mean actually attempting to teach short lessons to a small group of your friends or fellow students, or honest-to-goodness children or youths if you can get them. Ask your "students" to role-play the kind of students you want to teach, or let them be themselves, if you prefer.

The lessons can be short; six to ten minutes will do the trick in most cases. If possible, try to record the lessons on either audio or video tape and then take a good hard look at yourself as you try on individual teaching styles. We think your own evaluation of what you do is most valuable at this point, but don't let that stop you from pumping your "students," or anybody else, for reactions and suggestions.

It will take effort and organi- zation to manage this series of "practice lessons" or "micro- lessons," but our guess is that these may be your most significant experiences in the book. *)*

Self-evaluation

❚❚ After you teach a lesson, come back to this section.

What did you think of your teaching? It's your life—you need to decide if teaching should be a part of it. Remember, though, that you're not a pro. You're a beginner. So keep your evaluation in perspective. If you feel good about the lesson, great. If you feel badly, that doesn't necessarily make you a crummy teacher.

As you evaluate your teaching, consider the following questions:

1. Do you know what you'd do differently if you were to teach the lesson again? If you do, chalk it up to experience. If you don't, ask for help. Perhaps even reteach the lesson and see how it works out the second time.

2. Did something beyond your control spoil the lesson? Your friends didn't role-play well? Or the setting was so artificial that it would have thrown a pro?

3. Was it simply a bad choice of lesson for that particular style of teaching? Some content just doesn't lend itself to some purposes.

You may conclude that there was a serious problem with your teaching. But remember that this problem occurred in just one artificial test. Don't draw any conclusions until you've tried at least three lessons. Even then, you can't be sure. If you felt uncomfortable with the way you taught, you might eventually learn how to escape your discomforts. And if you felt comfortable in the practice lessons, you may soon find that you are tiring of the tasks all too quickly to become or remain an effective pro.

Even if you do decide that teaching is not for you, we hope you won't consider yourself a failure. For this book, success is deciding. If you feel you've made the right decision after openly examining the data, you've been successful. ❚❚

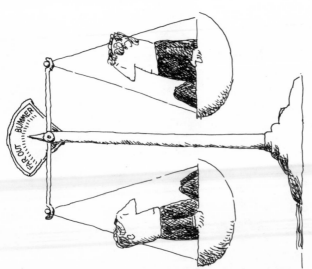

Presenting Subject Matter

" Have you ever taken a course containing material that you really wanted to learn? If you have, you probably found that the way the teacher taught was a good deal less important than it normally is. The teacher could be pretty dull, but you still found the experience worthwhile.

When we've been in those situations, we've found ourselves straining for structure and demanding forthright answers. Come on, lay that stuff on me. Don't mess around with any of that "What would you like to do today?" Just make the material complete, clear, and coherent.

When a teacher finds himself with a group of eager beavers, he had better be ready to lay out the subject matter in a concise and comprehensive manner. We refer to that most ancient of dirty words and most maligned of teaching acts: lecturing.

The problem with lecturing is that it's done too much. It's also done in the wrong places, with the wrong people, and for the wrong reasons. A productive lecture has two ingredients: a teacher who knows his stuff and can present it, and a student or group that wants to learn what the teacher knows. Simply pointing out how seldom these two conditions are satisfied, but how often the lecture is used, suggests the degree of malpractice we find.

We're all victims of our own experiences when it comes to lecturing, so we must fight off the tendency to use all the unhappy lecturing habits we've acquired: treating the lecture as a perfunctory act, a way to cover the book, a way to present material for testing, and/or a way to show kids how dumb they are.

Of course, lecturing must have something going for it or else it wouldn't have survived all these centuries."

Teaching is an art form and the lesson plan is its working sketch. As the soul of art is unity, that becomes the key to effective lesson planning. Whether the impression to be conveyed is an emotional or an intellectual one, it must be a unified impression. Any effective lecture or inquiry lesson has a totality of its own which is the result of its unity. Most beginning teachers and not a few veterans collapse in hopelessly fragmented lessons. Toward the conclusion of a lesson a teacher should be able to launch a peroration which might begin with the words: "So you see. . . ." And there should follow a conclusion or a series of conclusions made not only possible but *necessary* by the foregoing thirty minutes of work, whether done by the class or the teacher, or both. Rarely in the social studies or history classroom, at either the Ph.D. or junior high school level is such a thing possible. Far more common is the situation that ends with both bewildered students and reflective teacher asking themselves, after thirty minutes of holding forth, "So what?" Indeed many students no longer expect any unity. They have become inured to the haphazard intellectual or emotional bombardment that characterizes so much of our present day instruction and, were it not for the existence of their own random and chaotic notes, wouldn't realize they'd been to class. But for the bell system which punctuates the beginning and end of class, the instructor might go on forever. By tacit agreement students and teachers have accepted the bells as defining the development of whatever it was that they were doing. Stories are re-

10

Presenting Subject Matter: Doing It

peated of the instructors who stop mid-sentence on the bell, and who resume next class with the following word. I've known two who did just that. After twenty-five years of attending classes and ten years of watching colleagues teach, I can still count on one hand the number of teachers whose classroom presentation reflected some notion of unity. Parents have given up asking what was learned in school today. You can baffle a teacher by asking him what he taught. In either case the question is, to all intents and purposes, unanswerable. Well, it should not be so.

David F. Kellum

Wouldn't it be great, just once, to listen to the kind of lecture that Kellum describes? Maybe you've already been fortunate enough to have heard one or more. If so, we envy you.

An experience that allows you to try on the lecturing style and see how it fits.

A small-group experience. You'll need three or more people to role-play your students.

We think that for you to be good at presenting subject matter, you must master most, if not all, of the following four tasks. If you plan to lecture, we recommend you consider each of the four as you build your lesson.

1. Know your subject. Be something of an expert. Your expertise is what the kids are after. If they're not after that, forget about using this style.

2. At the beginning of the lesson, arouse the students' curiosity, stimulate their imagination, or capture their interest. A friend of ours calls this "mind-capture" and we think it's an apt descriptor for this task. For example, start a science lesson with a magical, inexplicable occurrence; a history lesson with a statement seemingly on contemporary society that turns out to have been written centuries ago. The point of mind capture is to make sure your students are asking questions before you try to give them answers.

3. Present your case. The product you are working for is much more than a simple string of "answers." It is student understanding. Structure a lecture as a logical, coherent, interesting procession of facts or principles, hopefully buttressed with lots of concrete examples. Putting it all together and producing student understanding is not easy. At every point, you must anticipate pitfalls in your students' minds; you need to do something resembling what the military calls "contingency planning." ("If this happens, I'm ready to respond in this way." "If that happens, I'll use this example." And so on.) And try not to be confusing or boring.

4. Have a finale. The presentation that you started "x" minutes ago has to achieve some sort of intellectually, maybe even aesthetically, satisfying closure. More than any other teaching style, good lecturing resembles good theatre. You want the climax of your presentation to come at the end. Ideally, the students' intellectual endeavors during your lecture should result in their experiencing either affirmation (Aha! I knew it!) or surprise (Well, I'll be damned!). Or, at the least, you need to close with a summary. As Kellum points out (page 47), you definitely don't want to end with the bell and the phrase, "We'll pick this up next time."

We've heard from time to time of lecturers who got standing ovations, but they are a very rare breed. Maybe like us, you're not part of that breed. The question is, whom are you going to try to emulate—Superteacher, or some of the mediocre content-coverers we've all somehow managed to survive?

Now, try to put together a lecture-presentation that is both an intellectual endeavor *and* a work of art. (Sounds like a dare, doesn't it?)

∎ ∎ ∎

Here's some space in which you can think through the lesson you plan to teach. You might also find the headings a useful guide for providing feedback to friends who elect to try on this style.

1. What is the subject matter, your goal of instruction?

_____
_____
_____
_____
_____
_____

2. What will be your starting gambit?

_____
_____
_____
_____
_____
_____

3. What examples, data, arguments will you use?

_____
_____
_____
_____
_____
_____

4. What will be your summation and/or finale?

_____
_____
_____
_____
_____
_____

5. Did the style, the lesson, work? What's your evaluation? (See page 46.)

_____
_____
_____
_____
_____
_____

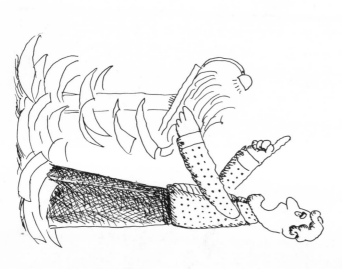

The new trend [in education] is rooted in Dewey and Neill and the progressive educators. Its modern advocates include such spokesmen as Paul Goodman, John Holt, Neil Postman, Herbert Kohl, and Edgar Friedenberg.

All of these new educational leaders surrender leadership to the children. John Holt . . . would not have teachers play a vital leadership role in changing and developing children; he would have each child determine his own educational goals—"School should be a place where children learn what they want to know, instead of what we think they ought to know."

Let me add here that I am in complete agreement with Holt when he accuses most schools—public schools, especially—of rigidity, irrelevance, unnecessary restrictions, lack of spontaneity, adult domination, and coerciveness. But then he throws up his hands. Just shake it all up, remove the teachers, abolish the teacher's leadership role in the classroom altogether, and thereby deny his responsibility in changing the current condition. He keeps stating: take it all off—and just that haphazardly. Regarding all learning as essentially the same, he ridicules the concept of curriculum as well as the teacher's leadership role. Because what is now taught in school is often irrelevant,

> **"** We're glad there are a few guys like Pearl around to help keep our view of education in balance. Maybe you'll find he does the same for you. **"**

> **"** We, or perhaps someone else reading this book someday, would be interested in the extent to which you see this part of the book stimulating these two types of learning: the extension of teaching "habits" you already have and the learning of new generalizations about teaching. Why don't you write your response right here? **"**

_____
_____
_____
_____
_____
_____
_____
_____
_____
_____
_____
_____
_____
_____

Jerome S. Bruner

The first object of any act of learning, over and beyond the pleasure it may give, is that it should serve us in the future. Learning should not only take us somewhere; it should allow us later to go further more easily. There are two ways in which learning serves the future. One is through its specific applicability to tasks that are highly similar to those we originally learned to perform. Psychologists refer to this phenomenon as specific transfer of training; perhaps it should be called the extension of habits or associations. Its utility appears to be limited in the main to what we usually speak of as skills. Having learned how to hammer nails, we are better able later to learn how to hammer tacks or chip wood. Learning in school undoubtedly creates skills of a kind that transfers to activities encountered later, either in school or after. A second way in which earlier learning renders later performance more efficient is through what is conveniently called nonspecific transfer or, more accurately, the transfer of principles and attitudes. In essence, it consists of learning initially not a skill but a general idea, which can then be used as a basis for recognizing subsequent problems as special cases of the idea originally mastered. This type of transfer is at the heart of the educational process—the continual broadening and deepening of knowledge in terms of basic and general ideas.

Holt concludes that it is impossible to identify relevance. And so he insists:

The most we can do is try to help, by letting him know roughly what is available and where he can look for it. Choosing what he wants to learn and what he does not is something he must do for himself. . . . In short, the school should be a great smorgasbord of intellectual, artistic, creative, and athletic activities from which each child could take whatever he wanted, and as much as he wanted or as little.

what is really possible for us to achieve through schools. John Holt exhibits an anti-intellectual distortion of equalitarianism. Because he could not eliminate fear of failure in the classroom, he assumes it cannot be done. Because what is now taught in school is irrelevant, he believes that it is impossible to identify relevance and teach it. I disagree! I believe, as I said before, that there is a body of knowledge to be taught to prevent racism and provincialism.

Arthur Pearl

I disagree. I believe that there is a body of knowledge to be taught and a position to be taken through it, and supported by it, against racism, against parochialism, against poverty and misery. It is important to remember once again that John Holt is a good man—at least by the criteria we all measure the goodness of a man. He agrees with me about most things. He is for peace and freedom, and against poverty. The problem is that his dissatisfactions have diverted his concentration so that he can only identify alternatives to what is. As a result, this relieves the teacher of responsibility for a better society once a student makes his choice to be a racist, a jingoist, a waster of resources, or a selfish accumulator of wealth.

Holt thinks that persons can be educated to be above these frailties "by creating in the school an atmosphere of freedom, respect, and trust within which true kindness and generosity can be expected to grow. It has little or nothing to do with content, curricula, or learning, and a great deal to do with the human heart and spirit." I have less faith in the undisciplined heart and spirit and less despair over

Jules Henry

School is an institution for drilling children in cultural orientations. Educationists have attempted to free the school from drill, but have failed because they have gotten lost among a multitude of phantasms—always choosing the most obvious "enemy" to attack. Furthermore, with every enemy destroyed, new ones are installed among the old fortifications—the enduring contradictory maze of the culture. Educators think that when they have made arithmetic or spelling into a game; made it unnecessary for children to "sit up straight"; defined the relation between teacher and children as democratic; and introduced plants, fish, and hamsters into schoolrooms, they have settled the problem of drill. They are mistaken.

Maybe that's why things like drill have endured over the centuries.

The true teacher is not the one who pours information into the student's head as through a funnel—the old-fashioned "disciplined" approach—or the one who regards all potentialities as already existing within the student and needing only to be pumped up—the newer "progressive" approach. It is the one who fosters genuine mutual contact and mutual trust, who experiences the other side of the relationship, and who helps his pupils realize, through the selection of the effective world, what it can mean to be a man. In the end education, too, centers on the problem of man. All education worthy of the name is education of character, writes Buber, and education of character takes place through the encounter with the image of man that the teacher brings before the pupil in the material he presents and in the way he stands behind this material.

"...and, we might add, through his genuine acceptance of each of his students as a unique, worth-while human being. A student, even one with a shaky self-image, confronted with this kind of teacher for an extended period of time begins to view himself in a more favorable light. As he comes to view himself as a "better" person, he begins to act as a better person. If he acts that way long enough, it becomes habitual. He becomes that better, more complete, more secure human being."

Helping Students Discuss

*We remember sitting once with a group of teachers watching a guy named Jerry demonstrate the use of the Magic Circle, a really useful curriculum for helping children deal with feelings. Jerry was great. He had third graders and the kids were so absorbed, sitting in that little circle on the floor, that the thirty of us surrounding them could have stood on our heads and we wouldn't have been noticed.

Jerry had each kid imagine that something he really wanted was in an imaginary box in front of him. Jerry described his own box carefully and then pretended to open the box and talk about how he felt. Jerry's box was big, two classrooms big and higher than the school! The box contained a fifty-foot two-masted sailboat. Jerry must have spent three or four minutes on an elaborate, enthusiastic description of the boat, choreographed with big sweeping gestures.

After all of the ten or so kids had opened their boxes, each saying what she or he wanted to be in it, Jerry asked one boy if he could remember what was in each person's box. The boy remembered every single item—except Jerry's. Now that probably wouldn't have been particularly astounding, except that Jerry had predicted it before the kids, whom he'd never seen before, were even brought in the room! It apparently happens all the time.*

Maurice Friedman

Well, this is a long way to make a short but very important point. We tune in on our peers better than we do on the other people in our lives. Our peers say things in our language, springing from our values, and they speak out of our experiences. They are relevant. Herein lies the major value and purpose of discussions, as well as of bull and rap sessions. They can unleash the forces locked up in peer relationships.

Right here and now we probably need to differentiate between the endeavor we're calling "discussion" and the familiar bull or rap session. About the only distinguishing standard that seems to make sense is the degree of struggle involved. If most of your students appear to be working at the cutting edge of their intellects or value systems, you can feel pretty secure about the worth of what's transpiring. Your students gossip and rap whether you're there or not. But they probably won't often engage in the struggle we call "discussion" without your help. It's too easy not to.

Facilitating discussions can be very tough. It's particularly difficult when you're trying to pack as much learning as you can into as many kids as you can in the time you've got with them. A dozen questions run through your head as you sit there trying to look casual and interested and really on top of things in a non-involved sort of

52

way. Are they running too far astray of the topic? Will this question I'm tempted to ask lead them deeper into the material, or will it just kill the exchange that's going on? A lot of kids seem interested...should I put them into small groups so more can talk? Why does Jane monopolize so damn much? Only ten minutes left...how can we possibly achieve any real closure? Dick Cavett, where are you now that I really need you?

See page 43 if that last plea makes no sense to you.

11

Helping Students Discuss: Doing It

A small-group experience. You'll need three or more people to role-play your students.

An experience that allows you to try on the discussion leader style and see how it fits.

We think that for you to be good at helping students discuss, you must master most, if not all, of the following six tasks. If you plan to lead a discussion, we recommend you consider each of the six as you build your lesson.

1. Set up ground rules. (Or you may opt not to set any.) Ground rules can be simple, like not raising hands to speak, talking directly to one another rather than always addressing remarks to you, the teacher, as though you were some sort of supreme information exchange. A ground rule may determine whether the discussion should evolve in small groups, perhaps pairs or trios, or in the large group. Ground rules can also be more subtle and complex, like getting your kids to begin to see the difference between having to understand someone else's point of view and having to accept it.

2. Ask questions. There are many ways of looking at question-asking. For example,

questions can be considered open (more than one answer) or closed (only one right answer). Both aren't always appropriate. Open questions seem to stimulate more discussion, probably because they increase the odds of a student having a "right" answer. Questions can also be thought of as initiating, as when one starts a new interchange or sets up a new idea, or as extending, as when one questions a student on a response that has been unclearly or incompletely stated. Both initiating and extending questions have their time and place.

3. Make statements. You can introduce information into a discussion, or express an opinion, or even become an adversary. But remember as a teacher you carry a lot of extra belt. You can crush some egos in a hurry if you aren't careful. Taking a stand is really a matter of style. One personality does it one way, one another. Try it out. See how it works for you.

4. Respond. You can encourage students to get involved, or reinforce their contributions, or tactfully inform them when you believe they're wrong. You can smile, nod, and attend to what students are saying.

5. Talk about the way you are talking, sometimes referred to as "processing." Have your students focus on the way they're going about their discussion. For example, people don't always listen to what someone else is saying. When this happens, it merits taking time out to get

them tuned in to each other. Lots of "nots" deserve this kind of time: not examining assumptions, not allowing some silent time for thinking, not allowing someone to take an unpopular stand, and so on.

6. Perhaps, shut up. Kids often have very good things to say to each other. At times like these, why not just keep your sailboats out of it? Sometimes the best teaching is to do nothing.

Now try to put together a good discussion lesson, one that engages your students in the struggle.

■
■
■

Here's some space in which you can think through the lesson you plan to teach. You might also find the headings a useful guide for providing feedback to friends who elect to try on this style.

1. How will you set up ground rules, if any?

_____
_____
_____
_____

2. What pivotal questions will you use?

_____
_____
_____
_____

3. & 4. What will be your role(s) in the discussion?

_____
_____
_____

5. What procedures will you use to process the lesson?

_____
_____
_____
_____
_____

6. How will you use teacher silence?

_____
_____
_____
_____
_____

7. Did the style, the lesson, work? What's your evaluation? (See page 46.)

_____
_____
_____
_____

54

" This is an interesting discussion because those reading it seem equally divided in their impression of its merits. About half see it as a free-wheeling gab-fest in which a bunch of kids with little verbal ability try to hash out an accurate recollection of <u>The Wizard of Oz</u>. The other half see it as unadulterated chaos, a bull session run amuck. We're still trying to figure out why individuals view this excerpt so differently. Maybe you can come up with an explanation.*"*

Big C's question was the catalyst for a great and memorable afternoon, one of those rare moments generated by chance, planned by no one, spontaneous and joyful, transcending the need for a teacher or a classroom, and making me once more think of <u>education</u> as something <u>alive</u> and <u>helpful</u>, instead of as a withered dream in need of formaldehyde. Oz took over the rest of the day. For a couple of minutes it was utter pandemonium. Fred introduced a moving argument in incomprehensible Fredese in favor of the proposition that water could evaporate witches. Prophet thought this was crap. He told Fred if he continued to think it was crap so. Fred told Prophet he would kick his butt if he continued to think it was crap. Mary mumbled something into her left hand about fire being better than water. Saul said that there ain't no sure way to kill a witch.

Cindy Lou's voice finally broke through the general upheaval of noise and offered to recite her King James Version of the story.

"O.K.," said I.

"There was this little girl who got blown away in a rainstorm," she started.

"That ain't the way it was," said Jimmy Sue.

"How was it then, you old ugly self?" Cindy Lou shot back.

"Ain't no rainstorm, sister."

"Damn right it was a rainstorm."

"No, girl, it was a tor-nay-do."

"Yeah," the class agreed, "it was a tor-nado."

"Same thing," claimed Cindy Lou.

"No, girl. Tor-nay-do take you head clean off," offered Mary.

"You tellin' the story, girl?" Cindy inquired menacingly of Jimmy Sue.

"No."

"Then you keep your mout' out of it."

"This girl got blown away by a wind and the house she was in hit a bad witch on the head and kill her dead. Then the girl and the little dog go marchin' down this yellow brick road 'til they meet this chicken lion who try to act tough."

"No," a chorus of voices shouted.

"No, what?" Cindy Lou asked.

"That girl don't meet no lion," said Samuel, in one of his first vocal contributions of the year.

"Sure she meets a lion."

"No, girl, first she sees the scarecrow. Ain't got no brains."

"Yeah, scarecrow first," the class agreed, acting out the chorus in this impromptu drama.

"You tell the story, cockeye."

"Call me cockeye and I bust your head,"

Samuel shouts, clenching his fists.

"Don't call Samuel cockeye, Cindy Lou."

"He is cockeye."

"Yeah, he cockeye," the chorus agrees.

"No," I say.

"I bust your head," Samuel warns the whole class.

"You cockeye," the class chants.

"The scarecrow first," says Richard. "Let me tell the story."

"Oh boy, Richard, give it to us."

Pat Conroy

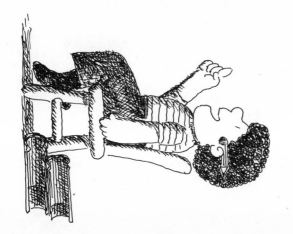

**We trust there'll be less dis-
agreement on the merits of this
discussion.**

"Ladies and gentlemen, we are concerned today with a special happening in our play *Death of a Salesman.* Willy, as we know, is always trying to impress people. And he thinks the way to impress people is by putting up a big front, being a showoff. In his attempts to impress people, he often has to tell lies. Some are small; most are relatively harmless, if we want to believe that any lie is relatively harmless. But Willy's lies are believed. *He* really believes them. To him they are not lies. For Willy it is easier to lie than to tell the truth. For our discussion period today let's consider the question: What makes it 'easier' to lie than to speak the truth? Anyone have any ideas on that subject?"

Silence. Looking at one another, at the floor, out the window. What catastrophic expectations they have. Who will break the silence first?

"Mr. Hillman, I think it's better to lie than to tell the truth if you're going to get hurt by it."

"You are saying that if you tell the truth you get punished anyway?"

"Yeah. So why tell the truth? You might get away with it."

"Ron tells lies all the time. He never tells the truth."

"What do you know?"

"I know you don't tell the truth."

"So what?"

"I don't know about you two at all. I try always to tell the truth."

"Are you telling us, Bonita, that you don't always tell the truth?"

"Yes, I don't think I do. I try, but some-

times I can't help it. But when I do, I go to church and ask for forgiveness."

"What keeps you from going to the person you lied to and telling them the truth and asking for forgiveness?"

"I couldn't do that. It wouldn't help them. Then maybe they would never need to know."

"Bonita, behind those thick glasses your beautiful face is searching, always searching. I see you fighting all your teachings. I see you wanting to join this group of kids your own age and live your own life. I see you hurting.

"Bonita doesn't even get to date yet."

"Why did you bring that in, Ramon?"

"That's none of your business."

"Well, it's true. Why don't you tell the truth?"

"O.K., so it is true. That's my business. I wish I could date, but my parents don't believe in it."

"But you have been out with boys. I've seen you out with boys."

"Sure I have. And I've got in trouble at home, too."

"Who cares about parents? What they don't know doesn't hurt them."

"They always find out. They won't let me date. Everyone else gets to date. I'm sixteen years old, and I can't date. I can't even walk home with a boy. Every time I get a boy friend he gets bored with me. Who wants to be with a girl he can only see at school?"

"If a boy really liked you, he wouldn't care.

Good old Lucy. Always the protectress. In your cage of family life and lack of "good "looks" and the bag dress they hang on you, you still find others to help.

"Not for a while, maybe. But five minutes in the hall between classes doesn't amount to much."

"What makes parents do that way, Mr. Hillman?"

"What would you do as a parent, Jim?"

"I ain't a parent."

"Do you plan on getting married some-day?"

"I probably will. Everyone else does."

"Well, it generally happens that when people get married they have children. O.K. So you're a parent. What would you do?"

"I know what I'd do."

"Bonita?"

"I would teach my children right. I will teach them right. And I'll trust them and I'll let them do what they want to do."

"But what if you believe they shouldn't do something they want to do?"

"Then I'll stop them."

"When we wrote on the question from the novel *Lord of the Flies*—you remember the book—that asked: 'What do you do if children don't obey their mother?', many of you wrote that you would lock them up and take any privileges away, and a great number of you said that you would beat them or otherwise physically punish them. Is that how you are going to handle your children?"

"I would talk to them. I would tell them why."

"But what happens if they still don't obey? What do you do to them?"

Aaron Hillman

" Can you accept what some kids say in a class discussion? As a teacher, must you accept? **"**

Robert E. Samples

Kari was the one student in the class who defended the heroine in Hawthorne's *The Scarlet Letter* for having the courage to be apart from the society. At the same time Kari damned her for her dishonesty to herself. The teacher was angry because virtue wasn't winning out in the analysis. Kari said virtue was in doing what *had* to be done, rather than "obeying like a starved rat the corridors of a maze somebody else built." The teacher was so frightened by Kari's argument that he gave her a "D" for her participation.

Teachers have always been somewhat ambivalent about what it is they do for a living. An excellent case in point concerns their conceptions of the human mind. For example, there is the type of teacher who believes he is in the lighting business. We may call him the Lamplighter. When he is asked what he is trying to do with his students, his reply is something like this: "I want to *illuminate* their minds, to allow some light to penetrate the darkness." Then there is the Gardener. He says, "I want to *cultivate* their minds, to fertilize them, so that the seeds I plant will flourish." There is also the Personnel Manager, who wants nothing more than to keep his students' minds busy, to make them efficient and industrious. The Muscle Builder wants to strengthen flabby minds, and the Bucket Filler wants to fill them up.

How should we talk about "the human mind" and our always imperfect attempts to do something to it? Shall we put on the lights or damp fertilizer or keep it busy or toughen it up or pump it full? Or maybe we should try, as the Potter does, to mold the mind? Or as the Dietician, to feed it? Or as the Builder, to provide it with a sturdy foundation?

Although we are sorely tempted, it is not our intention to ridicule any of these metaphors of the mind. After all, it is not possible to talk about "the mind" in any terms other than metaphorical. Even the words "the mind" are subtly metaphorical. Think of those words for a moment. Why *the* mind? Why a noun? Why a "thing"? As John Dewey and Arthur Bentley observed, we would come much closer to actuality if we spoke of "minding" (as a process) rather than of "the mind" (as a thing). . . .

The metaphor [we prefer is] "minding" as "meaning making." Before explaining what are the implications of this conception of the mind, we want to acknowledge where it comes from. Such acknowledgment must begin with Adelbert Ames, Jr. (And *who*, everybody asks, is Adelbert Ames, Jr.?) Unlike Marshall McLuhan, he never captured the attention of the press or intellectuals, and it is safe to say that not one teacher in 5,000 has ever heard his name. Yet, it is doubtful that any "educationist" of recent times has more impressive credentials. . . .

What is it that Ames seemed to prove? The first and most important fact uncovered by his perception studies is that *we do not get our perceptions from the "things" around us. Our perceptions come from us.* . . .

Secondly, it seems clear from the Ames studies that what we perceive is largely a function of our previous experiences, our assumptions, and our purposes (i.e., needs). . . .

Third, we are unlikely to alter our perceptions until and unless we are frustrated in our attempts to do something based on them. . . .

Fourth, since our perceptions come from us and our past experience, it is obvious that each individual will perceive what is "out there" in a unique way. . . .

Fifth, perception is, to a much greater extent than previously imagined, a function of the linguistic categories available to the perceiver. . . .

In the light of all this, perhaps you will understand why we prefer the metaphor "meaning making" to most of the metaphors of the mind that are operative in the schools. It is, to begin with, much less static than the others. It stresses a process view of minding, including the fact that "minding" is undergoing constant change. "Meaning making" also forces us to focus on the individuality and the uniqueness of the meaning *maker* (the *minder*). In most of the other metaphors there is an assumption of "sameness" in all learners. The "garden" to be cultivated, the

darkness to be lighted, the foundation to be built upon, the clay to be molded—there is always the implication that all learning will occur in the same way. The flowers will be the same color, the light will reveal the same room, the clay will take the same shape, and so on. Moreover, such metaphors imply boundaries, a limit to learning. How many flowers can a garden hold? How much water can a bucket take? What happens to the learner after his mind has been molded? How large can a building be, even if constructed on a solid foundation? The "meaning maker" has no such limitations. There is no end to his educative process. He continues to create new meanings, to make new transactions with his environment. . . .

We come then to the question "What difference does it all make?" It seems clear to us, that, if teachers *acted* as if their students were meaning makers, almost everything about the schooling process would change. For example, most school practices are based on the assumption that the student is fundamentally a *receiver*, that the object ("subject matter") from which the stimulus originates is all-important, and that the student has no choice but to see and understand the stimulus as "it" is. We now know that this assumption is false. To quote Earl Kelley:

Now it comes about that whatever we tell the learner, he will make something that is all his own out of it, and it will be different from what we held so dear and attempted to "transmit." He will build it into his own scheme of things, and relate it uniquely to what he already uniquely holds as experience. Thus he builds a world all his own, and what is really important is what he makes of what we tell him, not what we intended.

Helping Students Discover

▟▟ When people think of teaching, they usually envision one person (the knowledgeable one) dispensing answers (the knowledge) to another person. Teaching becomes equated with presenting subject matter. But so often it's dull for the student to sit there and listen to the results of another person's thinking. Besides, students of the presenting-type teacher may never learn how to find their own answers and therefore may never learn how to learn for themselves. Worse yet, they may forget how to ask their own questions.

These limitations lead some teachers to prefer the discovery approach. In the discovery approach, the students take a more active part in learning. They learn by trying to find answers to questions that the teacher has posed or that they themselves have raised.

Here are two examples of "guided discovery" lessons in which the teacher presents a specific problem to be solved and also gives "hints" to assist students in their problem-solving.

Example I Teacher writes on chalkboard:

$$a \times a \times a = a^3$$
$$b \times b = b^2$$
$$d \times d \times d \times d = d^4$$
$$e \times e \times f \times f \times f = e^2f^3$$

$$g \times g = ?$$
$$h \times h \times h \times h \times h = ?$$
$$i \times i \times j \times j = ?$$
$$k \times k \times k \times 1 \times 1 \times m \times m = ?$$
$$n \times n \times o = ?$$

Then, the teacher says, "Who can figure out some of these questions? Write down the answers you think you know and I'll come around and see how you're doing." Later, the teacher puts students into pairs or trios so those unable to solve the problems can get help.

Example II The teacher distributes a sheet of paper containing two descriptions of the same scene. The first description headed "Active Verbs" begins, "The boys ran to the tree and then abruptly screeched to a halt." The second description headed "Passive Verbs" begins, "The boys were going to the tree and then just as quickly stopped when they reached it." The teacher instructs all students to compare the two accounts and then to write a brief description of something they once experienced, perhaps in school, in each of the two styles. Students who seem stuck are offered an additional sheet that contains a column of active verbs and an adjacent column of equivalent passive verbs. After a bit, the teacher puts students into pairs or trios, to share papers and explain to each other how they approached their writing and why they approached it that way. Questions are answered on an individual basis and, at the end, for the whole class.

Discovery-type lessons are tricky to prepare, but they have a large payoff. Students not only learn the subject matter, but they also learn to think for themselves.

You'll have to plan carefully if you try a guided discovery lesson; you must generate a problem, make kids responsible for solving the problem, and then assist them in reviewing their endeavor. (We'll elaborate on these guidelines in the "Doing It" part of this style.)

A discovery lesson can be more or less structured, requiring larger or smaller inductive leaps by students and requiring more or less student independence, and still satisfy our definition of the "discovery style." For a lesson with less guidance, that is, with fewer clues than the examples above, you may need only to supply a provocative issue and/or equipment or materials students will need to find their own clues and data. The most "open" of discovery lessons, of course, is the lesson in which the teacher helps students clarify their questions and identify their means for dis-

covering answers to those questions.

Many teachers prefer what is sometimes called the "project method" of instruction, a method that we call an example of a long-term discovery lesson. In this method students are asked to work alone or with others on projects (building models, designing new cities, writing plays, investigating causes of delinquency, etc.) and are therefore engaging more extensively in discovery procedures. (We must say, though, that when teachers structure projects so that students merely copy pages from an encyclopedia, something much less demanding than discovery is taking place.)

A project method lesson likewise requires some structuring and planning; you must help kids find projects, have them write contracts for the projects, perpetuate student interest in project ideas, and then assist them in evaluating their endeavor. (Again, we'll elaborate on these guidelines in the "Doing It" part of this style.)

Whether he uses the structured guided discovery approach or the more open project approach, or a combination of both, a teacher is usually guaranteed more enthusiastic students. When success is not too elusive, students enjoy learning by discovery. It also provides an excellent opportunity for inquiry into the process of learning itself. "

It is the goal of inquiry development to produce an autonomous student whose inquiry is directed largely by the motivation of curiosity. It is the goal of the inquiry teacher to minimize the social-ego motivation of the student. He must do this by eliminating worry about approval and rewards. The student must feel secure in the knowledge that the teacher will support him, no matter what kind of questions he asks or what kind of theories he formulates. He must be released from worries about asking the kind of questions the teacher wants, finding the "right answers," or getting a good grade. When these worries are removed, his social-ego motivation will be minimized and he will be free to pursue open inquiry. The motivation of closure is used to push the dependent learner into inquiry, but even this kind of pressure should be reduced when the student is ready to inquire autonomously, directed only by his own curiosity.

Such autonomy is a prerequisite for healthy interpersonal relations. Self-direction must be firmly established before a student can enter into a joint creative effort with another person. Even the teacher-student relationship suffers if the student lacks autonomy, for the teacher is forced to take over and the student becomes accustomed to submitting to the plans of the teacher. This unhealthy relationship creates a dependency that will weaken the self-image of the student and in the long run will limit his capacity to lead a full and active intellectual life.

Conceptual Growth

. . . Conceptual growth is largely a matter of building new models from old. It is quite possible for a teacher to manipulate this process and lead students to form new concepts. The teacher can augment this kind of dialogue by bringing real objects and events to the student's attention. In this way the teacher enriches the student's background of experience to enable him to build even stronger concepts. Throughout this whole process the actual combination of models is arrived at by the learner himself. The teacher can guide and facilitate, but the act of concept formation itself is in the final analysis the act of the learner.

The teacher deliberately plans the sequence of events so that the learner emerges with a concept he didn't have before—a concept built of new pieces that the teacher helps to create through concrete experiences, and old pieces that are retrieved from the student's storage. . . .

In inquiry, where the student builds his own conceptual structures and tests them, one thing is certain: *Whatever concepts the student has at any given time are wholly meaningful to him, because they grew from his own thinking.*

We must now face the question of educational goals. If conceptual growth is stronger when it grows from inquiry, how can the teacher ensure that certain important and fundamental concepts *do* take form in the students' minds? Can the teacher assume that every student will inquire his way to all the fundamental concepts?

Of course not. The teacher must decide on his goal of the moment. If the primary goal is to be sure that the student has a *particular set of concepts*, then probably the best thing to do is use language to manipulate the thinking of the students until they seem to have the desired conceptual structure. If the teacher's objectives include building the skills of inquiry, it may be necessary to sacrifice so-called teaching efficiency. Efficiency is only meaningful with reference to some outcome. *It is not efficient to teach particular concepts if the goal is to build particular inquiry skills.* And, of course, *it is not efficient to teach inquiry skills if the goal is to build particular concepts in the students' minds.* The best solution is usually some combination of the two goals. *There is great merit in bringing appropriate didactic teaching into an inquiry session when the new concept organizers will increase the level of meaning.*

In an inquiry session *the teacher leads the students toward a particular concept only when the students are already seeking such a concept to account for their own observations.* Of course, care must be taken not to overdo this kind of instruction, lest the students become dependent on the teacher to step in with just the right set of organizers whenever they are temporarily at a loss. However, there is great value both for inquiry development and for conceptual growth in interspersing free inquiry with guided conceptual growth, particularly when the teacher watches for and uses the moment when the students truly need a concept—the moment of the teachable concept. . . .

[How Do You Know?]

If we want students not only to know *that* they know, but to know *what, how,* and *why* they know, time and effort must be spent on discussions of just what it means to know something. Raising the question "How do you know?" is relevant to the educational process at all levels.

By raising the question "How do you know?" teachers urge children to face up to the fact that knowledge is inferred from observations. Theories and generalizations are formulated on the basis of observations of the world, and in turn are tested by observations of objects and events. *Scientific inquiry is largely a matter of going back and forth between theorizing and data gathering.* Theories make it possible to decide which data to gather at any given time. The gathering of data otherwise might be meaningless and endless. The relevance of data can be determined only in the light of a particular theory. Children can learn what it means to have a theory. They are willing theorists and will speculate on theoretical issues with the slightest encouragement.

Inquiry is certainly not merely a technique for teaching subject matter. It is not a teaching method of any kind. It is much more. It is the fundamental means of human learning. All human knowledge comes through perception, analysis, inference, theorizing, and verification. Through these cognitive operations man constructs theories that enable him more powerfully to predict, control, and explain his environment. Inquiry is more than a method of science. Inquiry *is* science. It is at the very center of the scientific way of life.

J. Richard Suchman

12

Helping Students Discover: Doing It

An experience that allows you to try on the discovery learning style in one of two fairly distinct ways and see how it fits.

A small-group experience. You'll need three or more people to role-play your students.

In the guided discovery style, the strategies we employ to ask questions and help students search for answers are important. Using some very simple tactics can make your students more conscious of these strategies.

1. Generate a problem to solve. If your students don't have a problem, you'll have to help them find one, or present them with one. The problem need not be earth-shattering; much can be learned from very modest problems. But the problem must have intrigue for your students. It's the old mind-capture game we talked about earlier.

   Posing a problem can also have its zany side—for example, if you dumped a large bag of junk on the floor and asked each student, or small groups of students, to construct a Rube Goldberg machine (which doesn't have to work at all) that will save mankind. The idea here is to come up with a stimulus that allows a wide range of individual approaches.

2. Make kids responsible for solving the problem, and provide help and data only when needed. One way is to just make sure the problem is understood and then to withdraw, letting your students struggle with it independently. Another is to outline some basic steps they might use or simply to suggest some possible ones, being careful not to give or hint at the eventual outcomes of the steps. A third is to provide a list of clues (on a page, or in a whisper, via a student aide) that students can use when or if they need a clue. (Note: while the last two approaches probably enhance your students' chances of success, they also make them more dependent on you than does the first method in which you simply help them clarify the problem. Some students, however, will need more guidance than others.)

3. Help students "review" their endeavor by providing individual and group feedback. An important step because discovery doesn't make much sense without it. Your students need to be conscious of what they did and the relative success and effectiveness of the several strategies they tried (to be aware of what "works" in solving problems). This kind of thinking—reviewing what occurred, how it occurred, why it occurred, and whether it should have occurred—is often called "processing." In other words, you're helping your students become conscious of the strategies, values, ideas, and positions they are learning to use. In our Rube Goldberg problem, for example, the inventor of a money-making machine would seem to have a set of values different from those held by the inventor of a munitions-mulcher.

It would be difficult to have your students do much with a project method lesson given the constraints of our short lesson format. You could, however, initiate such an activity and adapt at least the first of the following guidelines to your microlesson.

1. Help students find projects and identify what they are after. You can assign projects and activities that you see as especially worthwhile and ask your students to complete them. Or you and the students jointly can select a group of projects and offer these as a cafeteria from which individuals or small groups can select what interests them. Or students can define and design their own projects and then request your approval before marching full steam ahead.

2. Have students write contracts, saying in outline form: what they plan to do, what they expect of you, and how they propose to be evaluated. You then approve the contracts, and ask each student to write on a public chart what he is working on during any given time period. Or you can ask him to turn in regular progress reports. Or you can trust him.

3. From time to time, suggest new project ideas to the class, hoping to arouse student interest. You can also help students, when that seems appropriate.

4. Assist students in evaluating their endeavor. Sometimes, what is learned may be of private importance to a student. At other times, what is learned merits sharing with interested classmates. Be ready and able to help students go either way with their projects.

■ ■ ■

Here's some space in which you can think through the lesson you plan to teach. You might also find the headings a useful guide for providing feedback to friends who elect to try on this style.

For a Guided Discovery Lesson:

1. What will be your role in generating the problem?

_____

_____

_____

_____

_____

2. How will the inquiry process be facilitated?

_____

_____

_____

_____

_____

3. What procedures will you use to process the lesson?

_____

_____

_____

_____

4. Did the style, the lesson, work? What's your evaluation? (See page 46.)

_____

_____

_____

_____

For a Project Method Lesson:

1. How will you help students find projects?

_____

_____

_____

_____

_____

2. How will you establish contracts?

_____

_____

_____

_____

3. How will you arouse student interest in project ideas?

_____

_____

_____

_____

_____

4. How will you assist students in evaluating their endeavor?

_____

_____

_____

_____

_____

_____

_____

_____

_____

5. Did the style, the lesson, work? What's your evaluation? (See page 46.)

Most of the students begin by glancing through the Problem Book section devoted to Problem Area I. One student is methodically reading the section from beginning to end. Several are skimming the section, looking at the pictures, examining the maps. Three boys have decided to locate Monument Valley on the large relief map of the United States. Their conversation deals with the problem of locating a place on a map that has no coordinate lines and no political boundaries.

S₁ : Let's find out why the water gets there and why it is dry here.

S₂ : Let's find it here (*pointing to the large relief map*). Hey, the states aren't marked. There aren't any names. Names . . . you gotta have names.

S₃ : No, we don't. We can tell if it is the right place by the mountains, rivers, and valleys. There ought to be a spot on the big map that looks like this map of the valley in the Problem Book.

S₁ : O.K. Now, where is Lake Tahoe?

S₃ : Here is Lake Tahoe.

S₁ : O.K. Then this would be the Colorado River.

S₂ : Then where is the San Juan River? It must be one of these curving ones that flows into the Colorado.

Meanwhile two other students are examining the stereo slide of the San Juan River. The teacher joins them.

S₄ : Hey! Get a load of this! You can see the river at the bottom.

There is no single, ideal approach to inquiry. Each student is free to come to grips with the problem in terms that are meaningful to him. Some people like' to have a broad base of data before they begin to theorize; others begin theorizing almost at once, revising their theories as they go. It helps to have class discussions about such strategies of inquiry after the children have experienced inquiry for a period of time.

Establishing a goal to give focus to inquiry.

Data source (relief map) presents new problem: How do you orient to maps that don't tell you explicitly what is where? How do you know where you are when you have only natural features to guide you? The students try out the strategy of using the familiar to place the un-familiar—a paradigm for all inquiry.

Some people get the most from pictures, some from numbers, and some from diagrams and charts. Data in many forms are presented in the books and kits.

Happiness is recognition!

S₅: And you can see how much water there used to be in the river.

This assumption is not valid, but finding this out for himself is part of inquiry. The teacher should not step in and "correct" the child, so that he will become independent of the teacher. Rather, the learner should retain his autonomy and with it the responsibility for checking out the accuracy of his own statements.

S₄: How can you tell?

S₅: The watermarks. The lines around the edge.

T: Have you seen the section on the San Juan River in the Problem Book?

Teacher facilitates by leading students to new and appropriate data source. Too much leading of this kind also can make students dependent.

S₅: No. What pages is it?

T: It starts on page 7.

Some students open their Problem Books and read. Others continue to look at the stereo slides.

S₆: Hey, look! It says the high watermark is fifty feet. But those lines are a lot higher than that. The whole canyon is probably more than a thousand feet.

The beginning of discrepancy. This forges a framework for inquiry.

S₇: But those could be old lines from when the river had more water a long time ago.

New possibilities to consider. Notice how group interaction can lead to the definition of problems.

S₈: Then what happened to the river? A little trickle like that couldn't have dug that giant ditch.

S₇: Maybe if it had enough time, it could.

S₆: I don't get why the river snakes around like that . . . the goosenecks. Why doesn't it just cut through the skinny part?

Still another problem. Each student can be dealing with the one that concerns him most.

One girl is sitting by herself reading about some of the monuments in her Problem Book. After twenty minutes or so, the teacher decides to talk with her to find out what she is thinking.

T: Are you beginning to get a picture in your mind about what Monument Valley is like?

> This student wants to build a comprehensive picture before moving on. Sometimes this approach is used as a dodge to escape becoming actively involved in inquiry. Such tactics temporarily serve a purpose for the individual and are ultimately abandoned when the student feels ready to engage in inquiry.

S₉: Well, it seems pretty dry and I sort of thought it was a desert. I guess it is, but I never thought deserts got cold. It says the temperature here gets below zero sometimes in the winter. But it is dry most of the time.

T: What about the monuments? Do they puzzle you?

> The teacher is eager to get inquiry started and is pushing too hard. If the student is puzzled and ready to engage, he will. Such probes limit the student's freedom and discourage initiative.

S₉: I never saw anything like that before except when we made towers out of dripping wet sand at the beach. They looked something like these things, only my towers weren't ever flat on top.

> The familiar—a possible bridge to the unfamiliar.

T: If you want, you may experiment at the sand table with dripping wet sand to see what happens.

> Teacher can make suggestions as long as they are accepted as such and not as directives.

S₉: I think I'll finish reading about the valley first. The monuments are all so different. But they all seem to have layers. I think it tells here what the layers are made of.

> Although the teacher can subtly manipulate with suggestions if he is not careful, this student has a strong will of his own, so the teacher feels free to make suggestions.

A group of three students has gathered around the table with the rock and mineral samples on it. After examining the profiles of the monuments in the Problem Book, they go into a discussion of the differences between various kinds of sedimentary rock. They turn to the rock samples to determine for themselves some of the differences.

S_{10}: Most of the rock seems to be sandstone, siltstone, mudstone, and shale, according to the book.

S_{11}: Here is a hunk of sandstone.

S_{10}: Shale is clay that has been pressed together. It always comes in thin, flat sheets.

S_{12}: It says on page 7 that siltstone and mudstone are similar to shale.

S_{11}: The slate seems harder than the sandstone. I can rub off little specks of sand from the sandstone, but the slate won't rub off.

S_{12}: Yeah, but it splits into sheets pretty easily.

S_{11}: *Well, look at the cross section in Figure 1-8. See . . . halfway up there is a layer of sandstone. Then there is shale right on top of that and then another layer of sandstone on top of the shale. The sandstone must be harder or the shale wouldn't start wearing back right above the sandstone. It seems like the sandstone is a kind of protection on top of softer stuff.*

S$_{10}$: All the monuments have places where the sides are straight up and down and other places where the slope is on an angle. Let's look and see if all the angle stuff is made of softer rock and the straight stuff is harder.

Analysis of data . . . .

leads to more specific data gathering.

S$_{12}$: It couldn't be what you said before, because there is sandstone in the straight layers and in the angle layers.

A useful confrontation . . .

S$_{11}$: Yeah, but where it is straight there is nothing but sandstone, and in the angle layers there is lots of stuff, a mixture of sandstone and other rock.

leads to further analysis.

S$_{12}$: But this sandstone sample isn't very hard. Why do its layers have straight sides?

Discrepancy—an inviting springboard to inquiry.

J. Richard Suchman

Lesson

Today you are going to learn how to evaluate one such series of numbers. What I mean by this is that if I give you a series like this (writes $1 + 2 + \ldots + 9 + 10$), then you should be able to find their sum without just adding all the numbers up. In other words, you should write an expression, a formula, that you can use to get the sum of this series or one like it.

(Teacher answers some student questions.)

Okay. What you need to do now is to figure out how to write a formula that will give you the sum of this series of numbers. (Points at series $1 + 2 + \ldots + 10$.) You'll need some scratch paper to work on. (Students get paper out.)

I'll give you a hint to get started. Try arranging numbers in groups. Yes, Darryl?

S: What are we supposed to do again?

T: Find a formula or a procedure that you can use to find the sum of that series of numbers. In other words, don't just add the numbers up, one plus two plus three and so on. Get a rule or procedure or formula that you can use to find the sum. Remember, try to group numbers together. (Teacher moves around room observing students' work.)

Okay. Several of you have grouped the numbers in pairs, putting the first two together, and the next two and so on. (Writes $(1 + 2) + (3 + 4) + (5 + 6) + (7 + 8) + (9 + 10)$ on board.)

$$3 + 7 + 11 + 15 + 19$$

T: That is a very interesting result, since the difference between the numbers is now four instead of one, and you have a series of numbers. But that doesn't seem to have led you anywhere. Why don't you try grouping the first and last numbers in the series together and see what happens? When you think you're on to something, raise your hand and we'll check it out. (Teacher moves around the room while students work. Several students raise their hands and teacher checks with them.)

Okay. Some. of you found that if you group the first and last numbers you always get 11. Teacher writes:

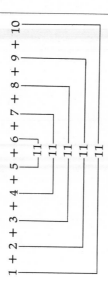

See if you can use that to find the sum of the series. Raise your hand when you do. (Several hands go up immediately. Teacher interacts with these students. Eventually, many hands have gone up.)

All right. You found that there are 5 pairs of 11, so the sum of that series is 5 times 11, or 55. Suppose we call the last number in the series "n." Now write a formula for the sum of this article. (Teacher observes a few students.)

Okay. You got $n + 1$, which is the 11 part, and now you need to get an expression for the number of pairs.

S: n over 2.

T: Why is that?

S: You have 10 numbers, so there are 5 pairs and n over 2 is 5.

T: That's right. So the formula is n over 2 times n plus 1.

S: Will that work if the series doesn't begin with one, or is it different like the other series?

T: It might not. We'd better check that out. First though, let's work out one more example and make sure we've all got the idea straight.

Edmund T. Emmer and Gregg B. Millett

When you are ready to teach this child geography, you get together your globes and your maps; and what machines they are! Why, instead of using all these representations, do you not begin by showing him the object itself, so as to let him know what you are talking of?

On some beautiful evening take the child to walk with you, in a place suitable for your purpose, where in the unobstructed horizon the setting sun can be plainly seen. Take a careful observation of all the objects marking the spot at which it goes down. When you go for an airing next day, return to this same place before the sun rises. You can see it announce itself by arrows of fire. The brightness increases; the east seems all aflame; from its glow you anticipate long beforehand the coming of day. Every moment you imagine you see it. At last it really does appear, a brilliant point which rises like a flash of lightning, and instantly fills all space. The veil of shadows is cast down and disappears. We know our dwelling-place once more, and

find it more beautiful than ever. The verdure has taken on fresh vigor during the night; transports with which it may be filled? And lastly, how can he be moved by the beautiful panorama of nature, if he does not know by it is revealed with its brilliant net-work of dew-drops, reflecting light and color to the eye, in the first golden rays of the new-born day. The full choir of birds, none silent, salute in concert the Father of life. Their warbling, still faint with the languor of a peaceful awakening, is now more lingering and sweet than at other hours of the day. All this fills the senses with a charm and freshness which seems to touch our inmost soul. No one can resist this enchanting hour, or behold with indifference a spectacle so grand, so beautiful, so full of all delight.

Carried away by such a sight, the teacher is eager to impart to the child his own enthusiasm, and thinks to arouse it by calling attention to what he himself feels. What folly! The drama of nature lives only in the heart; to see it, one must feel it. The child sees the objects, but not the relations that bind them together; he can make nothing of their harmony. The complex and momentary impression of all these sensations requires an experience he has never gained, and feelings he has never known. If he has never crossed the desert and felt its burning sands scorch his feet, the stifling reflection of the sun from its rock oppress him, how can he fully enjoy the coolness of a beautiful morning? How can the perfume of flowers, the cooling vapor of the dew, the sinking of his footstep in the soft and pleasant turf, enchant his senses? How can the singing of birds delight him, while the accents of love and pleasure are yet unknown? How can he see with transport the rise of so beautiful a

day, unless imagination can paint all the whose tender care it has been adorned?

Do not talk to the child about things he cannot understand. Let him hear from you no descriptions, no eloquence, no figurative language, no poetry. Sentiment and taste are just now out of the question. Continue to be clear, unaffected, and dispassionate; the time for using another language will come only too soon.

Educated in the spirit of our principles, accustomed to look for resources within himself, and to have recourse to others only when he finds himself really helpless, he will examine every new object for a long time without saying a word. He is thoughtful, and not disposed to ask questions. Be satisfied, therefore, with presenting objects at appropriate times and in appropriate ways. When you see his curiosity fairly at work, ask him some laconic question which will suggest its own answer.

On this occasion, having watched the sunrise from beginning to end with him, having made him notice the mountains and other neighboring objects on the same side, and allowed him to talk about them just as he pleases, be silent for a few minutes, as if in deep thought, and then say to him, "I think the sun set over there, and now it has risen over here. How can that be so?" Say no more; if he asks questions, do not answer them: speak of something else. Leave him to himself, and he will be certain to think the matter over.

To give the child the habit of attention and to impress him deeply with any truth affecting the senses, let him pass several restless days before he discovers that truth. If the one in question does not thus impress him, you may make him see it more clearly by reversing the problem. If he does not know how the sun passes from its setting to its rising, he at least does know how it travels from its rising to its setting; his eyes alone teach him this. Explain your first question by the second. If your pupil be not absolutely stupid, the analogy is so plain that he cannot escape it. This is his first lesson in cosmography. . . .

In general, never show the representation of a thing unless it be impossible to show the thing itself; for the sign absorbs the child's attention, and makes him lose sight of the thing signified. . . .

In investigating the laws of nature, always begin with the most common and most easily observed phenomena, and accustom your pupil not to consider these phenomena as reasons, but as facts. Taking a stone, I pretend to lay upon the air; opening my hand, the stone falls. Looking at Émile, who is watching my motions, I say to him, "Why did the stone fall?"

No child will hesitate in answering such a question, not even Émile, unless I have taken great care that he shall not know how. Any child will say that the stone falls because it is heavy. "And what does heavy mean?" "Whatever falls is heavy." Here my little philosopher is really at a stand. Whether this first lesson in experimental physics aids him in understanding that subject or not, will always be a practical lesson.

Let the child take nothing for granted because some one says it is so. Nothing is good to him but what he feels to be good. You think it far sighted to push him beyond his understanding of things, but you are mistaken. For the sake of arming him with weapons he does not know how to use, you take from one universal among men, common sense: you teach him to allow himself always to be led, never to be more than a machine in the hands of others. Then you will have him docile while he is young, you will make him a credulous dupe when he is a man. You are continually saying to him, "All I require of you is for your own good, but you cannot understand it yet. What does it matter to me whether you do what I require or not? You are doing it entirely for your own sake." With such fine speeches you are paving the way for some kind of trickster or fool,—some visionary babbler or charlatan,—who will entrap him or persuade him to adopt his own folly.

A man may be well acquainted with things whose utility a child cannot comprehend; but is it right, or even possible, for a child to learn what a man ought to know? Try to teach the child all that is useful to him now, and you will keep him busy all the time. Why would you injure the studies suitable to him at his age by giving him those of an age he may never attain? "But," you say, "will there be time for learning what he ought to know when the time to use it has already come?" I do not know; but I am sure that he cannot learn it sooner. For experience and feeling are our real teachers, and we never understand thoroughly what is best for us except from the circumstances of our case. A child knows that he will one day be a man. All the ideas of manhood that he can understand give us opportunities of teaching him; but of those he cannot understand he should remain in absolute ignorance. This entire book is only a continued demonstration of this principle of education.

Jean Jacques Rousseau

Every teacher has known the child whose sense of his own identity is so weak, his need to define himself so great, that he is emotionally driven to actions and reactions that are self-destructive. The integrity of the individual and his ability to learn depend upon a positive concept of the self.

Educators who daily encounter the traumatic experiences of poor minority youth must develop a method of approach responsive to the compelling needs of their student population. Certain basic hypotheses touching several areas of teacher-student-group relationships may be useful in formulating an effective approach.

These hypotheses are:

1. The student's self-concept is a significant factor in his ability to learn.
2. The student must be valued as an individual.
3. Every child wants to succeed.
4. The student's belief in himself must be nurtured if he is to grow emotionally and intellectually.
5. True learning will take place only if the student is an involved participant in the process.
6. The power structure and the learning situation must be understood and used to advantage because the child needs both the support of peers and the opportunity to differentiate himself from others.

Bennetta Washington

What, then, is the true meaning of preparation in the educational scheme? In the first place, it means that a person, young or old, gets out of his present experience all that there is in it for him at the time in which he has it. When preparation is made the controlling end, then the potentialities of the present are sacrificed to a supposititious future. When this happens, the actual preparation for the future is missed or distorted. The ideal of using the present simply to get ready for the future contradicts itself. It omits, and even shuts out, the very conditions by which a person can be prepared for his future. We always live at the time we live and not at some other time, and only by extracting at each present time the full meaning of each present experience are we prepared for doing the same thing in the future. This is the only preparation which in the long run amounts to anything.

All this means that attentive care must be devoted to the conditions which give each present experience a worthwhile meaning.

John Dewey

Tilford was the biggest guy in the class and it was pretty obvious that he greeted school with a healthy suspicion. He was the one that led the class in the exclamation, "You mean we're going *outside*? You mean outside of the *school*?" That we said we were going outside didn't seem to my colleague Dorothy Curtis and me to be such a source of amazement, but it certainly did to the class. They were ninth graders and it was a junior high school in a large city, and we were about to attempt to get a pilot approach to Environmental Studies under way. It seemed perfectly obvious to Dorothy and me that the best way to study an environment was to get out into it.

There was a moment of bewildering confusion when the students were asked to get their coats, as they had never before needed them until school was dismissed. The hall patrolmen glowered their disapproval at the students who babbled their confusion to each other amid their locker door version of the "Anvil Chorus." When they had finally gathered up their coats and returned to the room it occurred to someone to ask what we were going to do outside.

"We are going to go outside and photograph evidence of change."

"Photograph? You mean take pictures?"

"What are we gonna take pictures *with*?"

By this time Dorothy and I were un-

packing a half-dozen Polaroid Swinger cameras from a box we had carried in. I asked the students to divide up into five-man teams so that each team could have a camera. They quickly broke up into a reasonable facsimile of five-man teams, but the perfection of the symmetry was strongly influenced by personal friendships. There were six-man teams, three-man teams, and even one seven-man team. The students were all ready to argue the validity of their assemblage of teams but never had the chance to as we didn't complain about the unevenness of their grouping. Instead we passed out the cameras and film.

"Do you people know how to use these cameras?"

"Sure, man." And they reached out for them.

Armed with cameras and film, we left and locked the room, passed the glowering hall patrolmen, and proceeded out the locked school doors into the outside world. . . .

"Do you know how to load those cameras?"

"Yeah . . . sure."

With the students' assurance of expertise, Dorothy and I retreated to a neutral area and began an animated conversation that allowed us to watch the gaggle of confused students attempt to load the cameras. The frustration we experienced in trying to ignore the inept way these students proceeded with the task was excruciating. They had lied when they said they knew how to load the cameras, but they most vehemently wanted to succeed. Finally Tilford edged away from the group and approached us.

"This ain't the model I got at home."

"So?" I said.

"Can you load it for me?" he said.

"Sure." And I loaded the camera carefully, slowly, and even discovered I needed to check the procedure again so as to be sure it was correct. Tilford watched with a total kind of involvement. When I handed him the camera he went quickly back to the group and conducted an in-service course in loading Polaroid Swingers.

Everyone quickly became involved in taking pictures. They took pictures of each other, of the school grounds and of anything else that came into their minds. That is, everyone but Tilford. His leadership qualities were confined to getting everyone else going, but he wouldn't take a single picture of his own. When I asked him if he had taken any his answer was, "No . . . I'd just mess up."

"You'll what?"

"I'll just mess it up!" Tilford said. He looked at the ground. I grabbed as quickly as I could at the inadequate straws of my experience. I *knew* he could do it, but that suddenly became unimportant because I realized—*he didn't know he could do it!* I then became aware of the unused film in my right hand. I said as casually as I could:

"Hell, man . . . nobody can mess all this film up!"

It was as though everything became heavily weighted as in a dream and the world slowed to a stop. Tilford looked at me, then turned and took the camera from his group. He gestured to two girls and a boy and directed them into position, and then I think he smiled at me as he raised the camera to take their picture. I closed my eyes and prayed that if ever a picture turned out this one would . . . .

Currently a host of psychologists are vitally concerned with how people feel in the learning process. These psychologists, along with other varieties of social critics, have attacked the coercive institution called the school. Their argument is clear. They defend the students' right to "feel good" as well as to "know good." Some of those who have acted as spokesmen for this effort are John Holt, David Hawkins and Leonard Engle. All seemed to influence the pragmatic approach of Postman and Weingartner in their *Teaching as a Subversive Activity*. Their arguments can be summed up in the claim that school and what happens in it should be more compatible with the social and personal condition called *life*.

Meanwhile the ritualistic enterprise through which curriculum-makers inform young people of the structure of knowledge became known as the "new" in school. In addition, if it was "really new" its strategies and tactics were guided by cognitive psychologists who regimented not only what a person can know but how they can know it. All the while the murmuring group asking, "How do they feel?" began to get stronger.

Recently Dick Jones put a fine argument for the case in print with his *Fantasy and Feeling in Education*. Jones argued, as does Michael Polanyi in *The Tacit Dimension*, for that fantastic realm of intuitive knowledge that sculptures our preconscious thought processes. To put it more simply, we each have emotional-intuitive inputs into our lives as well as rational-logical inputs. Schools for generations have been concerned with that which was rational and logical. Jones and others are making a strong plea for allowing more access to the emotional and intuitive in the educational process. They argue that we should, in school as in life, allow the emotional self to be as apparent as the logical and rational self.

The sound of Tilford's camera shutter pealed like thunder above timberline. He seemed to take ages pulling the tab and picture pack from the Swinger. But when he did, I don't remember breathing for the ten seconds needed for the positive to develop. I swear he smiled at me before he stripped off his perfect portrait of Linda, Amelia and Ernie. He handed it to me with the pronouncement:

"How do you like that, man?"

"I guess that's pretty good." I grinned.

Arguments about what one can do to make a student feel better fall into two camps.

One group argues that, by predetermination, activities for the young can guide students into intellectual involvement that insures that the cognitive psychologists' intellectual progressions are met. These same theorists are convinced that the student's sense of self-worth is nourished by his ratio of success in conforming to the external intellectual criteria that they have in circular argument set up as standards for success.

The other camp is more suspicious. They argue that conformity to external criteria is a trivial indicator of personal success. This group argues that those qualities *inside* the child are more important than those outside the child. In essence their position is that, regardless of the nature of the external coercion, the important thing a child can know about himself is that which resists conforming for the purpose of sustaining personal honesty. The clichés put it this way: A child who knows himself will learn more capably than a child whose entire extrinsic response is toward adult coercion. That's a nice cliché, and it could easily be disproved if it weren't true. This internal or intrinsic group wants to see the fruition of the individual potential, aspiration and capacity in the presence of what happens to the child in the process of education.

As an example, students working in the presence of ambiguous assignments which require personal or intrinsic definition become quickly self-reliant. Their arguments become concerned with how to meet the constraints of the assignment as *they* see it, as opposed to how I (as teacher) see it. Upon getting involved in this fashion, the students all develop acumen in meeting the goals that each sets for himself.

The teacher's role is to focus on making each student reach in the direction in which he points. Since "change" provides conceptual as opposed to content constraints, the students have far greater degrees of freedom than otherwise. This tactic is compatible with the Environmental Studies approach. Ambiguity has a higher potential for relevance than does specificity. In the face of ambiguity concerning a conceptual topic (like "change"), a student has a far higher potential for serving his own (intrinsic) needs than he does if the teacher announces, "Go outside and get evidence of erosion." Erosion is content, whereas change is conceptual. Conceptual involvement is far less constraining than content.

Tilford then engaged in an activity that rejuvenated all my anxieties. He got involved with proving that the sun apparently moved. His technique was to go to the south side of the school and photograph the sun atop a steeple of a church adjacent to the school. He positioned himself so that the sun was directly aligned with the steeple. His next problem was to learn how to override the YES electric eye system of the camera so as to get an adequate picture of the sky and sun. He asked no one how to do this. It was all determined after a thoughtful stare at the camera mechanism. The proper adjustment was made and the picture was taken. It was beautiful. Intertwined among the lacy branches of November trees, the sun sat in a starburst pattern, perched upon the top of the church steeple. Immediately I wondered if Tilford would be clever enough to mark the point at which he took the photograph so he could return to it later. I almost started forward to tell him. But then he relieved my concern with a great smile across his face. . . .

Tilford (thirty minutes later) returned to the south side of the school. I had followed him and had promised myself that I would offer no cogent, adult, educated guidance (commonly called interference). I just stood there. Tilford looked at his first picture and sidled about on the sidewalk. Eventually he was happy with his position and he took the second picture of his sequence. He was sure he had photographic evidence the sun apparently changed its position in the sky.

I wanted, with my adult experience, to run up to Tilford and announce to him the names of the Greeks that had wrestled with the problems he had only moments ago confronted. I wanted to pour forth the rational verification of Tilford's intuition. I would have invoked the names of Eratosthenes, Ptolemy, Galileo, and even Brahe. But somehow I avoided the compulsion to inform Tilford that the brilliant insight he had just gained had preceded him by 2,000 years.

Somewhere down in my viscera I was able to avoid putting Tilford down by citing precedent. That history is replete with men who have thought our thoughts is no excuse for us to avoid thinking them. Minds explore independently of time. Only societies and historians are time-conscious.

The burning question is . . . *can curricula be written that can insure that we will create environments in which students can intrinsically emulate Eratosthenes, Ptolemy, Galileo and Brahe?* The evidence so far suggests that it is possible. We are hopeful that with appropriate admixtures of ambiguity and trust students will be able to re-create and procreate thought patterns that will accomplish two purposes. The first is that through involvement with actual and real environments the student can experience data sources that can promote the replication of classical scientific thought patterns. The second is that by utilizing primary sources of data, such as the actual environment, students will become more confident in themselves as instruments of inquiry.

The materials we hope to develop in the Environmental Studies program will reflect the notion that in true self-directed inquiry situations students have access to the entire process of research. Giving ambiguous directions such as, "Go out and photograph evidence of change," forces the student to begin the inquiry episode by making a series of decisions. He must decide on an operational definition of change, then decide what the evidence for that change is, and then attempt to photograph the evidence. Because "change" has more of a conceptual quality

as opposed to a content quality, the students' arenas of inquiry are less defined.

Such "forced" decision-making, in concert with the ambiguity of the assignment, quickly turns the effort into something that is more child-sponsored than teacher-sponsored. Although it is true that the initial assignment is a teacher-stated, extrinsically moderated directive, the students quickly take over.

Tilford's photographs were masterpieces of proof. By comparing the foregrounds of each of the pictures, it was clear that the branches of the trees were identically matched. He had returned to nearly the exact spot from which he had taken the first picture. I knew I wouldn't have attempted the same task without a tripod. In addition, the star-burst pattern of the sun had shifted appropriately to the right. Tilford had his proof.

The rest of Tilford's team used a variety of other techniques to prove the sun's apparent motion. He was active among the team members and assisted them in getting over hurdles of their own. They were all deeply engrossed in making marks on the sidewalk, photographing shadows and sketching shadow patterns on the side of the school building when a loud yell slammed down from above.

"Hey, you take my picture."

It came from one of several now open windows on the third floor of the sources of information. Even the cracks in sidewalks developed new meaning. In addition, they began alerting themselves to each other as people.

Did we succeed in any significant way? We cannot be sure, but we did feel pretty good when we discovered several members of the class *sneaking back into school to attend this one class each day.*

Robert E. Samples

---

school. Others chimed in with garishly animated gestures.

"Mee tooo."

"I'm beautiful."

"Look at me." It was obvious the teacher was out of the room, so I started to say something, but I was too slow!

"CLOSE THEM WINDOWS!" exploded from my right. It was Tilford. Let me tell you, THEM WINDOWS CLOSED. Tilford and some members of his group muttered among themselves about "them damn kids could queer this thing for us."

I didn't say anything. After the time we spent outside was finished we started back into the school. I noticed several of the class members picking up the debris from the Polaroid film wrappers. That's all they picked up, however. The school ground remained covered with trash and food wrappers, but they had picked up *their* mess.

All the students in the class accepted and demonstrated responsibility in a variety of ways. Other faculty members in the school had warned Dorothy and me that "these kids have no sense of responsibility. They will break or steal the cameras." Because of this we immediately gave the students the right to check out the cameras for home use. They could even take them home on weekends. We still have the original set of cameras . . . intact and working.

These early pilot efforts provided a basis for the work we are currently doing. With a sizable grant from the Polaroid Corporation, we equipped about 35 teachers in 20 cities across the country with pilot materials. At the briefing meetings we had with these teachers we were excited by the intensity of their concern about meeting the needs of the young. In our discussions we agreed that in free instructional environments the *real* needs of students would prevail. This had been proven in our experience with the inner-city ninth graders. None of these students asked questions about the management aspects of the class. No one wanted to know how we would grade. No one asked how lab reports should be filled in. No one asked about how he should organize his data. Instead they made all these decisions themselves and asked other kinds of questions such as these:

"How can I take two pictures on one?" (double exposure)

"How can I get pictures at night?"

"Where can I get a brick so I can find out how long it takes to wear down?"

"Where do they take all the garbage?"

"Can I take pictures of the stars to see if they move as fast as the sun?"

Somehow the experience left us with a warm conviction that school *can* be made more like life. The students had nurtured their interests and at the same time accumulated knowledge. By focusing on the immediate environment the students could return to their data sources if they needed more information. In doing so they began to be more alert to the nuances of strangeness in their commonplace environment. Bushes they had passed a hundred times became

The word "affect" is commonly thought of as a verb (e.g., something affects you); but "affect" is also a noun denoting that generic amalgam of feelings, emotions, and desires that resides in each of us. The degree to which affect determines a person's overt behavior varies greatly. At times, affective concerns may be at such low levels that they have no discernible impact on behavior. At other times, affective concerns may be so strong that the behavior they stimulate overpowers all efforts at self-control.

A teacher deals with affect in two general ways. First, he maintains an ongoing attitude of support, positive regard, and personal concern for his students. His actions say to them, "You are important to me; you are more to me than a homework doer or a test taker." Secondly, the teacher is not reluctant to discuss his students' affective concerns whenever they assume dominance of their thought and behavioral processes; in such cases, the teacher allows affect to become the subject matter (content) of the lesson.

Working with affect as content requires a commitment to a long established though seldom operationalized ordering of priorities that subordinates the acquisition of knowledge and the development of skills to the discussion of affective concerns whenever the latter become a dominant influence on classroom activity.

Tom Gregory

Dealing with Feelings

"The paraphrasing is probably a little trite, but, you really can't teach all of the people all of the time. Some of the people all of the time—yes. All of the people some of the time—maybe. But, all of the people all of the time—not even Superteacher pulls that off. What makes teaching so difficult and challenging is the human element. Teaching would be much easier if you didn't have to teach human beings. Humans have emotions. They love and they hate. They can feel irritable and resentful. And there are times when emotions, both pleasant and unpleasant ones, well up in an individual or a group, making concentration on Egypt or on binomials or even on the most exciting project difficult to impossible.

Sometimes the student's problem is so serious that a teacher can't help much, except maybe by letting the student know he's aware of it and that there's nothing abnormal about having a problem. Sometimes a student just needs to talk his feelings out and a teacher can become a person who listens, and who perhaps shares a time when he too had similar feelings.

Unfortunately, in the context of teaching, we generally lump all such incidents under the rubric of discipline. For most of us, "discipline" connotes all sorts of debilitating punishments like paddling, standing in the corner, or going to the principal's office. Worse yet the word "discipline" causes us to view such incidents as confrontations which teachers must win. When someone wins, someone else loses. The first step in avoiding this conflict is to be aware of it. Whatever else he is, a teacher can avoid being the nonperson who in effect says, "In my class you will not be human. You will not show emotions. All of you will do Egypt, or binomials, or whatever, at the time that I want them done.

For their own sanity, some teachers find it necessary to ignore all expressions of feelings or to squelch them immediately. Or they may set up a climate that strongly discourages such "disruptions" in the first place. Handling disruptive behavior is a tricky issue, too tricky to deal with adequately here. It is complicated by your purposes as a teacher, your stamina, your natural charisma, your tolerance for noise and distractions, the amount of student acquiescence you need to avoid feeling threatened, and the particular students with whom you are dealing, just to identify a few factors.

In the following experience we are focusing only on the style of teaching—or set of teaching acts—that enable a teacher to acknowledge and respond to student feelings and, ultimately, to help stu-

"dents cope with their feelings. These acts enable a teacher to deal with disruption and the associated emotions constructively (or at least nondestructively). How will you deal with feelings when they are disruptive?"

Mr. Brown: That Kenny! One of these days I'll kill him.

Mrs. Cohen: What has he done now?

Mr. Brown: Just tore his book up.

Mrs. Cohen: How come?

Mr. Brown: That's just it. I don't know. He's been working a lot better lately, untidy still, but better. And I went over to see how he was doing. They were writing a story, you know. I just suggested he try to keep the words touching the margin, and he jumped up in a great huff, tore his book in half, and threw it at me. Really, what can you do with a boy like that?

Mrs. Cohen: What did you do?

Mr. Brown: I told him to pick it up.

Mrs. Cohen: Did he?

Mr. Brown: Not likely. Just stood there and swore at me. Well I couldn't let that start again. I sent him to the office.

Mrs. Cohen: Did he go?

Mr. Brown: Yes, fortunately.

Mr. Brown is upset and he is puzzled. His relation with Kenny has obviously been improving of late and now, for apparently no reason, comes Kenny's outburst. At this point it would be usual to try to find the reasons for Kenny's outburst, whether it was provoked by Mr. Brown, and what Mr. Brown ought to have done. Let us suppose that the reasons could be discovered, it is very doubtful that they would really help Mr. Brown or Kenny. Instances are specific, and while perhaps over a period of time patterns of behavior are seen to emerge, nevertheless, the instance is unique, and it is precisely this with which Mr. Brown, and all teachers, have to cope. Reasons come in retrospect. They are not part of the happening as and when it occurs. So let us not try to probe and analyze the history of this incident, but take it as it is, and see where it is appropriate to go next. Mr. Brown seems indeed to have reacted in this way. Kenny tore his book, so now he must pick up the pieces. But this Kenny cannot do. Something for Kenny has been destroyed, and the literal pieces cannot be picked up until something inside Kenny can be reconstructed too. Thus there comes a point when Mr. Brown cannot go further in his relation with Kenny, and at that point he has to send Kenny away. It is precisely at that point that learning has to take place. It is the point at which Kenny has arrived, and he must be helped to go further. But there is apparently no conventional way Mr. Brown can give him that help. The point at which the student needs the teacher is the point at which the teacher is least able to help.

Anne and John Bremer

"We think the Bremers have a powerful idea when they talk about that crucial moment when a teacher thinks he has reached the limits of his ability to help a student and is left only with the question, "What more can I do?" If he can stop from throwing up his hands and turning his back on the student, if he can find one more way of responding, it may be the one more nudge that begins to break through the barricade and that allows him to help the student. Not incidentally, he too has learned something significant; he has grown as a teacher."

13

Dealing with Feelings: Doing It

An experience that allows you to try on the role of affective teacher—perhaps "helper" is a better decriptor for one using this style—and see how it fits.

A small-group experience. You'll need three or more people to role-play your students.

Dealing with feelings within our short lesson format requires that you use an entirely different approach to this lesson. Your "students" need to set up the incident in your absence. (Figuring out what the problem is, is half the fun.) Only one incident should occur in any one short lesson. It can be very subtle, like a student becoming increasingly bored or distracted, or very obvious, like a student doing or saying something that clearly implies some sort of problem. Positive expressions of feeling can also be incidents. In either case, your "student" must show his disinvolvement with the lesson and his involvement with his own behavior. Then you have to try to deal with the feelings generated.

Teacher: Bob, I've spoken to you twice already about your whispering while I'm speaking.

Bob: Bill just asked me a question.

T: But it seems to me you've been chatting all day. Is something the matter?

Bob: Nothin's the matter.

T: I feel awkward harping on this, but it really makes me angry when someone talks when I'm talking. I guess I feel insulted. Or perhaps, even teased. (Pause.) Can you tell me where you are with all this, Bob? (Silence.) I wonder what we can do? I sure don't like hassling with you. I feel like a nag. (Silence.) Well, let's put it aside for now. You look like you also feel it's a hassle. If I can think of anything we should do, I'll bring it up later. And, Bob, I want you to know that I'd be happy to talk with you alone at any time if you want me to. Now getting back to the lesson . . .

We suggest you consider these three approaches as you try to deal with your problem situation.

1. Clarify the problem. Who has it? Should you face it, or is it better left alone? Is it a temporary and non-serious issue that might disappear naturally? Is this student the only one involved, or is he the most obvious barometer of a general sentiment in the class?

   You may well need to collect this and other information. Too often, we act on premature judgments. Take your time. Perhaps, ask your students questions that will help you diagnose the best course of action. Remember that, at times, the best course of action may be to honor a student's need for privacy. Try to do so and still let him know you're quite willing

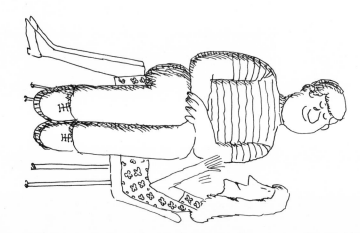

to help him in whatever way you can, whenever you can.

  Also bear in mind that very anti-social behavior sometimes occurs for very good reasons. Just because *how* a student has chosen to respond is inappropriate doesn't necessarily mean that *why* he is responding is unjustified. Try to avoid taking action until you have a clear picture of the problem.

2. Respond to the incident in a way that doesn't set the student up as a bad person, for that will probably make matters worse in the long run. (Don't make the situation a win-lose conflict between the two of you.) There are many ways to communicate disapproval of an act without communicating disapproval of a person. We'll suggest just three. Try to make one or more work for you.

a. You can empathize with the student. Try to understand and identify with what he is feeling and why he is feeling that way. Communicate that understanding to the student so he knows you understand. Then you might explore what you and he can do about the situation.

b. You can respect your students. Assume that each student is doing his best to act constructively within the context of his needs and perceptions. Assume that your students are willing to do what is best, if only they knew how to do it. This assumption won't always be accurate, but it's almost always the correct one to start with.

c. You can try to be genuine. Become more aware of your own feelings and how they affect your perceptions of and responses to situations. In many cases you can put your students at ease, and communicate your respect for them, by being honest and open about how you are presently feeling.

3. In some situations, extend the learning that takes place as a result of the incident. Not only can you help students become more conscious of their feelings and better able to verbalize them, but sometimes you can also bring them to a deeper understanding of these feelings. Not only can you assume that your students are trying to act constructively, but sometimes you can also help them find more mature ways of responding. Not only can you be aware of and describe your own feelings, but sometimes you can also move away from traditional role-defined behaviors and toward more fully human behaviors. But don't attempt to make a big lesson out of every little incident.

  Now, try to put together a creative lesson (in any style) and be ready to recognize, face, and perhaps reconcile any problem that makes it difficult for you to teach or for your students to learn during that lesson.

■ ■ ■

Here's some space in which you can review the lesson you have taught. You might also find the headings a useful guide for providing feedback to friends who elect to try on this style.

1. What was the problem?
_____
_____
_____
_____
_____

What kind of information did you collect?
_____
_____
_____
_____

2. How would you characterize your response?
_____
_____
_____
_____
_____

3. Did you extend the learning in any way?

4. Who learned what as a result of the incident?

5. Did the approach, the lesson, work? What's your evaluation? (See page 46.)

The realities of teaching—the overloaded classes, the endless demands, the sudden crises—make anger inevitable. Teachers need not apologize for their angry feelings. An effective teacher is neither a masochist nor a martyr. He does not play the role of a saint or act the part of an angel. He is aware of his human feelings and respects them. Though he cannot always be patient, he is always authentic. His response is genuine. His words fit his feelings. He does not hide his annoyance. He does not pretend patience. He does not demonstrate hypocrisy by acting nice when feeling nasty.

An enlightened teacher is not afraid of his anger because he has learned to express it without doing damage. He has mastered the secret of expressing anger without insult. Even under provocation he does not call children abusive names. He does not attack their character or offend their personality. He does not tell them whom they resemble and where they will end up.

When angry, an enlightened teacher remains real. He describes what he sees, what he feels, and what he expects. He attacks the problem, not the person. He knows that when angry, he is dealing with more elements than he can control. He protects himself and safeguards his students by using "I" messages.

"I am annoyed," "I am appalled," "I am furious" are safer statements than "You are a pest," "Look what you have done," "You are so stupid," "Who do you think you are?" . . . .

When teachers are angry, children are attentive. They listen to what is said. Teach-

ers have a unique opportunity to demonstrate good English. They can use their rich supply of English expressions to give vent to all nuances of anger: They can be uncomfortable, displeased, annoyed, irked, irritated, frustrated, aggravated, exasperated, livid, provoked, incensed, indignant, aghast, irate, angry, mad, furious, and enraged. They can be full of consternation, ire, and acrimony.

There are many more expressions of anger. Learning to use them is not easy, for the native tongue of lost tempers is insult. Yet, the salvation of communication between teacher and child depends on learning to express nuances of anger without nuances of insult. In learning this new method, teachers have a head start. Style flows from attitudes. Most teachers have the right attitudes and concern for children. All they need is a style of communication that demonstrates this concern.

Every teacher can develop an aversion to words that humiliate, acts that pain, and gestures that degrade. Even when enraged, a teacher can avoid the dictionary of denigration. These self-imposed restraints do not bring blandness of expression. On the contrary, they enhance a teacher's style. He learns to rely on a different tongue, one that voices anger vividly, fearlessly, and harmlessly. A teacher's motto is: Indignation—yes! Indignity—no!

Haim Ginott

83

I have taught in high school for ten years. During that time I have given assignments, among others, to a murderer, an evangelist, a pugilist, a thief, and an imbecile.

The murderer was a quiet little boy who sat on the front seat and regarded me with pale blue eyes; the evangelist, easily the most popular boy in school, had the lead in the junior play; the pugilist lounged by the window and let loose at intervals a raucous laugh that startled even the geraniums; the thief was a gay-hearted Lothario with a song on his lips; and the imbecile, a soft-eyed little animal seeking the shadows.

The murderer awaits death in the state penitentiary; the evangelist has lain a year now in the village churchyard; the pugilist lost an eye in a brawl in Hongkong; the thief, by standing on tiptoe, can see the windows of my room from the county jail; and the once gentle-eyed little moron beats his head against a padded wall in the state asylum.

All of these pupils once sat in my room, sat and looked at me gravely across worn brown desks. I must have been a great help to these pupils—I taught them the rhyming scheme of the Elizabethan sonnet and how to diagram a complex sentence.

Naomi J. White

The peculiar relation between teacher and pupil is an old mystery. If it is not like that between parent and child, lover and the beloved, master and servant, what is it? The terms "guide" and "midwife" are only two of many suggested to describe the essence of the relationship, and in some situations, such as the Socratic dialogue or the great research man and his graduate students, these metaphors are apt. But young pupils are not on journeys and are not pregnant with the kinds of ideas that require a Socratic midwife—at least it takes quite a stretch of the imagination to think of children's gropings in this way. In our time, perhaps, the professional-to-client relationship is more suggestive of what many in the educational enterprise seek. Students appreciate a relationship with someone who is concerned about them as individuals, but who does not consider them as psychological burdens or crutches. The occupant of such a role, however, needs not only time to think of pupils as individuals but also a theoretical understanding that does not confuse concern with sentimental identification. If his teaching resembles therapy, it cures through knowledge and insight. But first and last the teacher is responsible for instruction.

Harry S. White

We are teaching trivia.

Do not take my word. If you find the dose unpalatable, if you balk at the nauseous implications, try your pupils.

Watch the abler ones grow dull and apathetic, bored and lackluster, as they yawn and watch the clock over the stupid adventures of Muk-Muk the Eskimo Boy or Little Pedro from Argentina. Then, suddenly, as though opening an enchanted window upon a radiant pageant, give them the story of the wrath of Achilles. Let them stand with Casablanca upon the burning deck. Trek with them in spirit to the Yukon, and with glorious Buck let them answer the call of the wild. Place them upon the shot-swept shrouds of the *Bonhomme Richard*, and let them thrill to those words flashing like a rapier out of our past, "I have not yet begun to fight." Kneel with them behind the cotton bales at New Orleans with Andy Jackson at their side as the redcoats begin to emerge from the mist of the Louisiana swamps and the sullen guns of Lafitte begin to pound.

Watch their faces.

See the eyes brighten and the spirits ruffle. See the color come, the backs straighten, the arms go up. They dream, they live, they glow.

This is teaching. This is what you trained to do. You have done what any teacher worth his salt would mortgage his future to achieve, and you have set the ardent, selfless joy of learning flaming in those eager faces.

Thus you may hurl the eternal lie into the teeth of those who decry the significance of subject matter, who sneer at history and poetry and mythology and all those magical creations of the human mind which have raised man to a place a little lower than the gods.

Let us lift our heads. Let us say to these diluters of curricula, these emasculators of texts, these mutilators of our past, "We have had enough of you. The world is weary of you. The stage is ready for new actors. With your jargon of behaviorism and Gestalt and topological vectors and maturation levels, you have muddied the clear waters of childhood long enough. You have told us to teach the whole child, but you have made it impossible to teach him anything worth learning. Little by little you have picked the meat from the bones of Education and replaced it with Pablum. You have done your best to produce a race of barely literate savages."

Max Rafferty

PEANUTS

I'M WORRIED ABOUT A LITTLE BOY WHO SITS IN FRONT OF ME AT SCHOOL...

HE CRIES EVERY DAY... THIS AFTERNOON I TRIED TO HELP HIM.... I WHACKED HIM ONE ON THE ARM...

YOU WHACKED HIM ONE ON THE ARM?!

I THINK IT HELPED...

THERE'S NOTHING LIKE A LITTLE PHYSICAL PAIN TO TAKE YOUR MIND OFF YOUR EMOTIONAL PROBLEMS...

SCHULZ

He was aching to get to the faculty lunch-room for some coffee and a buttermilk doughnut, but when the period ended Janet Horner was at his desk saying, "Do you know why I didn't have my homework today?"

Her tone was challenging. She was smiling stiffly, as if trying to show every tooth she had, but Ernie could see the tears welling in her eyes.

"We have to do homework," said Ernie.

"I can't work in that place. I try hard, but it's impossible."

"What place?"

"Our house."

"What's wrong?"

Still smiling the forced, almost insane smile, as though she were about to scream, she said, "They're going to drive me out of my mind. I honestly don't know what to do."

Ernie sat down behind his desk, trying to forget the coffee. Janet sat down on the seat facing him.

"Who is trying to drive you out of your mind?"

"My crazy parents. Last night I was home, in my room, trying to do the assignment. They started an argument. I don't know what it was about, I never do, and I don't care, but then they came into my room and dragged me out and then they dragged my sister out of her room, and we're all in the living room, yelling at each other. The maid was in her room with ear plugs in, I guess. My mother runs into the den and brings out old income tax returns, for the past ten years, and starts shoving them in my sister's and my face, and then the old boy runs in and gets a stack of bills and shoves them in our faces."

"Why?"

"I don't know. They're loaded with loot. They really are. Every week they change the drapes and bedspreads in our rooms, so that we come home from school and never know if we're in the right room, and I've said a million times all I want is white. White! They've stuffed our closets so full of clothes I get a stomach-ache trying to decide what to wear to school, and whatever I choose, they think I should wear something else.

"Anyhow, we're there yelling at each other and they won't let me get back to my home-work. In the middle of all this, my mother says to me, 'Janet, you can have your tonsils out if you want to. Just pick a day and we'll arrange everything. Wouldn't you like to have your tonsils out?'"

"Have you been having trouble with your tonsils?" asked Ernie.

"No! She's crazy. So is he. You know what they did? They put a sound alarm on my windows. Not for burglars. For me! They don't want me to escape during the night. Lucky I have my own bathroom, because I ran in there and locked the door behind me, but they were outside yelling in, and who can study on a bathroom floor? That's where I finally went to sleep. And I want to get straight A's this semester. How am I going to do it?"

"I'd forget about school if I were you and run away from home."

As soon as he had said it, he was frightened, frightened at how easily he had said something. "Unprofessional" to a student. Her fierce smile faded and her face relaxed into something soft and sincere.

"That's the first time I ever heard honest advice from a teacher," she said.

Darryl Ponicsan

❚❚We can all help it not be the last. We think you'll find that David Nyberg's short statement on page 17 will really hit home now. Why don't you go back and read it once more?**❚❚**

Enriching Humanness

❚❚The teacher who wishes to enrich humanness in his classroom not only deals with subject matter but also sets up many other positive experiences. What Jerry did with the magic circle back on page 52 is one example of a teacher initiating a situation in which kids can grow. Some of the getting-acquainted activities we suggested in Part I of this book are others.

If you think that your job as a teacher is to do more than teach subject matter to kids—that it includes helping kids form more positive self-concepts and more effective interpersonal skills, for example—you will want to try on some of these teaching acts. These acts foster growth toward a more effective, fully functioning, self-actualizing humanness. Sometimes this means taking time to see that the day-to-day procedures we use in the classroom are the most pleasant (or least unpleasant). At other times it means switching the content from academics to ourselves as persons.

We like to do an exercise with our students that relates to this issue. Unfortunately it does not transfer into print very well, but we hope that by describing the exercise you'll be able to get the idea. Better yet: try following these directions with a friend and feel the idea.

Sit face to face, a few feet apart. One of you plays teacher; the other, student. The teacher holds up a piece of paper at arms length, so that he cannot see his student. The paper is your "subject matter." Now try talking to each other. Like most, you'll probably find that certain kinds of talk feel fairly comfortable. For example:

Teacher: How are you doing on _this_ (subject matter)?

Student: Not so well. I think if you could present _it_ differ-ently it would help.

Teacher: Would _it_ help if we looked at _it_ this way?

As long as the teacher focuses on how well the student is doing with _it_ and the student focuses on how well the teacher is teaching _it_, having an _it_ between you works out pretty well.

But now try talking about more personal matters, perhaps your worries or hopes, with _it_ still up there between you. You'll probably feel much more awkward.

Most teachers respond to this awkwardness by concluding that personal matters are inappro-priate. What we're suggesting is that they're not at all inappro-priate, that the problem exists because you're trying to function on a more personal level with that _it_ still between you. There are *times when it's asinine not to drop that damn piece of paper. That's what this style is all about—dropping traditional subject-related tasks from time to time and replacing them with interpersonal, process-related tasks. Or, referring to our little exercise, the equivalent of placing the piece of paper on the side. There's still an $\underline{it}$ there, but it's in a position where you can work on $\underline{it}$ together, or where the teacher can see the student work on $\underline{it}$ and help him the best he can, or where $\underline{it}$ can be ignored for a while, as we believe it should when something more central to the persons involved comes up.*"

14

Enriching Humanness: Doing It

An experience that allows you to try initiating experiences that will facilitate your students' personal growth and to see how this style fits.

A small-group experience. You'll need three or more people to role-play your students.

Developing a lesson that has the potential to enrich humanness may be difficult if you've had few such lessons "taught" you along the way. Here is one way to develop a lesson in this style.

1. First, create or borrow an experience that has the potential to allow students to examine, evaluate, or share an aspect of their humanness. (Once in a while it's even possible to have this experience relate to subject matter in some way, but that need not be a primary concern here.) Here are some examples:

   ■ Dig out an object from your pocket or wallet of which you are proud. Sit in small groups and share with others that one thing of which you're proud.
   ■ Which would be hardest for you: To be a prison guard? To be a routine assembly-line worker? To try to collect bad debts from poor people who bought encyclopedias? Each person writes down these three in the order that they would be hardest for him. Put the hardest first. Then compare the lists.
   ■ Who had a dream recently that they remember? How many remember a scary dream? Will anyone share a dream?
   ■ Sit in trios. Each person talks on the topic you call out. If each has already had a turn before you call out the next topic, just continue to discuss the issue informally. (Call out topics such as: Things I hate to do. Difficult problems I faced. The first time I rode a bike. Capital punishment.)

2. Engage your students in the experience and help them become comfortable with it. The key here is a supportive atmosphere, and perhaps a comment on the rationale for the experience—that it's useful to spend time once in a while getting to know ourselves and each other.

3. Help your students draw their own conclusions from the experience. Help each student establish his own personal meaning out of what has taken place, and be able to accept that meaning. Also help a student find ways of changing himself, if he concludes that that is important. Being supportive and non-judgmental is critical for these acts.

Alternatively, you could try an approach that does not make life or persons the content of the lesson, like those above, but that makes *process* the content. You might, for example, discuss with your students how well previous lessons have met their needs, or what kinds of feelings your teaching has generated in them, or what ambivalences they experienced as you taught. Or you might help them see how they could be more effective as learners in general. Or you might construct a lesson to show them the benefits of effective group work or cooperative learning.

Whatever you do, remember the aim is to enrich humanness, enhance the classroom atmosphere, or otherwise help people grow. Now, try to put together a short lesson in this style. See how it feels to you.

• • •

Here's some space in which you can think through the lesson you have taught. You might find the headings a useful guide for providing feedback to friends who elect to try on this style.

1. How did the experience allow your students to focus on their humanness?

_____
_____
_____
_____
_____
_____

2. How comfortable were your students
   with the experience?

_____
_____
_____

3. Were conclusions drawn?

_____
_____
_____

4. Did the style, the lesson, work? What's
   your evaluation? (See page 46.)

_____
_____
_____

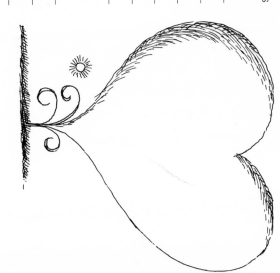

There are two notorious boxes.... One is the Quincy Box, which is a name school architects and school planners have given to the dimensions of the classrooms in the first fully graded American school, built in Quincy, Massachusetts: it is still determining the looks, functions, and character of schools in this country. The other is the Black Box, which is the name some psychologists have given to that part of us that somehow mediates between a stimulus and a response or between a sensory perception and an interpretation or between a sensory perception and a consequent extrasensory or asensory perception. In other words, it's what people actually do inside.

A third box is what people refer to when they say, "Don't get personal" or "My feelings have nothing to do with this; stick to the subject." I call this the Shadow Box. Some people think that only licensed medical or psychological persons should be privy to the contents of Shadow Boxes. These people are, of course, Shadow Boxers. They are the ones who have a suspicious view of their brothers and who believe that to be open among them is not only foolish but masochistic. The result is a boxed-in, self-protective person who is perceived by others as a predator, behind whose silent nervous gaze lies the mystery of his power. When will he pounce? Do not provoke him, fear him.

A Black Quincy Shadow Box is a typical American schoolroom, which has things going on inside that nobody understands and which is full of people who are afraid of each other but won't admit it.

What are the mysteries of this triply closed box and what skills and knowledge do we need to open it?

David Nyberg

"What courage do we need, David? What courage?"

Teachers have been accused of not caring about the emotional difficulties of their pupils (a deficiency in philetics) and that this deficiency is the major obstacle to pupils' wanting to learn. Even if this were true, which I doubt, it does not follow that the care and concern a teacher ought to have for a pupil is that of a doctor (mental or physical) for a patient. Bad tonsils may also make a pupil hostile to learning, but the teacher is not therefore charged with removing the tonsils before trying to teach arithmetic; yet something quite analogous is expected in mental and psychic indispositions. The care and concern that can be demanded of a teacher is for the pupil as a learner, a potential learner; the frustrations he is accountable for are the frustrations caused by inappropriate tasks; and the major character malformation the pupil has the right to be protected from is that which results from being allowed to get away with much less than he can really do.

"...and, if we are to believe Broudy, the teacher is allowed to get away with teaching much less than he really can."

Harry S. Broudy

Feelings are essentially unteachable. They can not be passed along from teacher to learner in the way that information is transmitted. Nor can the learner acquire them by pursuing them directly as he might acquire understanding by study. Feelings are almost always the consequence of something—of success or failure, of duty done or duty ignored, of danger encountered or danger escaped. Further, good feelings (and bad feelings also, fortunately) are seldom if ever permanent possessions. They tend to be highly ephemeral. The surest prediction that one can make when he feels particularly good, strong, wise, or happy is that sooner or later he is going to feel bad, weak, foolish, or sad. In these circumstances it is hardly surprising that feelings are difficult to teach.

Nor do they need to be taught. A new-born infant has, or quickly develops, a full complement of them—pain, rage, satiety, drowsiness, vitality, joy, love, and all the rest. Experience may attach these feelings to new objects. It may teach the wisdom of curbing the expression of certain feelings at inappropriate times or in inappropriate ways. And while such attachments and curbings may be desirable, and may be seen as part of the task of the school, they hardly qualify as one of its major missions.

The school has in fact a much more important educational mission than affective education, one which in the current cultural climate and educational fashion is being badly neglected. I refer to moral education—the inculcation in the young of the accumulated moral wisdom of the race. Some of our young people have been allowed to grow up as virtual moral illiterates. And as Joseph Junell points out . . . we are paying a heavy price for this neglect as the youth of our society become alienated, turn to revolt, and threaten the destruction of our social fabric.

Robert L. Ebel

As we reconsider the second paragraph of this reading, we endorse Ebel's notion of the importance of experience in helping us cope with our feelings. But can we leave the nature and number of those expe-riences to chance? And should we ignore those experiences that occur spontaneously before our very eyes? Can we pretend we've dropped our feelings in a box at the schoolyard gate, to be picked up as we exit at day's end?

Finding the right balance is never easy; there will always be a certain tension between two groups of educational objectives—those concerned with individual growth and fulfillment, and those concerned with the transmission of specific skills, intellectual disciplines, and bodies of knowledge—and finding the "right" balance is neither easy nor obvious. In the older American progressive schools, the balance certainly needed to be tipped toward the cognitive; in most of American schools today, as Geoffrey Caston of the Schools Council, a leading figure in curriculum reform in England, argues, on the basis of extensive visits, "the need is to tip it very strongly back toward the affective." In doing so, there is a risk of tipping too far; fortunately, the people in charge of most of the current experiments in informal education seem to be well aware of the danger.

Charles E. Silberman

15

Drawing Conclusions

A way to build on the "trying on" experiences you've had in this part of the book.

A small-group experience. Requires about thirty minutes. The participants should be the "students" who observed or participated in at least one of your lessons.

We've presented you with five different styles of teaching. We hope you've looked at yourself as a teacher in the context of at least three of them. That may not be very much data, but it's better than no data. How has your image of yourself as a teacher changed as a result of these experiences? Or if it remained the same, how has your image been reinforced? In what ways has the image become more clearly drawn? You might find the following experience helpful as you consider these questions. As you proceed, bear in mind our earlier caution against thinking of yourself or your friends exclusively in terms of one or two styles.

1 Write down a list of statements that you think describe you as a teacher. Then, number the statements according to how accurately they reflect your image. Number "1" the statement you feel is most accurate—down

the line to the last statement, the one you're least sure of. Make two or three copies of your list.

2 Get together with one or more friends who have been a part of your teaching group, and distribute copies of your lists.

3 Read all the lists. Add statements about each person's teaching that you think may have been overlooked. Then try to help the person relate any add-on statements to his sure-unsure continuum.

4 Sit as a group and listen as each person answers the following questions: Did others see you as a teacher in ways that you were largely unaware of? Did others make very different kinds of statements than you did? Did you and/or others describe you largely in terms of weaknesses or in terms of strengths? Did you and/or others describe you more as a person or as a teacher? Did you and/or others focus on how you handle subject matter, or on how you relate to students, or . . .? What, if any, conclusions can you draw from this experience?

Let me use this example also to show you why you cannot tell the difference between the good ones and the poor ones on the basis of the methods which they use. Take two teachers, each of whom believes children are "able." Now one of these teachers, because she believes the children are able, makes them work real hard because she knows they can and the message that gets through is, She thinks I can. She is tough. Here is another teacher who also believes the children are able, but she says to them, "You know that is an interesting idea, why don't you take the rest of the afternoon to work on it by yourself?" She is a softy. Now here are two widely different methods, both of them used by good teachers. The important question is not what they are doing but the *message that is conveyed* by what they are doing, and the message comes from their beliefs, not what they did. In each case the same message gets through, "She thinks I can, she has confidence in me. She believes I am able." The important question we have to look at is the message that is conveyed by what people do rather than the things which they say.

There is an old Indian saying, "What you do speaks so loudly, I can't hear what you say." And that is true; the beliefs you have betray you in spite of yourself. Not long ago I was listening to a psychiatrist who was talking about the difficulties he had with some kinds of patients who came to his office. "I don't seem to be getting the kind of results that you people are getting," he said. "I believe in the same kind of therapy that you do. I believe in the dignity and integrity of my clients and I believe that the client

ought to be helped to find his own answers," and so on. Then, when he was through with all this, he said, "I have great difficulty in *making my patients understand*." His real belief shows in spite of the fact that he knows the right words to say. His behavior is a function of the belief system which he has.

In research after research the good helpers all turn out to believe people are able and dependable and friendly and worthy and dignified and persons of integrity and value. The poor ones come out on the other side of that picture. You might ask yourself, do I really believe that people are really dependable?

Arthur Combs

Well..do you? You might find it valuable to go back to page 52 after reading Combs and sample again Friedman's ideas about man's image of man. It may mean even more to you now.

IV

People and Things That Help and Hurt

Do you function best inside or outside the system (any system)?

Can you put up with "people"—kids, parents, professionals?

Can you put up with "things"—the institution of school?

Can you find realistic ways to make schools better?

" Teachers don't work alone. They work with many other people. Some of these people allow them and even help them become better people and better teachers. Some don't. The question is, can you find ways to beneficially tap the kids and parents and other administrators that are available, willing, and able to help you? And conversely, can you find ways to coexist with these people if you find them personally dysfunctional? Or are you, as Cleaver put it, likely to become part of the problem rather than part of the solution? In this part we put together a "people" section with the hope that it would help you begin to sort out these kinds of personal and professional issues.

Then there is the issue of "the school". We wish we could wave a magic wand and eliminate whatever repressiveness the institution of school fosters. We can't–of course and maybe we don't need to. Some schools are really very pleasant places in which to teach and learn, but others aren't. Whatever the case, becoming a good teacher involves picking a spot where you can become a good teacher. In this part we put together a "things" section with the hope it would help you to pick that school. Or find out that no such school exists—for you anyway.

We'll try to depict the reality of the "people" and the "things" as it exists, in all its diversity, in the schools. Teaching at times has its romantic side. It is delightful suddenly to realize that you've had a big impact on some students, or that a student really looks up to you or trusts you. Somehow though, that doesn't happen enough. Or all the other pains that can be a part of teaching too often blind us to those good things. Whatever the cause, teaching very often seems to be just plain, hard, unrewarding work. It may help you, as you decide about teaching, to view the job stripped clean of much of the romance that can enshroud it. We'll try to help you do that in this part.

What we're really trying to impress upon you here is the importance of measuring yourself, your abilities and limitations, your values and aspirations, against all the people and forces, both positive and negative, that are part and parcel of teaching. You've seen a lot of schools and the people in them. But that view has been mainly through a student's eyes. The view from the other side of the desk can be very different, and it may be useful for you to develop it here.

If you want more than the clarity that comes from casual dabbling with ideas in this part, you might write some "I learned" statements as you go along, when an insight comes to you, perhaps about the kind of school you would like to work in, or what you want to do as a teacher, or not do, or how you want to react to people or educational forces.

Keep the sentences in a notebook, changing them, adding to the list as new personal conclusions (however tentative) emerge. Or write them on these pages, as they occur to you. Then, from time to time, you might sit with one or two friends and share your thoughts.

Move into this part with a notebook in hand, capturing your personal learnings. What you want to remember—about people and things that can help and hurt teachers (you)—can yield a useful harvest when the time comes for you to decide about teaching. **"**

It takes a mathematical wizard to handle the money that is placed on a first-grade teacher's desk almost any morning. I am not conceited, but I can do it. . . .

The first graders came in loaded with cash. They knew the routine. One by one, they came by the left side of my desk, each clutching a fistful of money and notes from mother.

Jimmy was first in line. He had two $5 bills pinned to a note from his mother. The note said he had two day's milk money already paid (left over from last week), but he wanted to buy a lunch ticket for $3, pay another $3 for his pictures, give 10¢ to the Multiple Sclerosis Fund, pay $1 for his school supplies, pay three day's milk money, and buy three tickets to the AAUW plays for $1.50. A postscript asked me to keep the change until the end of the day.

I took all the change from my purse and laid it on my desk. I was surely going to need it. I made the proper change for Jimmy, and wrote down in my little book where every cent was to go. There! So far, good!

Susan came around to the right side of my desk. "Teacher, did you like the earrings I brought you Friday?"

"Please get back in line, Susan." I was too busy making change to look up.

Linda was next in line with a $5 bill. Linda didn't have a note, because she knew where her money was to go. "Teacher, I want to pay $3 for my pictures, 30¢ for lunch today, buy the three tickets to the plays, and give the rest to you for the school supplies." Adding mentally, I said, "But that's not enough—" Linda interrupted, "Mother says I don't use a dollar's worth of paper a month anyway."

I gasped and took the money. That line looked endless, and I didn't have time to explain about school supply money right now. Besides, we had sent home letters at the beginning of school explaining what that money was to be spent for.

Janice was next. She didn't have any money except her dollar for school supplies. But she said, "Mrs. Brummett, Mommy said you were wrong about my IOU Friday. I did, too, have 30¢. I laid it right here on your desk on top of a book.

I stared and tried to remember. Well, maybe she did.

Now came Richard. His money was in an envelope. His mother wrote instructions as to where his money was to go. Then she added that his morning milk was already paid for a month. I looked it up. It was, indeed.

"Mrs. Brummett, did you really like those earrings I brought you?" Susan had slipped up to my right again.

"Yes, I did. But we'll discuss that later, Susan." I sounded cross even to myself.

Just then, the school secretary called me on the loud speaker. "Mrs. Brummett, did you turn in your Red Cross money last Friday?" Holding up my hand, I stopped the first-grade line. Did I turn it in? I couldn't remember, but I searched the middle drawer of my desk. In the thumbtacks box I found three dimes and eleven pennies. I put these in an envelope, along with two dimes I found lying loose, and sent them to the office.

Now Edward's voice rang out loud and clear. "Teacher, can I call Mother?"

Again I didn't look up. "May I?" I corrected him. "No, you may not call your mother." I kept making change.

"But, Teacher, look!"

Sensing the urgency in Edward's voice, I looked. A red rash covered his face and neck. Too rushed to risk even a teacher's diagnosis, I wrote him a note to use the telephone. I was red-faced myself by now, but finally I breathed a sigh of relief. At last, the end. Every child and his money was accounted for.

Now, to distribute the money. There was one envelope for the play money, another for the Multiple Sclerosis Fund, and still another for the lunch tickets. . . .

Beatrice Brummett

❚❚ We understand that a minor in accounting is now recommended for all elementary education majors. **❚❚**

People . . . . .

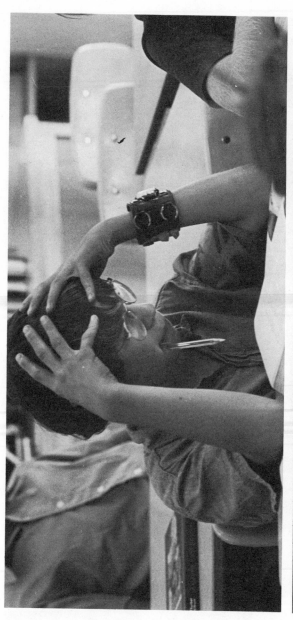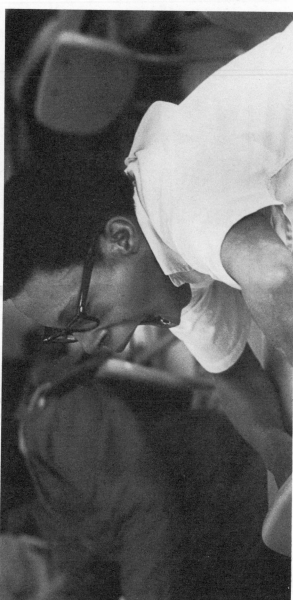

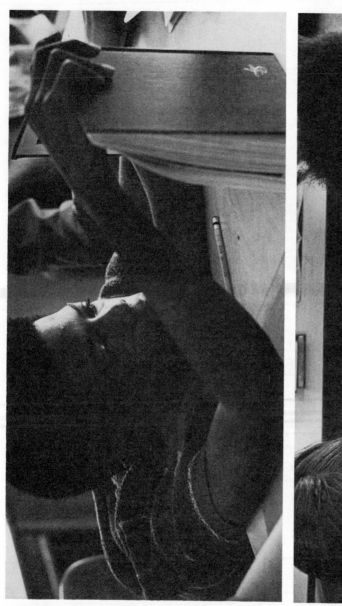
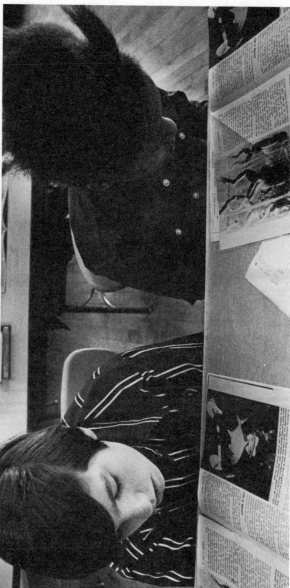

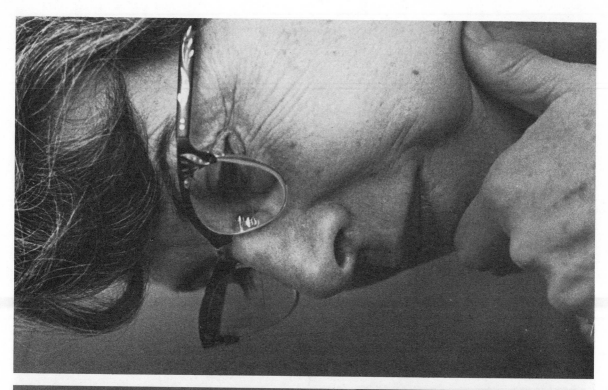

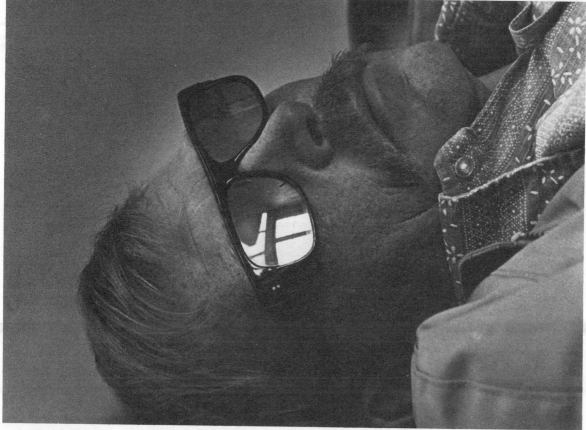

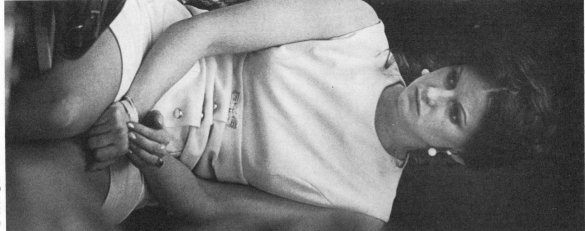

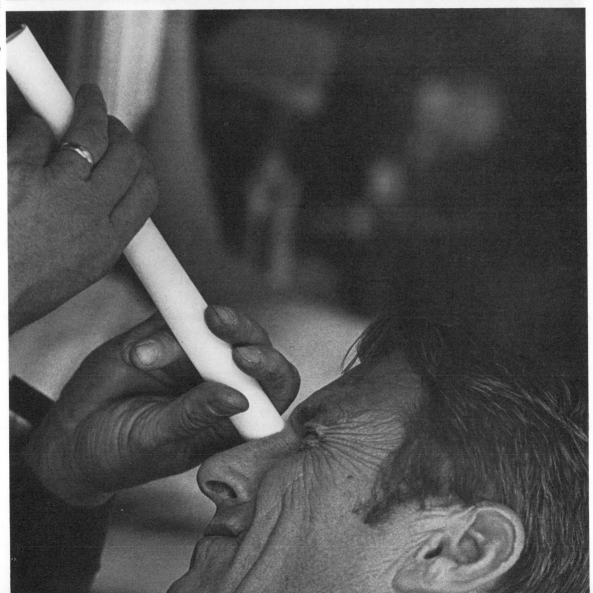

16

What'll We Say After We've Said, "Hello"?

An experience of being with a young person that promotes a relationship of equality and openness because you are prohibited from using customary adult strategies for controlling conversations.

A self-directed experience. Requires little or no group time.

To get a better sense of what younger people are like and how you feel with them, try spending from one hour to one day with a young person of about the age you think you'd like to teach.

There's one basic rule: You can't ask questions. The question is often the adult's tool for directing a child's mind. In that sense, to question is to control. Without the power of asking questions, we are more likely to see where children are and to hear what they are saying. And, incidentally, we are in a better position to answer *their* questions.

Find a young person with whom you can spend time. The group might gather kids from neighbors and relatives and exchange them, so that each person is paired with someone he does not know. Oftentimes, arrangements

for this experience can be made through a local school or through another institution that serves young people.

What we're suggesting is, indeed, a tough task. You might find it useful to think of two or three ways to begin the conversation without asking a question. Would you be comfortable first in saying something about yourself? Or remaining silent and letting your new friend take the lead? Or dropping all pretense by saying, "I'm trying to learn about teaching and about myself and about you. To do that, I've decided to try to talk with you without asking any questions. Silly, but that's what I'd like to try. I think I may have trouble doing it without some help from you."

...

After such a non-questioning interaction with a young person, share your experiences and perceptions with some friends.

- How many found it very difficult to keep from asking questions?
- How many succeeded in asking absolutely no questions?
- How many felt uncomfortable with their young person?
- How many felt very comfortable?
- How many learned from the experience?
- What did you learn?

Helps

A smile
Handshakes
Compliments
A kiss
When others are
  happy it makes
  you happy
A laugh
A note or card to
  let you know
  others are
  thinking of you
The right tone of
  voice
A telephone call
A nod of the head
Spankings
An excuse to do
  what you want
  to do

Hurts

When somebody
  snubs you
Interruptions
People staring at
  you
Discourtesy
A stern look
An evil eye
Sneers
Spankings
Talking behind
  your back
When someone
  tells on you
Being hit by
  somebody
Saying bad things
  about you
Being ignored

Jacqueline Murphy
What Helps and Hurts
(according to seventh-grade students)

Miss Murphy,
how did you get
attention when
you were
young and how
do you get it
now

Jane

Please Read

The person in front
of me is cutting some
farts I can not
stand it

" Well, teacher, what do you do
now? **"**

Kari obviously has begun to reject elements of the role that she has inherited. She watches fads drift like culture clouds across the scene. She sees paisley print blouses give way to ragged tennis shoes. None of these elements of controlled change apply, for they are not relevant to her. She appears strange to the conformity-cloistered society around her, for it sees her respond to herself rather than to its collective voice. She creates a guilt in the cliché-makers which they transform to resentment for their own self-preservation. They decide that she is the element of abnormality and ply her toward the norm. Her resistance is interpreted as immaturity and stubbornness that must be overcome. . . .

In a line of poetry she once wrote, Kari claimed that "Before you can love you must know how to walk in the snow leaving no tracks." She knew the thrill of dashing chaotically through a virgin field of snow. In addition, she knew the excited fulfillment of willing abstinence. Both of these ideas were synthesized into the beautiful statement that applied to all love.

Kari is sixteen and growing up. . . . We need the Karis, all of them, but how can they be saved?

Robert E. Samples

1. walk barefoot
2. play my harp
3. fly kites
4. spend money
5. get high
6. feel the wind
7. talk to people
8. give myself to others
9. cook
10. wear freaky clothes to straight places
11. touch
12. laugh
13. hitchhike
14. meet new people
15. run through the woods
16. read
17. talk politics
18. eat chocolate mandarin sherbet
19. help
20. be me

A fourteen-year-old boy's response to, "Make a list of 20 things you like to do."

17

Shadowing a Student

An informative way to look at a student and a school and the way they interact.

A self-directed experience. Requires one school day, plus some group time to interact with others.

This is a rather simple but surprisingly enlightening activity. Get permission from a school to follow one of its students through an entire school day. A sample procedure for the day:

- Arrive at the school at least fifteen minutes before its starting time.
- Pick a student at random from the school's files and copy down his schedule for the day.
- Go to the student's first-period class.
- Ask the teacher to identify your student for you.
- Do your best not to let the student know that you're following him.
- As unobtrusively as possible, follow the student throughout the entire day, including lunch.
- Every ten minutes, jot down a brief answer to two questions: What's going on in the room at that point in time? What is your student doing? (See page 110 for an example.)
- At the end of the day, introduce yourself

to your student and ask him whatever questions you think will further your understanding of the student, his behavior, and the school. Show the student your log if he's interested and let him tell you what was *really* going on.

• • •

Share your experiences with others in your group who have also shadowed a student.

- What most surprised you from the day's experience?
- What conclusions do you draw about the impact of the school on your student?
- To what degree was the student involved with school life?
- What implications for you as teachers are suggested by the sum total of your several experiences?

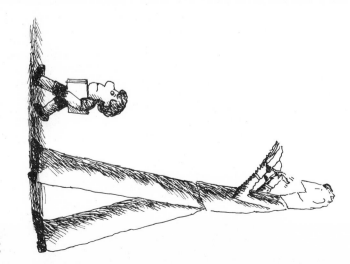

Time & Location	Behavior	Environment
9:40 Science Mr. M.	Bob sat quietly, listened, and followed directions.	Teacher, Mr. M., also homeroom teacher, started by going over science vocabulary on board. Quick review. Pleasant. Joked with students.
	Passive participation. Bites lips, fingernails.	Text assignment, pages 336–73. (Read: "How Do Living Things Reproduce Without Seeds?") Room rich in students' work. Science current events, charts, much NDEA equipment. Well-equipped. Went over new words before the reading began.
9:50	Sat, listened.	Interrupted to read notices. Teacher decided which words would be "strange." Bulbs, stems, roots. Almost twenty minutes devoted to explanation of new words. Filmstrip: *Kinds of Plants*. Used student operator. Reviewed some work covered last year.
10:00 Science	Cleaned eyeglasses. Listened. Seemed to have difficulty *seeing*. Kept adjusting glasses. Stretched, yawned, smiled at teacher's humor. Rested head on desk. Stretched out legs. Slumped further down in seat.	Teacher, with pointer, pointed out highlights of filmstrip frames. Explained—answered questions. Skipped frames involving reading. Instead the teacher explained. Teacher admitted he did not know whether ____ had a nucleus; said he would find out.
10:10	Answered questions asked by the teacher. (One-word answers.) Stretched after filmstrip. Looked at projector and boy rewinding the filmstrip. Talked awhile to two boys near him.	Mushrooms and toadstools. One student described the differences. Teacher asked, "Is this 100 percent true?" Asked if there were any questions. Noise—teacher became firm.

Time & Location	Behavior	Environment
10:20 Art Mr. S.	Picked up box of colored pencils to work with. Outlined large face with pointed hat on head. Hat looked like a pagoda perched on head.	Teacher wearing "shop" apron; sleeves rolled up. He is a young man; appeared not to be interested in his work. Did not seem to like students. Seemed more interested in having everyone busy, quiet, and following directions. Students entered room and took their seats. Mr. S. said, "This is going to be a general drawing period. Those of you who are not finished with woodcuts, work on them. The rest of you try to finish a picture. Stay away from pastels. If you finish ahead of time, use the rest of the period for study. I want to see everyone working this period."
10:30	Bob worked bent over, very close to his paper. Shared pencils with boy sitting in front of him. Bob worked very slowly; carefully studied his efforts, then did a little more. Compared drawing with boy in front of him.	"Who told you to move?" the teacher shouted across the room to a student who had moved. Students went to front of room for materials. A little noise. Teacher blew whistle for order. About six students asked where the compasses were. Teacher replied, "They've either been broken or stolen." Some students doing woodcraft. Some worked with water colors; some developed geometrical designs; some worked with colored pencils and crayons. Little display of students' work around room.

Time & Location	Behavior	Environment
10:40 Art	Bob's drawing was turning out to be the head of a clown. (Circus coming to town today; students being dismissed early to attend.) Talked to boy in front of him. Continued to draw. Seems to enjoy what he is doing. The face of the clown is a laughing one. Very thick lenses (Bob's glasses). At times his head is no more than 4 to 5 inches from the paper.	Teacher continued to bark orders. He leaned on a table at the rear of the room. Once or twice he walked around the room. (One boy was not doing art. Instead he was copying a book report which he had borrowed from a girl in another class.) Girls giggled; teacher shouted, "Come on, girls; let's not be silly back there." (At this point the teacher was sitting at his desk working on a design on a sheet of paper.)
10:50	After finishing basic picture, Bob kept adding a thing or two every once in a while. Bob sits quietly and does not bother anyone. He puts ears on the face he has drawn. Returned pencils to the supply cabinet. Was friendly at the supply cabinet with another student who was there.	Teacher seemed to have it in for several students. Teacher blew whistle again for order, glared at everyone and said, "The period's not over yet." (Seems as though he is mad at the world.) Teacher helped one boy with a woodcut. Blew whistle again and said, "Everybody stop now. Clean up and put your names on your papers. Let's go right now, everybody."

Time & Location	Behavior	Environment
11:10 Social Studies Mrs. A.	Yawning Sat quietly (first row) and listened attentively. Nodded in response to question.	Mrs. A. was very neat, well-dressed and attractive. Film projector was set up for a showing. Preparation for the film consisted of a very brief teacher-led discussion. Film was about oil, one of the natural resources. Teacher interrupted her speech by shouting at a student in the rear of the room, "You may be removed, you know." The film was entitled, "Spindletop" and was the (romantic) story of Michael Lucas and the first oil well. It was a Dupont film—one of the "Cavalcade of America" series.

John H. Lounsbury and Jean V. Marani

113

Hi, teach!

Looka her! She's a teacher?

Who she?

Is this 304? Are you Mr. Barringer?

No. I'm Miss Barrett.

I'm supposed to have Mr. Barringer.

I'm Miss Barrett.

You the teacher? You so young.

Hey she's cute! Hey, teach, can I be in your class?

Please don't block the doorway. Please come in.

Good afternoon, Miss Barnet.

Miss Barrett. My name is on the blackboard. Good morning.

O, no! A *dame* for homeroom?

You want I should slug him, teach?

Is this homeroom period?

Yes. Sit down, please.

I don't belong here.

We gonna have you all term? Are you a regular or a sub?

There's not enough chairs!

Take any seat at all.

Hey, where do we sit?

Is this 309?

Someone swiped the pass. Can I have a pass?

What's your name?

My name is on the board.

I can't read your writing.

I gotta go to the nurse. I'm dying.

Don't believe him, teach. He ain't dying!

Can I sharpen my pencil in the office?

Why don't you leave the teacher alone, you bums?

Can we sit on the radiator? That's what we did last term.

Hi, teach! You the homeroom?

Pipe down, you morons! Don't you see the teacher's trying to say something?

Please sit down. I'd like to—

Hey, the bell just rung!

How come Mrs. Singer's not here? She was in this room last term.

When do we go home?

The first day of school, he wants to go home already!

That bell is your signal to come to order. Will you please—

Can I have a pass to a drink of water?

You want me to alphabetize for you?

What room is this?

This is room 304. My name is on the board: Miss Barrett. I'll have you for homeroom all term, and I hope to meet some of you in my English classes. Now, someone once said that first impressions—

English! No wonder!

Who needs it?

You give homework?

First impressions, they say, are lasting. What do we base our first—Yes? Do you belong in this class? No. Mr. McHabe wants Ferone right away.

Who?

McHabe.

Whom does he want?

Joe Ferone.

Is Joe Ferone here?

Him? That's a laugh?

He'll show up when he feels like it.

Put down that window-pole, please. We all know that first impressions—Yes?

Is this 304?

Yes. You're late.

I'm not late. I'm absent.

You are?

I was absent all last term.

Well—sit down.

I can't. I'm dropping out. You're supposed to sign my Book Clearance from last term.

Do you owe any books?

I'm not on the Blacklist! That's a yellow slip. This here is a green!

Hey, isn't the pass back yet?

Quit your shoving!

He started it, teach!

I'd like you to come to order, please. I'm afraid we won't have time for the discussion on first impressions I had planned. I'm passing out—

Hey, she's passing out!

Give her air!

Bel Kaufman

❝ Honestly, we've never known anyone who had a first day like this. But then, maybe it's just that they so seldom survive with enough mental faculties to tell the tale. ❞

" Scattered through the pages of this part you'll find a series of school memos. Schools differ greatly in the kind of professional relationships they foster. We don't have the space to represent the various hues of that spectrum, but we thought you would find it informative, perhaps even entertaining, to view at least one American high school through the eyes of its professional staff. Without further comment, we offer up these examples. **"**

September 14, 1972

To: Teachers
From: Principal
Subject: For Your Information

1. Some teachers are forgetting to read the morning announcements when you first get them. I have students listed in the bulletin that we want to see in the office first period.
2. We are trying to get this attendance settled down so we will be checking students when they are marked one period or two.
3. Keep on these kids. Don't take anything off of them. Some of them are getting a little brazen.
4. This is the first full week of school and most of us know it too.

September 15, 1972

1. Sally Gordon, Jean Baumgartner, and Sandy Gellar will be checked on. Skipping????--also Jane Archer.
2. There is smoking in the upstairs and downstairs restrooms. Teachers should be making spot checks on this.

September 18, 1972

1. There is smoking going on in the restrooms upstairs. Teachers on the top floor should check this at times. Let's see if we can stop this. I hate to have to lock up these rooms.
2. Jane Archer will not be allowed any passes at any time and no library privileges for the rest of the year unless I sign the pass.

September 20, 1972

1. When a student is absent from your class, are you asking for an admit slip before he or she gets into your class? Keep a close check on this! Students know what teachers don't check on the Admit Slip.
2. Herbert Tucker kicked out for three days for skipping. Must bring his parents back before I will admit him to class.
3. Peter Henshaw should not be given a pass at anytime. This also goes for Sam Berry unless I sign it.
4. Lesson Plan books are due Friday.

Across My Desk

Parents speak of the modern generation as if they had nothing to do with it.

If you keep your mind sufficiently open, people will throw a lot of rubbish in it.

Vote for the man who promises least; he'll be the least disappointing.

Constant use will wear out anything--especially friends.

We spared the rod and wound up with the beat generation.

Some things aren't worth arguing about.

There is no right way of doing something wrong.

There is no failure--except in giving up.

It's the extra effort that counts for success.

115

I

What did you learn in school today,
Dear little boy of mine?
What did you learn in school today,
Dear little boy of mine?
I learned that Washington never told a lie,
I learned that soldiers seldom die,
I learned that everybody's free,
That's what the teacher said to me,
And that's what I learned in school today,
That's what I learned in school.

II

What did you learn in school today,
Dear little boy of mine?
What did you learn in school today,
Dear little boy of mine?
I learned that policemen are my friends,
I learned that justice never ends,
I learned that murderers die for their crimes,
Even if we make a mistake sometimes,
And that's what I learned in school today,
That's what I learned in school.

III

What did you learn in school today,
Dear little boy of mine?
What did you learn in school today,
Dear little boy of mine?
I learned our government must be strong,
It's always right and never wrong,
Our leaders are the finest men,
And we elect them again and again,
And that's what I learned in school today,
That's what I learned in school.

IV

What did you learn in school today,
Dear little boy of mine?
What did you learn in school today,
Dear little boy of mine?
I learned that war is not so bad,
I learned about the great ones we have had,
We fought in Germany and in France,
And someday I might get my chance,
And that's what I learned in school today,
That's what I learned in school.

Tom Paxton

We were in our morning meeting and Michael was giving his report about what he planned to do that day. Suddenly seven-year-old Jeff burst in, shattering the silence, yelling, BOY, IT IS QUIET IN HERE!

I motioned him over, told him quietly that we were planning the day and that I would like him to sit beside me. To my amazement he sat quietly, very close to me for about 10 minutes. (His usual reaction is to bolt and run.)

After awhile he got restless, left my side, and walked among the others sitting on the floor. At one point he was fooling with Vic. Vic asked him to sit down next to him. Jeff said, "No" and started to walk away. Vic reached out and put his arm around Jeff's legs. Jeff allowed himself to be swept up and held himself firmly, snugly between Vic's legs. He sat still for awhile. He looked happy, secure. Then he got up on Vic's shoulders and wrapped his arms around Vic's head.

The meeting wore on. Jeff began clearing his throat and looking to Eric and Brian to pick up the cue. They did. I caught Jeff's eye and he stopped for a minute or so. Then he started again. I looked evenly at him and said to the group that we might now draw things to a close. Jeff brightened and bolted.

Jacqueline Murphy

116

18

Helping One Student

An extended experience with one student enabling you to see the degree of impact you can have on an individual over time.

A self-directed experience. Requires an hour or two a week for several months.

One of the ways we learn about ourselves as teachers is to try to make some assessment of the degree of impact we have on a student over an extended period of time. Shorter encounters serve some valuable functions, but figuring out just what you've accomplished in short-term situations is often difficult.

So we suggest you collect more in-depth information about yourself as a teacher by working continuously with at least one student for several months, perhaps as a tutor. Don't limit your view of your role to simply that of teaching subject matter however. Consider the potential that exists for enriching human-ness in other ways—for example, by being a counselor or a big brother/sister, or by raising non-academic issues for discussion.

Finding a student to tutor is relatively easy. Many schools will welcome your services. You might also consider other sources for young people: community agencies that can hook you up with kids that are on probation or are physically handicapped or come from broken homes or are shut-ins or have psychological problems. Or consider a neighbor-child you'd like to know better.

What kind of a student could you help most—from whom could you learn most about yourself as a teacher? Track that person down and establish a relationship.

• • •

During and after your helping experience, consider these questions:

- At what times do you feel most at ease with your student?

- Does anything about you or about your student seem to hamper the development of your relationship? Is it beyond your control? Can it be changed?

- About what proportion of your time together is spent on teaching your student subject matter and what proportion is devoted to just talking or doing things together? How comfortable do you feel about this apportionment?

- As a result of your experience, what are you learning about yourself as a person and as a teacher?

In one of the schools in the outskirts of Atlanta a very lovely girl was teaching first grade. This young woman had beautiful long hair which she was accustomed to wearing in a pony tail down to the middle of her back. She wore her hair this way the first three days of the school year. Then, on Thursday, she decided to do it differently. She did it up in a bun on top of her head, and went to teach her first grade. Well, one of her little boys came, looked in her room, and did not recognize his teacher. That sometimes happens when a woman changes her hairdo. So the little boy was lost, all by himself out in the hall.

Soon, along came a supervisor who said, "What's the trouble?" He said, "I can't find my teacher." The supervisor then asked "What's your teacher's name?" Well, he did not know, so she said, "What room are you in?" but he did not know that either. He had looked in there and it was not the right place. So she said, "Well, come on. Let's see if we can find her," and they started down the hall together, the little boy and the supervisor, hand in hand. She opened the doors of several rooms without much luck. Finally, they came to the room where this young woman was teaching. As they opened the door the young teacher turned, saw the supervisor with the little boy standing in the doorway and said, "Why, Joey, it's so good to see you, son. We were wondering where you were. Do come in. We've missed you so." The little boy pulled out of the supervisor's hand and threw himself into the teacher's arms. She gave him a hug, a pat on the fanny, and he trotted to his seat.

While the supervisor was telling me this story, she and I were riding along in a car. She said to me, "Art, I said a prayer for that teacher, she knew what was important. She thought little boys were important!" We got to kicking this around; suppose she had not thought little boys were important, suppose she thought supervisors were important? In that case she would have said, "Why, good morning, Miss K., we've been hoping you would come and see us, haven't we, boys and girls?" And the little boy would have been ignored. Or she might have thought that the lesson was important. In that case she would have said, "Well, Joey, for heaven's sakes, where have you been? Come in here and get to work." Or she might have thought that the discipline was important. In that case she would have said, "Joey, you know very well when you are late you must go to the office and get a permit. Now run right down there and get it." But she didn't. She behaved in terms of what she believed was important, and so it is for each of us.

Arthur Combs

" There's a happy kind of discomfort that a teacher experiences from time to time. It happens when you've been open enough with your students for them to feel comfortable disclosing their feelings about you. It's the uneasiness that results when you are suddenly reminded of how much you can teach, for good or for bad, by simply being you. **"**

Cindy Taylor   111 words

Miss Murphy I feel that you are a hero because you have your own beliefs and I feel that you want and try to be yourself. I respect you for that. I feel that a person who wants to be themself should be respected and that they can express their feelings much better than people who try to act or be like someone they are not. Miss Murphy have people ever try to change you. I don't see why anyone would want to change you. May if ~~they~~ they were trying to say you had a fault they ~~did~~ didn't like. But ~~it~~ to me to change you would be a mistake.

of the school? How does teaching affect the rest of your life?

- Ask your teacher what things he would, in retrospect, have liked an experienced teacher to have told him when he embarked on his teaching career.
- Ask your teacher what made him stay in teaching.
- Ask him to recall what he remembers about you as a student.

19

Teacher Talk

An easy way to collect useful, valid, and perhaps unexpected information about teaching kids in school.

A self-directed experience. Requires an hour or so out of a trip home.

Sometime when you're back home, why don't you look up one of your favorite teachers and ask him if he would mind sitting down and talking to you informally about teaching? If you feel reluctant, fearing that your teacher might view your request as an imposition, know that this is rarely the case. Most teachers really enjoy seeing their former students; it's one of the ways they can realize a sense of accomplishment. And, if the teacher is one of your favorite people, chances are good that you are one of his favorite people too. So why not give it a try?

Before you get together, think about how you can best learn from the experience. Only you can decide, but one of the following approaches may give you some ideas:

- Go into the meeting with a list of prepared questions, focusing on areas about which you'd like more information.
- Find out the answers to some personal issues. What's it like to be a teacher outside

❚❚ This is from a book written by a bunch of Italian peasant boys who would have been dropouts or push-outs in the Italian school system. A caring priest changed all that by starting an alternative school for them. This is only one of many eloquent statements they make about school in their book Letter to a Teacher, written as a tribute to their teacher-priest. **❚❚**

The Schoolboys of Barbiana

Teachers are like priests and whores. They have to fall in love in a hurry with anybody who comes their way. Afterward there is no time to cry. The world is an immense family. There are so many others to serve.

Then said a teacher, Speak to us of Teaching.

And he said:

No man can reveal to you aught but that which already lies half asleep in the dawning of your knowledge.

The teacher who talks in the shadow of the temple, among his followers, gives not of his wisdom but rather of his faith and his lovingness.

If he is indeed wise he does not bid you enter the house of his wisdom, but rather leads you to the threshold of your own mind.

The astronomer may speak to you of his understanding of space, but he cannot give you his understanding.

The musician may sing to you of the rhythm which is in all space but he cannot give you the ear which arrests the rhythm nor the voice that echoes it.

And he who is versed in the science of numbers can tell of the regions of weight and measure, but he cannot conduct you thither.

For the vision of one man lends not its wings to another man.

And even as each one of you stands alone in God's knowledge, so must each one of you be alone in his knowledge of God and in his understanding of the earth.

Kahlil Gibran

❚❚ Sounds like "meaning making." You might go back and check Postman and Weingartner's ideas on page 57 to see if you agree. **❚❚**

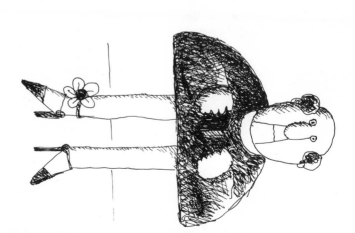

Reading the behavior of another or sensing the appropriate thing to do is not always easy. Knowing how another person feels is much more difficult than is apparent. Sensitive responses are not necessarily available. But more importantly, a person may not recognize what he has to do.

A teacher had just returned from a long day at school. He was tired and emotionally drained. Taking an easy chair in his living room, he turned his attention to the evening newspaper. Although he had warmly greeted his family, his three-year-old daughter found her way to his side. She took the remaining space in his chair, whispering, "Daddy, I love you."

He replied, "I know you do," thinking, "that's sweet."

Within a few seconds, she insisted, "Daddy, I love you so much."

With that restatement, he exclaimed, "I love you, too, honey."

Now she snuggled up much closer, making it most difficult for him to read the paper. He didn't want to turn away from her in his chair, although it would have made reading easier. He knew this movement might be interpreted as rejection. So he remained in his somewhat uncomfortable position.

At this moment she gave him a kiss on the cheek and was almost sitting in his lap. Softly, she said, "Daddy, I missed you."

"Sugar, I missed you too," he repeated. By now the paper was completely disarrayed in his hands and he hadn't the faintest notion of what he was reading. He turned his full attention to her, gave her a squeeze, and put his right arm around her. Responding to those silent cues, she remained still and quiet. In that second, he wondered if he was going to be able to read the paper at all.

A moment before, his adolescent son had entered the room to sit nearby. He realized that his son was there but he chose not to acknowledge his presence. Without knowing how, he somehow realized that his son knew what was going on. For a brief second he didn't know what to do. But the paper no longer seemed important. He decided to look at his son without appearing gushy and with a glance that suggested, we men stick together. Winking back, his son expressed without a word, "Dad, we know you had a long day, but we want to be with you." Except for a quick, few sensitive seconds, he could have missed it all.

Charles M. Galloway

An Aside on the Power of the School to Socialize Young Teachers

❚❚ We see a strong inclination for each group of prospective teachers to view themselves as the vanguard, the new beginning, the first teachers who want change. It's easy to understand how this happens. Their thinking seems to go like this:

"We see serious problems in schools. We must be the first people to perceive and appreciate these problems; otherwise, the teachers out there would already be working on them. So we'll have to change things. We'll have to initiate the educational renaissance. We'll have to kick the phoenix in the butt and get him flying."

Alas, those teachers "out there" who seem so readily to accept the status-quo were once where you're at now. A lot of them saw the need for change. They sat in the same classes, with the same profs, maybe even read some of the same books, and had the same discussions. They really did, honest. Look at all the stuff carved on the desks. They did that!

So what happened? Undoubtedly, the most important thing that happened to them was that they began teaching. For most of us, that seems to be about all it takes. Schools are very good at changing people. Not just kids, but teachers. Even principals. The process is very effective because it's so pervasive and subtle.

It's pervasive to the extent that everything and everybody reinforces conformity: other teachers do, and even kids do. Kids have learned the old game too well to want to risk learning yours. It's easier to change you. Besides it's more fun. So they try. They measure your actions against your words. They pick and pry and do their best to unearth that residue of the archetypal teacher they rightly suspect is buried inside everyone. In no other way do students so regularly succeed in school. And, accordingly, in no other way do new teachers so regularly fail.

The process is also devastatingly subtle. New teachers sometimes imagine themselves embarking on a crusade to save freedom and wisdom and curiosity and creativity and whatever. They might even succeed if the "enemy" were all that obvious. It isn't. Rather what new teachers find upon entering school are a bunch of pretty nice people. They've got their problems and hangups, but who hasn't? And they really seem to want to help make the new teacher's first few days easier. The old pros volunteer much advice to the rookie. Nobody orders you to do this or that. Nobody even has the hint of adversary about him. You don't even know it's happening. The process may start with simply letting the kids take you apart. When you're a little groggy and hanging on the ropes,

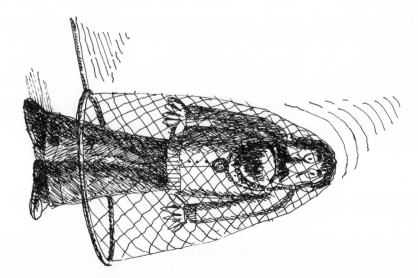

the old pros step in and tell you what <u>really</u> works. What really works, of course, is the same old game, the one the kids are used to. You begin to become just like those other teachers. The kids begin to feel comfortable with you; other teachers begin to feel comfortable with you; parents begin to feel comfortable with you; and worst of all, you begin to feel comfortable with you. And it's so hard to get up from a comfortable bed.

So beware. Beware of pragmatism; sometimes the wrong things work. Beware of old pros; although some of their ideas are best, some aren't. Beware of kids. If anybody strikes you as being terrible in your new school, it's likely to be the students; they'll go to great lengths to test you. And beware of the steady march of time. Without frequent self-evaluation, time can steadily erode the best of ideals. While you're at it, you probably ought to beware of listening too carefully to a couple of writers who haven't taught in public school classrooms for too many years. The veil of impotence and futility that regularly enshrouds so many public school teachers has been almost completely lifted from our shoulders.

You've got to build a filter that will allow you to embrace the good and ignore the bad. That filter is sometimes called a personal philosophy of teaching. Without it, you'll be a lamb going to the slaughter.

"Communities differ dramatically in the implied constraints they place on their teachers' extra-school life. We doubt that the black picture Reichart paints exists in more than a diminishing minority of our nation's communities. But we feel that minority is still large enough to warrant this entry."

With every national magazine and most newspapers featuring stories about education daily, weekly, and monthly, there is so much exposure to the varieties of views about teaching and the teacher that no teacher would be sane who did not recognize that his professional world is not his private world and that his would-be private world is also a part of his public world. It comes as no surprise that the type and style of life the teacher leads is a matter for concern to others and this does result in pressures upon him.

It is not as much of a problem for those within the conforming patterns as for those outside them. For example, it is perfectly all right to be an unmarried female schoolteacher as long as one fits the conforming pattern of the spinster type who does not care for men, who manages not to look at pornography much less pose for it, who can balance seeming obliviousness to masculine urges with the ability to tell little boys how to use urinals. The unmarried female teacher is generally expected to be a virginal type, sexless amoeba who decided to make other people's little children her life, using her bed for sleep and not for play. If the world wonders whether or not she ever had the experience of such play, whether or not she ever knew fulfillment and decides she must have, since she is such a warm, feminine woman, then it is best discovered that the experience is mixed with its sorrow, like the loss of a love in the war just before the walk down the aisle. On the other hand, if the unmarried female teacher is too young and too attractive she needs to be careful. She will do well to appear to be serious toward one fellow, probably one she cannot marry until he has finished school at which time she will help put him through medical school. This will serve better than for her to be just looking around. She needs to avoid the impression that she dates too much and that she is too physical when she does date. She needs to avoid wearing clothes that are too seductive because teachers are supposed to be restrained and are expected to project the portrait of one who is more involved with books than with glands. If the unmarried female teacher was once married it is so much better if the lack of husband is due to death rather than divorce. If divorced, she would do well to let it be known that she tried to save the marriage, that the spouse was absolutely vicious, and that she suffered with so much valor and so much dignity that were it not so long in coming she could be nominated for sainthood.

The female teacher should be all woman but not too much woman, giving but not being given unless under conventional circumstances. She should be warm but never hot. She should be loving but loved only under conventional circumstances. She should be well dressed and never too un-dressed, soft of tongue but not too soft of limb, polite, practical, and preferably not too plump.

For the male teacher there are image prob-lems as well. Since men are supposed to be men he should have the right to have sex but he had better be discreet about it. Far better that his premarital encounters have the look of the marriage search and that his dates be the comfortable non-flamboyant type, girls of good reputation who do not look bed-oriented. If married the male teacher would do well to get some children into the act as soon as possible so everyone will be able to attest to his happy married state. If no chil-dren do come along, it might be a good idea to adopt some to show what a pillar of the community he is, what good values he dem-onstrates. If not married, and unable to pro-ject the man-searching-for-a-mate image, the male teacher would do well to assume as sexless an image as possible, the psycho-logical eunuch demeanor wherein all of his energies go into teaching and so none are left over for hanky-panky. He should appear as though he is healthy with sex but not too much craving it. It should appear that al-though he has had experiences, he has ac-cepted the responsibility of controlling new ones forever more. No sensual adventurer he. Not one for too much sex, but just enough. He should inspire students to look beyond his own needs and functions and not to arouse any curiosities.

He would do well to be just as predictable, tidy, and cautious about many other things: about where he goes; about what and how much he drinks; about what he says; about what clothing he wears, not too faddish and not too expensive.

In short, teachers should be as close to superhuman as possible, relieved of as many human foibles as is believable. And you know, it is a wonderful teacher who is able to be all of that and teach too. They are the ones who can live beyond reproach, who can be extensions beyond the obvious and soar into majesties of deed and word. But not all are so qualified, and those who are not will feel the pressures of subjective judgment concerning their actions, their styles, their rights, their tolerances, their denials. Although it is coming to be a trend in some places to be more concerned about the performance of the teacher than about his personal affairs, civil liberty being what it is, the expectation that the teacher be a "safe person" is still very much prev-alent, however humorously one may treat the image required. It is still a preferred con-dition. When teachers are able to impress parents with the image of their being safe, exempted from physical needs, super beings who live off the air, who do not form waste and dispose only of knowledge and humor, smiles and sweetness, sunlight's creatures who exude goodness, asking for nothing but to love children and to be given large class-rooms with a desk for every child.

Sanford Reichart

Advice to a Teacher New to Edison School

by Mrs. G. Ilnitski

When planning your first day's activities, everything should be done to make your first day of class run smoothly. Try to plan your first day so that all of your time will be spent actively working with the children. Here are some suggestions for things that can be done on orientation day to expedite this:

1. Put a set of books on each desk. All books excepting readers and arithmetic books should be in this group. If your books have numbers written inside the covers, see that each set has the same numbers. If not, on the first day, be prepared to write in ink, the names of the children in each book. Upper class children may write their own names. Also, see that your room number is in each book. If the book is subsequently lost, it can easily be returned to your room.

2. Put up at least one welcoming bulletin board—more if time permits.

3. Check your supplies. You should have at least one package each of composition paper, arithmetic paper, manila paper, and ditto paper. You should also have a working pencil sharpener, ditto masters, a few sharpened pencils, and assorted crayons.

4. Check your attendance sheet and progress sheet. I fill in an index card for each child on my list. I also jot down suggested reading and arithmetic levels on this card. If time permits, compare this information with the information on the cumulative record cards. Check the conduct marks. Arrange these cards in temporary reading groups. This will help you when you are testing for your reading groups.

5. If time permits and your children are from a previous class in Edison School, contact the former teachers and ask them about specific children, especially those with poor conduct marks.

6. Write a complete teaching plan covering your first day.

7. Make up a few ditto masters in reading and arithmetic and run them off.

8. Read and implement all bulletins from the office.

First Day of Class

Much confusion can be avoided if you have your routines well planned. I would suggest the following:

1. Greet children as they enter the room and tell them to take any seat. Encourage them to look through the books, but advise them not to exchange them.

2. Have opening exercises.

3. Look over your class. Reseat the children. I usually alternate a boy and a girl, etc. You will be changing their seats many times throughout the school year.

4. Fill out a seating plan.

5. If the books are numbered, jot on your index cards the numbers of the books each child has.

6. Assign lockers and jot down locker numbers.

7. Have a concrete plan for the day.

First Weeks

1. Be firm. The children will think you are weak if you allow them to be noisy, inattentive, or disrespectful.

2. Have classroom activities that involve the minimum of movement. Tell children you expect them to remain in their seats unless given permission to do otherwise. To implement this, don't recognize children who come to your desk.

3. Tell children exactly what you expect from them. Example: "put all food in your lockers." "Don't bring briefcases into this room."

4. If class is noisy, stop teaching. Don't teach an unsettled class. Make a point of not resuming your teaching until you have every child's attention. You will find the children who are cooperative will force the uncooperative children to fall in line.

5. Tell children what time they are expected to arrive at school. I always insist that my children be in line at 9:45 and 12:45. This is before the bell rings. If you insist on these times, you'll find most of them will arrive on time. Again, other members of the class will discipline them.

6. Make a point of sending for the parents of recalcitrant children immediately. You should see these parents in the early weeks of the school year. Don't hesitate to send for and see a parent several times. Parents tire of coming to school and thus put pressure on their children to conform.

7. Plan your day so that the children will have quiet periods followed by active periods.

8. Be lavish with your praise. Let the children know that although you may not approve of their behavior, you love them and will stand by them at all times.

9. Be fair in your judgments. Play no favorites.

10. Don't hesitate to ask experienced teachers for advice. They are delighted to give it.

11. Enter in informal conversations with the other teachers. You can learn a lot in this way.

12. Practice routines for going to gym and fire drill behavior.

13. Be flexible. Always have "instant seat work" on hand. The office, on occasion, sends unexpected clerical work for you to do. Or, gym might be cancelled. Or, a parent may come to see you unexpectedly.

14. If you have door duty, be there on time.

15. Attend all faculty meetings.

8. Tell the children what kind of behavior you expect at recess time and lunch time. Have them practice routines of lining up in an orderly manner.

9. Anticipate interruptions from the office. New children will be assigned to your room throughout the week. Place these children in the group with the minimum of confusion.

10. Before the end of the day, have the children copy from the chalk-board a list of supplies they should bring from home. The following are suggestions: pencils, ball-point pen, notebook and paper, crayons, gym clothes, workbook money, etc.

16. Use your school preparation time wisely. These are the times between 8:30 and 8:50 and your library free period. At this time, place work on the chalkboard, run off ditto masters, or set up your audio-visual equipment. Struggling with a non-working movie projector before a classroom of children could disrupt your class for the rest of the day.

17. Change seats of children who are antagonistic or too friendly towards their neighbors.

18. Don't plan a field trip until you have reasonable control of your class. Don't take a discipline problem on a field trip unless his parent comes along to watch him.

19. Remember, most accidents can be avoided. Anticipate these situations and be alert.

Specific Problems and Possible Solutions

Problem— Children are unruly before classtime.
Solution—Put work on the board for the children to do as they enter the room. Perhaps a few arithmetic examples or a few scrambled spelling words for the children to do.

Problem— Children are chewing gum.
Solution—Make a game of going around the room with several paper towels and have the children place gum in same. If a child is still chewing gum (after above), take any gum you find in his pockets and desk. Put the gum in an envelope and tell him to have his mother come for it.

Problem— Children are fighting.
Solution—Get the facts and send the children to the office.

Problem— A child is constantly talking, bothering other children, is hyperactive, or is inattentive or withdrawn.
Solution—The work might be too difficult. The child may not understand the directions. The child might have a physical handicap. Try changing his seat. Try giving him special attention. Try giving him an interesting responsibility. Check his records to see if he was this way with former teachers. Discuss the problem with his parent or the nurse. If serious, consult the principal.

Problem— A child is accused of stealing.
Solution—If you saw it, take the item from the child and return it to the owner. If you're not sure but suspect the child, let the office handle it. Be slow to accuse a child of stealing.

Problem— You feel things are really getting out of hand.
Solution—Discuss in depth with the principal. Discipline problems alone do not indicate that you are a poor teacher. Some factors leading to poor discipline lie much deeper than the classroom situation.

Eighth period I was involved with this dumb class which was supposed to achieve adding and subtracting before it got out of the eighth grade and went to high school. Could the class achieve it? No sir. Given an adding problem to add, most of the dumb class couldn't add it. Those who did add it hadn't any notion of whether or not they'd added it correctly, even if they had. They asked me Is this right? Is this right? This ain't right, is it? What's the answer? If you don't know whether it's right or not, I'd say, then you aren't adding it. Is this right? screamed four kids, rushing me waving papers. Boy, this dumb class can't learn, I'd say to myself. Not a very sophisticated remark, perhaps.

For a while I would drop in on the Tierra Firma bowling alley, since Jay and Jack were always dying to go there. One day I ran into the dumbest kid in the dumb class. Rather, he came up to us as we were playing this baseball slot machine. Jay and Jack were not defeating the machine, to say the least, and as a result had put in another dime each time they wanted to play again. Well the dumb kid showed us how to lift the front legs of the machine in just the right way so that the machine would run up a big score without tilting, enough for ten or so free games, all by itself. After it did that, he told us, you could go ahead and really play it for fun. Jay and Jack were pretty impressed; they thought this dumb kid was a genius. Those big kids in your school sure are smart, was how Jack put it.

Well, as Jay and Jack happily set out to strike out and pop-up to the infield on the machine for those free games, the dumb kid and I walked around and watched the bowlers and had a smoke and talked. In the end, of course, I asked him what he was doing around there. He was getting ready to go to work, he told me. Fooling around until five, when he started. What did he do? I kept score, he told me. For the leagues. He kept score for two teams at once. He made fifteen bucks for a couple of hours. He thought it was a great job, making fifteen bucks for something he liked to do anyway, perhaps would have done for nothing, just to be able to do it.

He was keeping score. Two teams, four people on each, eight bowling scores at once. Adding quickly, not making any mistakes (for no one was going to put up with errors), following the rather complicated process of scoring in the game of bowling. Get a spare, score ten plus whatever you get on the next ball, score a strike, then ten plus whatever you get on the next two balls; imagine the man gets three strikes in a row and two spares and you are the scorer, plus you are dealing with seven other guys all striking or sparing or neither one . . . The bowling league is not a welfare organization nor part of Headstart or anything like that and wasn't interested in giving some dumb kid a chance to improve himself by fucking up their bowling scores. No, they were giving this smart kid who had proved to be fast and accurate fifteen dollars because they could use a good scorer.

I figured I had this particular dumb kid now. Back in eighth period I lectured him on how smart he was to be a league scorer in bowling. I pried admissions from the other boys, about how they had paper routes and made change. I made the girls confess that when they went to buy stuff they didn't have any difficulty deciding if those shoes cost $10.95 or whether it meant $109.50 or whether it meant $1.09 or how much change they'd get back from a twenty. Naturally I then handed out bowling-score problems and paper-route change-making problems and buying-shoes problems, and naturally everyone could choose which ones they wanted to solve, and naturally the result was that all the dumb kids immediately rushed me yelling Is this right? I don't know how to do it! What's the answer? This ain't right, is it? and What's my grade? The girls who bought shoes for $10.95 with a $20 bill came up with $400.15 for change and wanted to know if that was right? The brilliant league scorer couldn't decide whether two strikes and a third frame of eight amounted to eighteen or twenty-eight or whether it was one hundred eight and one half.

The reason they can't learn is because they are the dumb class. No other reason. Is adding difficult? No. It is the dumb class which is difficult. Are the teachers a dumb class? Well, we are supposed to teach kids to "read, write, cipher and sing," according to an old phrase. Can we do it? Mostly not. Is it difficult? Not at all. We can't do it because we are a dumb class, which by definition can't do it, whatever it is.

❝ Recently, considerable research has indicated the power of teacher expectancies to help or hinder student learning. Perhaps, when schools put kids in smart, average, and dumb classes, they make it impossible for even a teacher with positive expectancies to break through the dumb class's self-fulfilling prophecy of failure. ❞

James Herndon

In the working class suburbs of major cities, not to mention vast rural areas in the Midwest and the South and the Southwest, one finds a great degree of satisfaction among parents with what is going on in the schools. A greater degree of communion, I would almost call it, between parents and the teachers.

Teachers, you know, are working-class people. Teachers are essentially white-collar workers economically. They are struggling very hard to make a limited income. And a lot of the parents, too, work very hard all day. They come home quite tired and they have all they can do to have supper and go to sleep. They are only too happy to have their children just get along in school in order that they may get by, graduate and then get on to a job. They're not thinking about a fancy university education. They don't have the money for it and often don't have the ambition for it or the sense that it is possible or maybe even desirable. They have a different attitude toward what life is all about.

Yet these families do want their children to learn well the skills, to learn well how to get a trade and to be prepared well for the job market. They are ambitious for their children to rise in the world of blue-collar workers and white-collar workers. Many of these parents I have found are basically satisfied with the kind of education their children are getting....

I think it would be nice for some of our educational critics to talk with telephone operators, with secretaries, factory workers, construction workers, gas station owners, to find out how they felt about going to school and how they feel now as parents about the education of their children, and what they want for their children and indeed what their children want from schools and teachers. I see an absence of that. I see an absence of fundamental anthropological or ethnographic data.

Robert Coles

20

Three Teachers

A simple way to learn about teachers and teaching.

A self-directed experience. Requires about ten minutes.

We'd like you to recall three teachers. The first should be one of the very best teachers you've ever had; another, one of the very worst ones you've ever had; the third, one of your average teachers. Under each heading below, list the characteristics, *both strengths and weaknesses*, of each of your three teachers. Be careful to describe specific people. Avoid generalized composites.

Your Best Teacher

_____
_____
_____
_____
_____
_____
_____

Your Average Teacher

_____
_____
_____
_____
_____
_____
_____

Your Worst Teacher

_____
_____
_____
_____
_____
_____
_____

▪ ▪ ▪

- What conclusions do you draw?
- What separates the men from the boys (the women from the girls)?
- All teachers, even our best ones, have weaknesses. Good teachers usually compensate with some outstanding traits. Is this true of your good teacher?
- Imagine some future student making a list of your characteristics, you as his teacher. What do you think he'd list as your strengths and weaknesses? Under which of the three headings do you think that list would appear?

" These next three statements by Coles, Wolfe, and Borton hang together very well for us. Maybe they will for you, too. **"**

I've also seen schools in Appalachia, one-room schoolhouses that are marvelous places, where mountain children come in contact with very fine and thoughtful, beautifully idealistic schoolteachers of the old-fashioned schoolmarm variety, who have opened up the whole world to them. Who have used materials that many of us from the upper-middle-class suburbs might consider inadequate. But in the hands of these teachers, an old copy of a *National Geographic*, an out-of-date map, a book that many of us would consider corny, can be used to bring those children not only into the 20th century but into the whole world around us. These teachers weren't necessarily the ones who were highly accredited by schools of education, teachers who had taken all kinds of audio-visual courses. They weren't necessarily teachers who had read a lot of educational or social criticism. They were teachers who had a real capacity for firmness and toughness with their children, as well as affection.

Robert Coles

During the years Mrs. Roberts taught me she exercised an influence that is inestimable on almost every particular of my life and thought.

With the other boys of my age I know she did the same. We turned instinctively to this lady for her advice and direction and we trusted to it unfalteringly.

I think that kind of relation is one of the profoundest experiences of anyone's life,—I put the relation of a fine teacher to a student just below the relation of a mother to her son and I don't think I could say more than this.

Thomas Wolfe

Stack a man against a machine and immediately the man begins to sound defensive—with good reason. Whatever subject the man teaches the machine can be programmed to teach. The man's knowledge is limited by heredity, personal upbringing, and education; the machine can carry programs built by the most brilliant men in each field, and is limited only by the amount of patience which multibillion-dollar corporations are willing to expend in preparing programs.

And yet we, the flesh-and-blood teachers, feel we have something to give. It is not subject knowledge, or even the ability to structure that knowledge according to its most fundamental principles. The machine may do that better than we. It is not the ability to adapt the subject to the students' own level—the computers may someday be programmed to diagnose each student every day, branch him according to his own cognitive style, retrace the areas he has had difficulty in, and then steer him gracefully into new material. What we human teachers have to give, ultimately, is ourselves—our own love for life and for our subject and our ability to respond to the personal concerns of our students.

We have ourselves to give, and that is a great deal. Within any teacher, within any person, there is infinite complexity, ability to respond, to exchange ideas, and to change personality. The common teacher is not common at all; he is bulging with talent, with energy, and with understanding.

Terry Borton

21

Visit to a Teachers' Lounge

One way to get a feel for the teacher's view of schooling.

A self-directed activity requiring an hour or two of time.

This is an easy one. Simply get permission to sit in a teachers' lounge and listen; find out when the lounge will be frequented by a large number of teachers and arrange to visit during that time. You'll probably feel a little strange entering this inner sanctum. If need be, introduce yourself, "I'm planning to become a teacher and trying to see the job from as many angles as I can. Would you mind if I just hang around awhile?" They won't. Your major problem will probably be to avoid the old pro-rookie talk game we mentioned earlier. Try not to be the center of attention.

Here are some ways to view the action:

- How do teachers look? Act?
- What is talked about?
- Who is talked about?
- Can you imagine the discussions taking place if administrators were present? If parents were present? If kids were present? What effect, if any, does your presence have?

TEACHER'S MEETING   September 6, 1972   8:00 a.m.

Roll was taken. All teachers were present except Mrs. Taylor who was excused. Mr. Stevens and Miss Gurstmier were excused at 8:10 for morning hall duty. Mr. Stone said that some teachers were wondering why the meetings could not be held after school. He explained that he felt it best to have them first thing in the morning and get them over with since teachers generally do not want to be held down to meetings when school is out. An agenda was issued prior to the meeting and the following points were discussed.

1. Girls going braless. Dress Code.—The girls are to wear bras. They will be told in the P.E. classes. The girls should be sent to Mr. Stone, unless there is some doubt; then send them to Mrs. Alexander, the Girls' P.E. teacher, for a check. If asked where this is covered by the dress code, refer the student to article number 13.

2. Warning Letters—Six Weeks.—Mr. Stone believes that the first six weeks warning letters are due too soon to be able to make a proper judgment of the student; therefore, do not do more than make warning letters for those students you know to be particular problems from the start, such as disciplinary problems.

3. Check on windows, shades, lights, and lock doors.—Mr. Stone said he had not noticed too much lack in this yet, but reminded the teachers that this is their responsibility and should not be left for the school janitors. It is most important that if a teacher comes to the school at night that all outside doors are locked and checked before leaving.

4. Review of Course of Study.—Mr. Stone named the teachers who have failed to turn in the work. Teachers were reminded that this is past due, and is due now.

5. Attendance taking—All teachers should turn in chair counts when asked. These are important to Mr. Stone and are not just busy work for the teachers. Checking attendance is very important since it means a lot to school funding. It has been a big problem in the office to keep track. Do take roll with special attention.

6. Class and Organization meetings must be set up by sponsors—not students—two days prior to meeting. A list of students present must be turned into office at the conclusion of the meeting.—This has been tried already by a student, and he wasn't even the president of the class.

7. Reading of Announcements—When teachers read the announcements in the morning, Mr. Stone requested that they look for the names of the students that he wants to see in his office and read this first. This is important since he would like to clear up the problem and get them back to class, and also he can take care of this one particular job all at one time and get it over with.

8. Program cards to be filled out Thursday first period—Teachers should know the number of each class in their room and secure the right number of cards. Green—freshmen, yellow—sophomores, orange—juniors, and white—seniors. This year there was some information added on the back which the student was to fill out. This is for in case of emergency treatment. Students should print.

9. GAA meeting scheduled last thirty minutes of ninth hour tomorrow.

10. Correction of Student Council meeting schedule—A meeting was not scheduled for October by mistake. Add two meetings to the calendar, October 8, third period and October 23, seventh period.

Respectfully submitted,

Mary Bracken

I've seen such a range of teachers all over this nation—teachers in, say, Boston, where I've spent a lot of time, in Appalachia, or the rural South, or even in the schools for migrant children—that when I read some of the criticism of teachers I wonder which teachers they're talking about. Many are not only hard-working men and women but men and women of real sensitivity and compassion and concern and idealism and devotion and patience. And one also encounters, sometimes within the same school building, teachers of indifference and callousness, and sometimes outright meanness. But this is the problem of human beings in all professions. And that is why I stress the importance of recognizing the particularity of people.

Robert Coles

" For us, Coles' observations fits very well with what Combs had to say on page 93. "

Longing to tell off unreasonable parents who blame you for Susie's low grades? Fed up because you spend lunch period quieting your pupils rather than quieting your nerves?

Threatening to walk out of the next faculty meeting if the principal does nothing but read off duplicated notes again?

Aching to upend the fire extinguisher in the teachers' lounge and get rid of the smoke and the gossip at the same time?

If you answered yes to any of these questions, you have common cause with some of the more than a thousand educators who have written to the *Journal's* "It Burns Me Up!" column since September. Almost 6 percent flared up about the parents of pupils, over 14 percent about working conditions, over 18 percent about the upper echelon (from supervisors to school boards), almost 40 percent about other teachers, and over 20 percent about miscellaneous irritants.

Less than 1 percent found fault with their pupils; indeed, concern for giving children the best possible education seems to be the chief underlying motivation for the complaints against others.

Parents

Among those who criticized parents was an elementary principal from Maryland who wryly admits, "I can't fight biology—children need parents." Many teachers feel that although parents neglect or fail to see children's needs, they expect the teacher "to do more and more, while they do less and less."

One common complaint is that parents

blame the teacher if the child does poorly at school. A West Virginia teacher tells of a conference in which a mother expressed displeasure with her son's grades and then said, "Could you see that Billy does his homework at noon or sometime at school? I just can't get him to do it at home."

A mother who plans to return to teaching charges that parents send a sick child to school just so he will have a perfect attendance record or so that the mother can keep her appointment with the hairdresser.

Other shortcomings attributed to parents include readiness to believe children's tales about teachers, thoughtlessness in calling teachers at any time or place, and misconception about the work of the school.

Working Conditions

Parents are a relatively minor problem compared with poor working conditions. "Lunch period has always been the hardest part of my day's work," maintains an Alabaman who has been teaching forty-two years. Writes a Kentucky critic of this fringe liability, "I know of no other worker, day laborer or white collar, who doesn't have a chance to eat lunch away from his job, in some place of peace and quiet, if he so desires."

From all over the country, from both elementary and secondary teachers have come similar outcries. Pointing to both a physical and emotional need for a few minutes away from their classes, some teachers call for the use of teachers' aides.

Another debit in teaching is the great time robbery—lack of enough time free from students and other assignments to prepare lessons, grade papers, or set up equipment. It is not so much the hours spent on work for the classroom that teachers begrudge; they object to the time taken from teaching duties and given over to handling lunch money, filling out triplicate records, or taking tickets at ball games. A South Dakota teacher longs for the day when, "relieved of time-consuming menial tasks, the teacher can direct all her proficiency and skills to each student and his special needs."

One of the greatest classroom annoyances is interruption, whether by unscheduled assemblies pre-empting tests, janitorial repairs made while class is in session, or P.A. announcements which destroy continuity of thought. A California teacher sputtered about "little children constantly knocking down my door with earth-shattering messages that could never wait until recess or lunch."

The difficulty of keeping students in the classroom gets some teachers' dander up. An Ohio teacher asks, "Why must I share my class time with the guidance counselor, the speech therapist, the band director, the school nurse, the librarian, the vocal music resource teacher, and the basketball coach? . . . One teacher in our building has only one half hour during the entire week when all her pupils are present!"

Affronts to personal and professional dignity generate more fire among those doing a slow burn than poor facilities or even low salaries. As a beginning teacher from Georgia said, "One of the greatest disillusionments is to realize that even though teachers are part of a profession, they are not treated in a professional manner. Teachers' hours are regulated, meetings are required whether of benefit or not, and policies which affect the teacher directly or indirectly are changed without consulting with the teachers. We are dealt with in an unprofessional manner by parents, principals, supervisors, and other administrators."

An Illinois teacher sizzles over the insult to his professional integrity in not being able to get into his school to work on weekends. He comments "Janitors, cooks, secretaries (fine fellows all) have keys. Little league coaches and Brownie troop leaders (may their tribe increase) seemingly enter at will. Do we also serve who stand outside and wait?"

Administrators

While many teachers are unhappy about working conditions, even more complain about the people they blame for these and other problems. An elementary teacher from Oregon sums up several teachers' sentiments about administrators: "We feel we are treated like children, not as trusted professionals."

Some teachers paint their principals as being unpleasantly paternalistic; others portray them as dictatorial. A Minnesota teacher charges, "This entire autocracy is generally disguised under the cloak of committees, which, in my experience, either begin as rubber stamps of the administration or become so out of the human desire to survive."

An Oklahoma teacher lists half a dozen grievances against her principal, including the fact that he does not allow teachers off the school grounds at noon without permission. A Pennsylvania teacher protests being "held in detention" after school every day even though most of the students leave immediately, claiming she usually has no reason for staying. Several teachers chafe because principals restrict use of new methods and materials.

Another sore spot is the evaluation of classroom performance by supervisors and principals. Laments a New Mexico teacher, "Too many administrators resort to rating teachers on personality or on the quietness—not discipline, but quietness!—of his classroom. The laboratory with movement and sound is usually rated as 'discipline poor,' whereas a non-laboratory class next door is rated 'very good' because everyone may be sleeping."

Some contributors report that principals, superintendents, and school boards try to exercise authority over personal as well as professional activities. "Teacher participation in politics and community projects is being stressed in all of the education journals," writes a Kansas teacher. "This sounds good on paper, but practice it, and your job may be in jeopardy."

On the other side of the coin, administrators take a few licks at teachers they consider lazy, incompetent, undedicated. Administrators, too, complain about their bosses. After detailing the lack of qualifications of some school board members, an Iowa superintendent calls for a state law "to establish a few desirable minimum standards for membership on boards of education."

Other Teachers

Judging by the comments, what upsets teachers more than anything else is other teachers, particularly those encountered in the faculty lounges. The lounges in many schools seem to be in constant danger of spontaneous combustion. Notes a California teacher, "Faculty lounges are notoriously ugly places. Perhaps that is why so many ugly things happen there. Students are torn to pieces. Teachers are torn to astonishingly smaller pieces, unless they happen to be present. Students, teachers, then administrators. This last group really gets it. Everyone who has ever been to college knows how to teach English or run an American public school."

Another teacher opines, "What our profession needs is a good five-cent muzzle." Gossip about students raises more temperatures than gossip about the faculty. Most frequently condemned are teachers who discuss confidential information about students or their families or make remarks likely to prejudice other teachers against students.

Neophyte teachers are disturbed by lounge lectures like the cynical advice which a beginning teacher in Oregon reports receiving. "You're working too hard. Take it easy. Your students don't care; why beat your brains out for nothing?"

Some vocational teachers, librarians, and guidance counselors have special beefs about other teachers. A New Hampshire home economics teacher bemoans the lack of consideration of teachers who regard her department as a school tailoring shop and send

in students needing buttons sewed on, zippers fixed, or holes patched. A business-education teacher from Tennessee is irked because teachers load her down with extra typing. Several librarians and counselors are angry about filling in for anyone absent, including the secretary.

An English teacher from Washington state was irate when he found that students were being assigned themes as punishment by the coach, the math teacher, the student-faculty traffic court, the discipline committee, and the city traffic court judge.

The war between the sexes still wages on some fronts. Generally, men accuse women of being less devoted to their jobs than they might be, and women object when men receive higher pay.

The charge of S. K. H. (November *Journal*) that married women use home responsibilities as an excuse to shirk professional duties provoked a number of heated rebuttals. A Maryland teacher wrote, "True, a mother usually does have to give Saturday to her family rather than to a convention. But she may be the same one who another day opens her home to the faculty picnic, or shows the French Club how to make coq au vin for their dinner."

An Ohio teacher claims that men not only do less work than women but they get paid more for it. "Why is it," she asks, "that nearly every man on the staff not too old to move has the title *coach* tacked after his name? They use this as an excuse not to do the things the rest of us have to do: hall duty, late bus duty, selling tickets, taking tickets, attending meetings, ad nauseum. It also adds

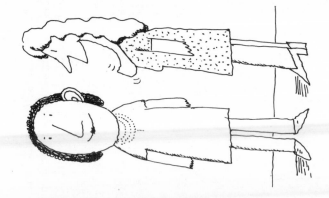

between $200 to $1,000 extra to their salary for the extra hours required. Then they are given lighter work loads to make up for the extra hours."

A Kansas teacher answers those who argue that men should be paid more because they have families to provide for: "I believe in being paid for what we produce at school, not what we produce at home!"

One of the most frequently cited failings of teachers of both sexes is discourtesy at meetings. According to complainants from over a dozen states, some teachers indulge in things they won't let their students do: arrive late, talk during speeches, leave early, grumble over decisions which they did not oppose openly, and play hooky.

NEA Journal

❚❚ People do help and hurt. In some ways helping and hurting go hand in hand.

We look at teaching as helping. To help someone, you must trust and respect him, be open to him—and by being so, you've made yourself vulnerable to being hurt. You won't be hurt often, but it will happen enough to tempt you to become guarded, aloof, and remote. You can yield to the temptation, and it would be hard to blame you; many teachers do just that. Being a good teacher, like being a good person, requires courage. Each of us has to determine the extent to which he possesses that kind of courage. Each of us has to find his own way to muster that courage when he finds it wanting. Each of us must ultimately decide how whole a teacher he can become.

How much are you willing to risk hurt in order to help? ❚❚

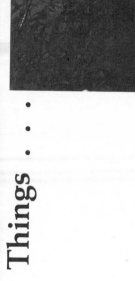

Things . . . .

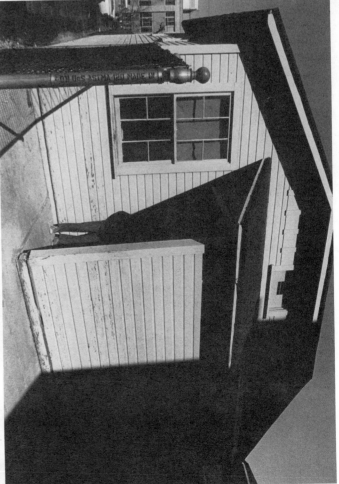

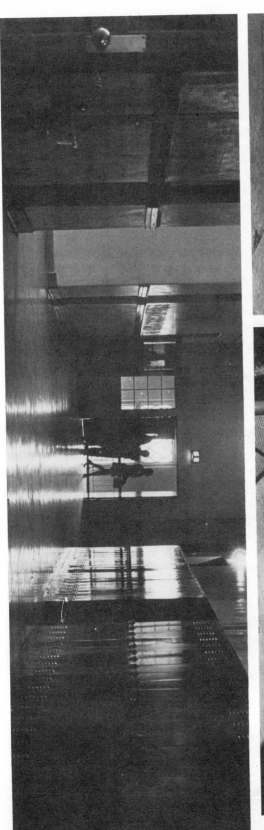

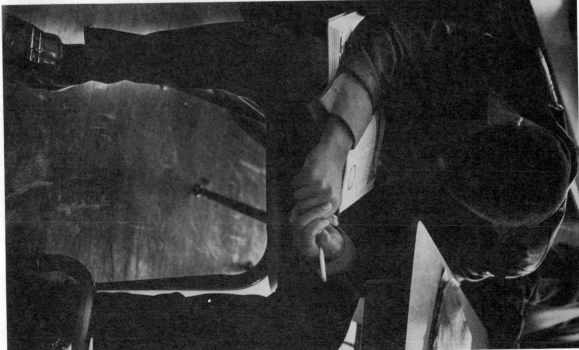

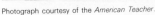
Photograph courtesy of the *American Teacher*.

SOCIAL WORKER

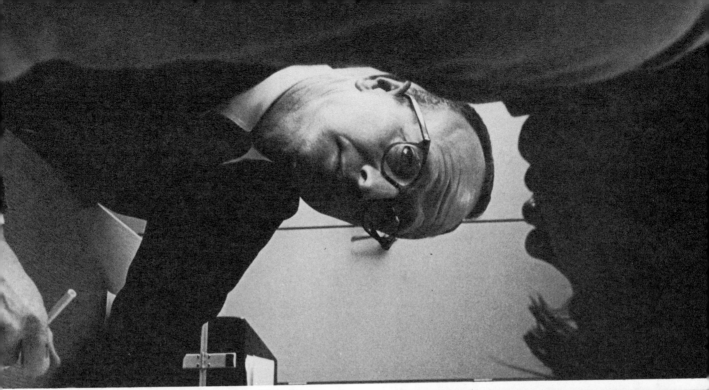

Photographs by Michael Sexton, *Who Is the School?* © 1973. The Westminster Press.

22

Will the Real School Please Stand Up?

An observation of the reality of a school—to see to what extent the goals of schools are reflected in their daily activities.

A self-directed experience. Requires little or no group time.

A teacher is told that his job is "to promote mutual respect and cooperation with the ideals of democracy in an interdependent and dynamic world," and there he stands, facing a new class, for the first time. How does he begin? Usually by taking attendance.

Goal statements often fail to guide a teacher, most often because the statements are too abstract—merely strings of words. The action implications, from the vantage point of a teacher engaged in day-to-day classroom management, are anything but apparent.

But goal statements fail for other reasons too. Sometimes they fail because current problems sop up all the time.

Example 1: A school wants to help students learn to think for themselves and to handle self-direction responsibly. But the school is even more desirous of keeping everyday operations from becoming disorderly. Consequently, the school staff works hard at fostering com-

pliance to school rules and never gets around to fostering responsible self-direction.

Example 2: Teachers want students to learn the big ideas, the meaningful concepts and generalizations of the culture. But the basic facts are seen as a requisite to the big ideas—so much of a prerequisite that few teachers have time even to finish the basics, much less to contemplate the big ideas.

We'd like you to look for gaps between school goals and school reality, either in one particular school or for schools in general. Work alone or in pairs.

1 Identify the Goals

If you focus on one school, obtain a copy of the school's philosophy or objectives. The office of the Board of Education, the superintendent of schools, or the principal usually will make it readily available.

If you want to look at schools in general, check the objectives or school philosophies of several schools. This section reprints some (page 150). You may wish to augment these philosophies with objectives and philosophies you find in education texts or curriculum guides, available in college libraries. In any case, your first step is to identify a few of the most important, or frequently professed, school goals.

2 Observe Reality

The second step is to compare the goals with the day-to-day reality of schools.

You can make this comparison informally, by visiting a school and carefully observing what goes on. You might, for example, check the tests students take to find out what teachers consider important. Also, study the report cards or other forms that go home to parents. Or ask students what is on their minds as they go through the school day, or what matters in that particular building, or what they personally are trying to accomplish in school. Ask who students most admire: the scholars, the sports stars, or the most popular students. Pick a school objective and, by comparing older students with younger students, assess the school's progress with that objective. Check the school board minutes or visit a school board meeting to see what is discussed.

...

One useful way to capitalize on what you learn is to make two lists. The first contains examples of congruence between school reality and the professed goals. The second list contains the examples of incongruence that you observe; order this list so that the most obvious, blatant incongruence you observe appears first and the most subtle, last. Compare your findings with one or two others.

- What do the lists say about schools?
- Why do we think schools function as they do?
- On the basis of the way they operate, what are schools for?
- Do these comparisons have implications for you as a teacher?

If you're one of those who know you have to go to school, and you know that the school you're going to doesn't suit you, then you know that it's nice to have alternative schools. Here's an example: The school I was going to had a dress code, and there were people there who didn't mind. They could get plenty of the right kind of clothes. I couldn't. Along with the dress code was a personality code for those who could see it. I could see it in my own, immature way—if you weren't suited to the school's "in" crowd, you didn't want to fit in with anybody. But you kept trying and failing and eventually decided to drop out, not going at all.

Then I heard about Metro Youth Education Center. It's really like a haven for dropouts. That may be a corny thing to say, but there are reasons for calling it that. You can come here, even if you're past your high school years, to get that high school diploma, and it's a small enough school that it's easy to forget about whether or not you are popular. You get kind of a "homey" feeling instead. If there are personal problems you can't clear up, which keep you from being interested in extra-curricular activities and which keep you from moving along with the regular high school's pace, well, the alternative school could be just your thing.

Some people may be too mature to stay in a high school that treats them like children. They just want the freedom that the alternative school offers, and if they're really mature, they don't abuse it but enjoy it. Then again, there are the people who are immature when they come here, and it becomes a challenge to stay with the books.

A Student in a Public Alternative School

1. A Philosophy of a Small City School System

To educate means to "bring out". To begin this process of leading a student into certain paths, we must first instill in our students healthful attitudes of self and family acceptance. As educators, we believe that we must develop in each individual the ability to understand the rights and duties of a citizen; to respect the rights of others; to fulfill his obligations as a member of the community, the state and the nation. In addition, we believe it is our task to provide each child the tools for meeting with calmness and composure life situations whether favorable or unfavorable for him. At the same time, agreeing that it is impossible to teach all on any subject, we, nevertheless, recognize the great importance of encouraging the development of such habits and skills and mastery of such knowledge as will make it possible for the student to pursue his vocation. We believe that our principal trust as educators is to provide the student with that guidance and counsel which will best prepare him for his future responsibilities to himself and to the society in which he lives. Education for our students should insure that each child will be helped (1) to realize his full potential, (2) to take his place in society as a happy, useful, productive citizen and (3) to contribute something of value to his world.

2. The Objectives of a Large Urban School

1. Students should be taught to understand and appraise the democratic institutions of the United States.
2. They should be taught the privileges and responsibilities of American citizenship.
3. They should be given a knowledge and appreciation of the many cultures of the world in order to deepen their understanding of our pluralistic society and to foster respect for human dignity.
4. Students and teachers should be given the opportunity to experience the diversity of integrated education.
5. Students should be given opportunity for democratic participation in school activities.
6. They should be provided programs which recognize their individual differences without specific identification which may be psychologically damaging.
7. They should be taught the skills of inquiry and research, as well as basic intellectual skills.
8. They should be encouraged to be creative in their thinking and to make decisions based on cultivated judgments.
9. They should be realistically challenged to learn and to perform to the best of their abilities, setting excellence as their goal in any work they undertake.
10. They should be taught to conduct themselves in a socially acceptable and reasonable manner.

3. The Program of an Established Private School

Beginning School

Children enter at three, four, or five years of age, and remain until ready for first grade. The half day program is held in an imaginative school laboratory called the Beehive. The child who comes here finds pleasure, intellectual stimulation, and friends who will support the social, artistic, and learning activities he is ready to try. The Beginning School is the first step in the educational process, not merely a play school or day care center.

Lower School

Mastery of the art of communication is the single most important task in grades 1 through 6. Teachers strive by example, and through curricular patterns, to establish learning habits that stimulate curiosity, generate a desire for excellence, as well as creating awareness of the environment, developing willingness to accept responsibility for one's actions, and respecting each other's right to be different. As the child progresses, each success is applauded and each failure turned into a learning experience.

Middle School

In grades 7 and 8 the emphasis is on helping each student further his intellectual commitment. With fewer rules and more freedom he learns to respect independence and human dignity, in himself and others. The flexibility of the academic and activity program gives each student increased responsibility for his own education, and presents opportunities for the student to progress as rapidly as he is adequately prepared. He may begin Upper School work during these years.

Upper School

Small classes, teachers who are vitally interested in teaching, an informal atmosphere where independent thought and exchange of ideas are encouraged—all these describe the approach to learning in grades 9-12. Individual aptitudes and self-expression are developed through varied curriculum offerings in English, history, language, mathematics, science, and the arts. Honors work is available in all areas. Teachers work closely in class and individual conference as well as through a faculty advisory program, to help students develop habits of thoroughness and penetration in critical evaluation in recitation, papers, independent projects and creative endeavor. Emphasizing further its belief in a process of continuous growth of intellectual capacity, the Upper School encourages a quality of preparation that enables its students to attend colleges of their choice.

4. The Program of a New Unit in a Large Urban School System

Consider, if you will, a school that uses the entire city as its classroom—where the resources of businesses, community organizations, labor and cultural institutions become the center of learning for the students. Certified teachers help the students draw on and use the practical knowledge of skilled experts in various fields.

This brief statement describes what educators call a "school without walls"; without walls because the classroom and the learning experiences that take place in it are not confined by physical structural walls and because the quantity and quality of the knowledge communicated is not "walled in" by inflexible guidelines.

The purpose of this new high school is to provide an alternative educational opportunity for those secondary students who are dissatisfied with the traditional school program. The school will have a special appeal for the student who is seeking a maximum degree of flexibility in his studies, active participation in decisions involving his education and responsibility for his own education. Students will be involved in the planning-teaching-learning process.

The school will operate on a twelve-month plan with ten-week quarters followed by three-week vacation periods. Some of the advantages of this plan are:

1. Shorter sessions should help students maintain a greater degree of interest and enthusiasm.

2. We will have access to community resources that are only available during the summer.

3. Three week intervals between learning periods will provide the staff with the opportunity to carry out in-depth written evaluations of the program, make changes, if needed, and develop new resources and learning units.

Initially, the school will have a student body of 150 eleventh-grade students drawn from all sections of the city and representing the academic, racial, and economic diversity of the city's public high school youth. The faculty will be composed of experienced and highly competent personnel selected to implement this creative program.

The curriculum will consist of a variety of instructional experiences which will be jointly planned by the staff and students, relying on regular feedback and input from parents. Community resources will be utilized so that many of the instructional activities will occur away from the school's home base. Students will be provided with funds for their transportation by the school.

Parents will be contacted at regular intervals during the quarter and will receive an in-depth written evaluation at the end of each quarter. The staff at the school views grades as a positive factor. Grades should not be used as punishment but as encouragement. To reinforce this philosophy, students will be evaluated by the following grading system: A, B, credit, or no credit. Future educational plans will not be hindered by this change in the grading system.

5. The Program of a New Private Alternative High School

Learning: A Mode of Living

Our name is more than a name for a school. It is a philosophy of learning and an attitude about the way people relate to one another and to the world. Our school is an environment which will foster the skill/attitudes necessary for becoming an autonomous learner or a self-actualizing person. We believe that learning thrives best where learners are free to pursue personal interests; where creativity is actively fostered; where the integration of all subjects is emphasized; where people are in vital contact with their feelings and the feelings of others; where learners are in active contact with their social and physical environment; where independence and self-motivation is coupled with a sense of responsibility for one's own decisions and their consequences; and where cooperation and consideration of others is a way of life.

Curriculum: The Course Is Where the Runner Runs

Our axiom, that learning is a mode of living, fosters an environment in which one can become aware of one's real interests and at the same time become aware of the interrelations between all ways of approaching reality. Since the precise content of what an individual or the group as a whole studies will depend on the direction of individual interest and the nature of the group experiences, we cannot satisfy in advance your curiosity about what will be studied. However, there will be qualified people available at all times to assist and direct learners in the pursuit of their interests. These interests may be pursued in an exhaustive and rigorous academic manner or directed toward more immediate practical or aesthetic ends *depending on the needs and interests of the individual.* The experience will be one of freedom but not without form.

Who Is a Teacher?

The roles of teacher and learner should be fluidly interchanged if learning is to be an authentically human activity. The staff consists of four core faculty available to the students on a twenty-four hour a day basis. There will be a second group of over thirty resource persons that will work with learners on specific projects and a third group that will be available for general consultation and the development of specialized skills. The role of the core faculty is to foster the basic skill/attitudes, namely, reasoning, media, and communication skills; why and how to be in vital contact with one's self and the surrounding world; and why and how to activate one's imagination and fantasy. With this format we feel that any student will be exposed to the fullest range of educational experience which may, according to the individual, lead to further study, travel or a profession.

Excerpted from literature of public, private, and alternative schools

Our school may look like a little green army building, but you sure can't judge a book by its cover in this case. I mean we don't have a football team and if you're looking for a pep club, you're going to have to look pretty hard because we don't have one. But we do have one heck of a place to grow.

By growing, I mean not just physically but mentally as well. As far as growth academically, it is obviously better because you are not forced to keep up with someone else's standards. You work at your own speed. Therefore, there are no hassles about competing with each other, which actually has no place in learning anyway. Aside from that, you also learn a lot about life. You probably won't know everything there is to know about life when you leave here, but you will be so much more familiar with a few words, such as honesty, understanding and hopefulness.

We have our problems, but at least ours are out in the open. Take for instance when auto-mechanics was not offered to girls here. There was a petition sent around, signed by all the girls and given to our principal. He is now in the process of getting the auto-mechanics class opened to us girls. We currently have a petition going around for more vending machines which we need badly. But I have confidence that our need is going to be recognized and fulfilled. The people here are not unreasonable. Really, you learn to deal with problems openly and honestly.

One other good thing that bothers a few kids, is that when you attend this school, you don't come to win a popularity contest. You come to learn! I've heard this school being accused of unfriendliness. That's not true at all. We are not constantly worried about who's going out with "Mr. All American" and we don't hold any "who's most likely to succeed" contests. The lack of these things do seem to bother some kids though.

See, our school is different. The teachers are different here. The kids who attend this school are different. (Even the janitor is different, you won't find another one like him in the whole state.) That difference stems from the way our school is run. We have a certain quality I don't think you find in too many schools. In other words, this is a part of my life I wouldn't give up for anything.

A Student in a Public Alternative School

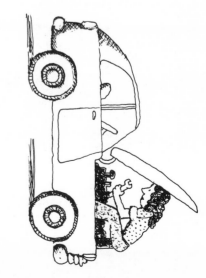

" There's a whole research area in education that focuses on "incidental learning," learning that just kind of happens in schools. Here are some examples that may remind you of some parts of your incidental education that you need to unlearn to be the kind of teacher you want to be. **"**

" One of the incidental things we learn in school is that the everyday common-sense kind of learning that occurs outside of school doesn't count. **"**

We confront . . . a most difficult problem in education: helping students to *unlearn* much of what they "know." Josh Billings said it almost a century ago: "The trouble ain't that people are ignorant; it's that they 'know' so much that ain't so." What are some of the things these students know that "ain't so"? Well, for example, they "know" that 1) the more "content" a person "knows," the better teacher he is; 2) that "content" is best "imparted" via a "course of study"; 3) that "content" is best kept "pure" by departmentalizing instruction; 4) that "content" or "subject matter" has a "logical structure" or "logical sequence" that dictates how the "content" should be "imparted"; 5) that bigger schools are better than smaller schools; 6) that smaller classes are better than bigger classes; 7) that "homogeneous grouping" (with students "grouped" on the basis of some real or fancied similarity) makes the learning of subjects more efficient; 8) that classes must be held for "periods" of about an hour in length, five days a week, for about 15 weeks in order for a "course" in a "subject" to happen.*

It comes as a shock to the students that there is *no evidence to support any of these contentions.* On the contrary, there is massive evidence to confute them. It takes some doing, however, to help students to recognize the fact that most of their deeply internalized assumptions about "education" are based on misinformation rather than information.

Neil Postman and Charles Weingartner

*See Ben M. Harris, "Ten Myths That Have Led Education Astray," *The Nation's Schools*, April 1962.

Flax is what school is all about. In my own old-fashioned geography books I went to various countries in the company of Bedouin and Greek and Turkish kids and the thing that most remains in my mind now about those imaginary kids is that they always grew flax. I myself put flax on my maps alongside corn and wheat and coal; I wrote down flax to answer questions about the products of countries. I never knew what flax was, but I knew that if I kept it in mind and wrote it down a lot and raised my hand and said it a lot, I would be making it.

Flax is actually a slender erect plant with a blue flower, the seeds of which are used to make linseed oil. Linen is made from the fiber of the stalk. I know this now because I've just looked it up in the dictionary. It is quite possible that it does grow in all those countries like the book and my test papers said. But beyond that, a thing like flax has an important place in a school. Unlike corn, say, which in L.A. we could drive out and see in fields and buy from roadside stands and take home and eat, unlike wheat or cotton or potatoes, I think you could live your entire life in America and never see or even hear of flax, never know about it or need to know about it. Only in the school, only from the geography book, only from the teacher, could you learn about flax.

It showed you how smart the school was, for one thing. For another, it showed you what Learning precisely was; corn, for example, wasn't Learning precisely because you *could* go out and see it in the fields and buy it from roadside stands and take it home and shuck it and eat it and your mother and father could tell you about how they used to grow corn and how to tell fresh corn and about names of corn like Country Gentleman, which my father preferred. You could do all that without ever going to school and so it didn't count. Finally, it showed the school who among the students was willing and able to keep flax in mind, to raise his hand and say it aloud, to write it down, and put its name on maps. So that in the cumulative records of each child the teacher could write down for the next teacher the information that

Child reads flax, writes down flax   *Leader.*
  and says flax.
Child sometimes remembers flax.   *Nice kid.*
Child can't remember flax.   *Child is
    black
    and/or
    deprived.*
Child digs flax, but inadvertently   *Brain-
  says "chili-dog" instead.   damaged?*
Child don't dig flax a-tall.   *Reluctant
    learner.*

I think you could make up an entirely new Achievement Test, doing away with expensive and tedious vocabulary and graphs and reading comprehension, doing away with special pencils for IBM scoring and doing away with filling in all those rows. Just pass out a sheet with the word *flax* printed on it in big letters and count the seconds it took for a kid to raise his hand. That would tell you everything that an Achievement Test is designed to tell you.

Even in the Victory Gardens of 1942 America (where such an outlandish name as *Swiss Chard* became part of my experience, growing non-stop in the back yard), no one was ever known to grow flax, no one saw flax sprouting under the eucalyptus trees, no newspaper articles were written about anyone raising flax in the vacant lots, no war hero mentioned flax as contributing to the war effort. It remained, like Learning, a monopoly of the schools.

James Herndon

There are four operating principles of the Open Classroom. First, the room itself is decentralized: an open, flexible space divided into functional areas, rather than one fixed, homogeneous unit. Second, the children are free for much of the time to explore this room, individually or in groups, and to choose their own activities. Third, the environment is rich in learning resources, including plenty of concrete materials, as well as books and other media. Fourth, the teacher and her aides work most of the time with individual children or two or three, hardly ever presenting the same material to the class as a whole.

The teachers begin with the assumption that the children want to learn and will learn in their fashion; learning is rooted in first-hand experience so that teaching becomes the encouragement and enhancement of each child's own thrust toward mastery and understanding. Respect for and trust in the child are perhaps the most basic principles underlying the Open Classroom.

From the application of these principles derive the most notable characteristics of learning in such a classroom: a general atmosphere of excitement; virtually complete flexibility in the curriculum; interpenetration of the various subjects and skills; emphasis on learning rather than teaching; focus on each child's thinking and problem-solving processes, and on his ability to communicate with others; and freedom and responsibility for the children.

From the moment you walk in the door of such a classroom, the difference from the conventional procedures is striking. In most classrooms rows of desks or tables and chairs face the front of the room, where the teacher is simultaneously presenting material and controlling the class; the children are either quietly engaged by what the teacher is doing, surreptitiously communicating, daydreaming, or fooling. Even in classrooms using innovative materials, such as the Individually Prescribed Instruction, in which each student works on a math sheet prescribed for his particular level of achievement, the basic pattern is one in which all the children do the same thing at the same time, sitting at their desks with the teacher watching from up front.

But in an Open Classroom, there is none of this. There is no up front, and one doesn't know where to look to find the teacher or her desk. She is usually to be found working intensively with one or two children, or if things are going as they should, often standing unobtrusively aside but observing each child's activities with great diligence. There are no desks and few chairs—fewer than the number of children. And the children are everywhere: sprawled on the floor, in groups in the corners, alone on chairs or pillows, out in the hall, or outside in the playground if it's good weather.

"The children are working on fractions." This kind of description of what's going on in a class, which comes so easily in a conventional situation, can never be applied to an Open Classroom. Each child uses the room differently, according to his own interests, concerns, and feelings on a particular day.

How does the day proceed? As they arrive,

the students check the Chore Chart to see what their housekeeping responsibility is for the day. They take turns doing such chores as bringing up the milk, watering the plants, cleaning the animal cage, mixing new paints, sharpening pencils, taking attendance.

Many Open Classroom teachers call a general meeting after the children arrive, focusing on some interesting experiment several children did the day before, something brought from home, an unusual item in the newspaper, or a sentence she has written on the board to be corrected by the class. The children squat on their haunches or sit cross-legged in whatever area most comfortably holds the whole group.

After the meeting, children choose the areas in which they would like to begin their day. Some prefer to start quietly reading, curled up in the overstuffed chairs. Some like to get their assigned work out of the way first, but others may not have a choice if the teacher has noticed, for instance, that they have been neglecting math or need work in punctuation, and she tells them that they should start the day working with her. Soon the room is full of action, used as it will be for the remainder of the day, unless some special visitor or specialist focuses the group's attention for a special activity.

The layout of the room supports the program. An aerial view of a typical second-grade class in the middle of a morning would show that the room is divided into six sections, defined by open bookshelves that hold appropriate equipment, all of which is easily accessible to the children.

The child is free to choose, but whatever choice he makes he will be confronted with a wealth of opportunities for exploration and discovery. In the math section is everything he can use to measure and figure, including the Cuisenaire rods, balance scales, rulers and a stop watch, workbooks, and counting games such as Sorry and Pokerino. Similar riches await him in the language arts section, where he can read, make a tape recording or type, write, and play word-games and puzzles; or in the arts area with its paints, clay, dyes, and sand. Other corners are devoted to science, music, and blocks.

The child's freedom, autonomy, and independence—as well as his responsibility—are epitomized by the largest and most elaborate of the many charts and pictures around the room. It is the "Activity Chart," and it lists by word and appropriate picture all the possible activities in the room: from reading, typing, playground, painting, right through to visiting and gerbils. Next to each are several hooks, on which the child hangs his name tag to indicate what he's doing. A simple device, but it says much about the respect for the child and the relationship between the child, the teacher, and the room. The equivalent in the conventional classroom is the notorious Delaney Book, still widely used, which represents each student by a little card tucked in a slot corresponding to his desk position, fixing the child in a constrained position, with the teacher clearly in charge.

In the Open Classroom, each child's day is distinctive and different from every other day. To give him a sense of his progress, each child may keep a diary, which is also

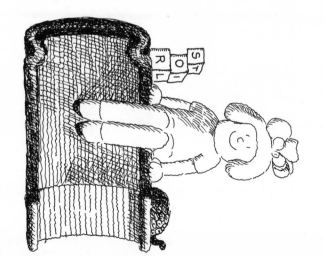

used to communicate to the teacher. Some typical entries indicate the flow of activity, and the frustrations and concerns of the children:

Today I read *Horton the Elephant.* I began the green series in SRA. Ollie helped me with the words in the *Horton* book. I helped John and Sara make a staircase with the Cuisenaire rods.

I played in the Block Corner most of the day. We were making a suspension bridge. We talked a lot about our water tower and how it got flooded by Jimmy and what we should charge for a toll. I'll do my math tomorrow. Okay?

We had a turtle race today. Mrs. White taught me how to break words down. I can read words, but I can't break them down. We timed the turtles with the stopwatch. They tried to climb over the side of the box.

We're making a book of fables like "How the Snake Lost His Legs"; "How the Elephant Got His Trunk"; "How José got to be a Genius"; "How I Got to Be Invisible."

The variety of the activities mentioned in the diaries suggests the highlights of each child's day, but many educators and most parents find it difficult to define clearly what is being learned at any one moment and are usually resistant to the idea that a relaxed and unpressured atmosphere can stimulate serious work. . . .

In the present climate of American education, the Open Classroom approach sometimes seems like a flower too fragile to survive. The demands on the schools today are harsh and often narrow. Many black parents demand measurable reading achievement and other test scores to assure that they are no longer being given short shrift. At the same time, white parents are often concerned that the schools continue to give their children an advantage in status over someone else's children.

In such a climate, the Open Classroom seems precariously based on a kind of trust little evident in education today. Teachers must trust children's imagination, feelings, curiosity, and natural desire to explore and understand their world. They also must learn to trust themselves—to be willing to gamble that they can retain the children's interest and respect once they relinquish the external means of control: testing, threats, demerits, petty rules, and rituals. School administrators, in turn, must trust teachers enough to permit them to run a classroom that is not rigidly organized and controlled but, rather, is bustling, messy, flexible, and impulsive. Parents must trust school people to do well by their children, without the assurance provided by a classroom atmosphere recognizable from their own childhoods and validated, however emptily, by standardized tests.

Much recent experience suggests that the basis for trust such as this may not exist in American education at present. But perhaps the existence of classrooms where learning based on such trust is taking place will itself help create the beginnings of a new climate.

Beatrice and Ronald Gross

The first object of any school must be to equip the student with the tools of learning. . . .

The second object of any school—and this is vital to a democratic community—should be to open new worlds to the young, to get them out of the rut of the place and time in which they were born. Whatever the charms of the neighborhood school, whatever the pleasures of touring one's native city, whatever the allure of the present, emphasis upon the immediate environment and its current condition must narrow the mind and prevent understanding of the wider national or world community and any real comprehension of the present. Hence those who would center education on the interests of children and on their surroundings, though these critics may seem up-to-date, are working contrary to the demands contemporary society is making upon any educational system.

The third object of any educational institution must be to get the young to understand their cultural heritage. This, too, is in the interest of the individual and the community. The individual ought to see himself in the community, a community having a tradition, which perhaps ought to be rejected, but not unless it is first understood. Comprehension of the cultural heritage is the means by which the bonds uniting the community are strengthened. The public school is the only agency that can be entrusted with this obligation. Its performance cannot be left to chance.

Robert M. Hutchins

Today, nowhere in the world are there elders who know what the children know, no matter how remote and simple the societies are in which the children live. In the past there were always some elders who knew more than any children in terms of their experience of having grown up within a cultural system. Today there are none. It is not only that parents are no longer guides, but that there are no guides, whether one seeks them in one's own country or abroad. There are no elders who know what those who have been reared within the last twenty years know about the world into which they were born.

The elders are separated from them by the fact that they, too, are a strangely isolated generation. No generation has ever known, experienced, and incorporated such rapid changes, watched the sources of power, the means of communication, the definition of humanity, the limits of their explorable universe, the certainties of a known and limited world, the fundamental imperatives of life and death—all change before their eyes. They know more about change than any generation has ever known and so stand, over, against, and vastly alienated, from the young, who by the very nature of their position, have had to reject their elders' past.

Just as the early Americans had to teach themselves not to daydream of the past but concentrate on the present, and so in turn taught their children not to daydream but to act, so today's elders have to treat their own past as incommunicable, and teach their children, even in the midst of lamenting that it is so, not to ask, because they can never understand. We have to realize that no other generation will ever experience what we have experienced. In this sense we must recognize that we have no descendants, as our children have no forbears.

Margaret Mead

1. Most people do not want to be hungry; they cherish the value of *sufficient nourishment*.

2. Most people do not want to be cold or ragged; they cherish the value of *adequate dress*.

3. Most people do not want uncontrolled exposure, either to the elements or to people; they cherish the value of *shelter and privacy*.

4. Most people do not want celibacy; they cherish the value of *erotic expression and celebration*.

5. Most people do not want illness; they cherish the value of *physiological and mental health*.

6. Most people do not want chronic economic insecurity; they cherish the value of *steady work, steady income*.

7. Most people do not want loneliness; they cherish the value of *companionship, mutual devotion, belongingness*.

8. Most people do not want indifference; they cherish the value of *recognition, appreciation, status*.

9. Most people do not want constant monotony, routine, or drudgery; they cherish the value of *novelty, curiosity, variation, recreation, adventure, growth, creativity*.

10. Most people do not want ignorance; they cherish the value of *literacy, skill, information*.

11. Most people do not want to be continually dominated; they cherish the value of *participation, sharing*.

12. Most people do not want bewilderment; they cherish the value of *fairly immediate meaning, significance, order, direction*.

Theodore Brameld

" So why are schools the way they are? "

Once upon a time, the animals decided they must do something heroic to meet the problems of "a new world," so they organized a school. They adopted an activity curriculum consisting of running, climbing, swimming, and flying and, to make it easier to administer, all the animals took all the subjects.

The duck was excellent in swimming, better in fact than his instructor, and made passing grades in flying, but he was very poor in running. Since he was slow in running, he had to stay after school and also drop swimming to practice running. This was kept up until his web feet were badly worn and he was only average in swimming. But average was acceptable in school, so nobody worried about that except the duck.

The rabbit started at the top of the class in running, but had a nervous breakdown because of so much make-up work in swimming.

The squirrel was excellent in climbing until he developed frustration in the flying class where his teacher made him start from the ground-up instead of from the tree-top-down. He also developed charley horses from over-exertion and then got C in climbing and D in running.

The eagle was a problem child and was disciplined severely. In the climbing class he beat all the others to the top of the tree, but insisted on using his own way to get there.

At the end of the year, an abnormal eel that could swim exceedingly well, and also run, climb, and fly a little held the highest average and was valedictorian.

The prairie dogs stayed out of school and fought the tax levy because the administration would not add digging and burrowing to the curriculum. They apprenticed their children to a badger and later joined the groundhogs and gophers to start a successful private school.

Does this fable have a moral?

G. H. Reavis

Fable of the Animal School

The result of teaching small parts of a large number of subjects is the passive reception of disconnected ideas, not illumined with any spark of vitality. Let the main ideas which are introduced into a child's education be few and important, and let them be thrown into every combination possible. The child should make them his own, and should understand their application here and now in the circumstances of his actual life. From the very beginning of his education, the child should experience the joy of discovery. The discovery which he has to make, is that general ideas give an understanding of that stream of events which pours through his life, which is his life. By understanding I mean more than a mere logical analysis, though that is included. I mean "understanding" in the sense in which it is used in the French proverb, "To understand all, is to forgive all." Pedants sneer at an education which is useful. But if education is not useful, what is it? Is it a talent, to be hidden away in a napkin? Of course, education should be useful, whatever your aim in life. It was useful to Saint Augustine and it was useful to Napoleon. It is useful, because understanding is useful.

Alfred North Whitehead

Hey kid! Are they teaching you how to keep self-trust and pride alive?
Or are they telling you 2 + 2 = 4 Dummy,
NOT 5.

Hey kid! Are they teaching you how to SEE
and HEAR and SMELL and TASTE?
Or are they telling you:
"This is a classroom, WITH NO TIME TO WASTE!"

Hey kid! Are they teaching you how to learn
and how to discover?
Or are they telling you:
"If you don't know, keep it under cover."

Hey kid! Are they teaching you how to grow
and how to die?
Or are they telling you how to "fit in" and
get by?

Hey kid! Are they teaching you how to love
and how to give?
Or are they telling you to GET AHEAD?
"After all, that's the only way you can LIVE!"

Hey kid! Are they teaching you your manhood and the joys of loving a wife?
Or are they telling you that human plumbing
is all there is to life?

Hey kid! Are they teaching you how to
master YOUR life of endless quests?
Or are they telling you:
"DON'T TRY AND CHANGE IT! WE HAVE DONE OUR
BEST!"

John Harold Halcrow

Hey Kid! What Are They Teaching You?

161

The major obstacle on the way to a society that truly educates was well defined by a black friend of mine in Chicago, who told me that our imagination was "all schooled up." We permit the state to ascertain the universal educational deficiencies of its citizens and establish one specialized agency to treat them. We thus share in the delusion that we can distinguish between what is necessary education for others and what is not, just as former generations established laws which defined what was sacred and what was profane.

Ivan Illich

❞ Which is why he wants to de-school society and let people do their learning wherever they choose.❞

May 18, 1973

To: Teachers

From: Mr. Stone

Subject: For Your Information

1. Mrs. Veal and Mrs. Stone have hall duty this week.

2. Mr. Ashby has detention this week. Don Bent and Bruce DeCosta will be serving detention plus others.

3. The library will close Monday. This will give Mrs. Riley a chance to get all books checked in.

4. Seniors will turn in books on Wednesday. If they owe any money, get this list to me Thursday morning by 8:30. This also goes for library.

5. We will put the canvas down on the gym floor Wednesday and leave it down till end of school so P.E. Teachers plan accordingly.

6. Semester tests start Thursday. No passes are to be issued at any time. Keep these kids out of hallway.

7. Jim Porter kicked out for three days for fighting.

8. Paul Singer kicked out for rest of the year.

9. No School on Friday or Monday. Baccalaureate Service Sunday at 8:00 sharp in the high school gym.

10. It is later than you think. We are about to wind up another school year. The next two weeks will be the toughest. Keep those students in line.

11. Water guns are here and they are going to go along with the person pulling the trigger. Send them to my office and I will take care of the shooter. Check to see that they get to my "Gun Control" office.

12. No weather forecast. I give up on weekend weather. My concerns are to get school out with all of us working hard to keep control of these students.

13. Martin Collins and Alex Wilson will lead the Seniors at Baccalaureate and Commencement so when they finish their semester tests, let them come to the gym.

162

There is an important fact about a student's life that teachers and parents often prefer not to talk about, at least not in front of students. This is the fact that young people have to be in school, whether they want to be or not. In this regard students have something in common with the members of two other of our social institutions that have involuntary attendance: prisons and mental hospitals. The analogy, though dramatic, is not intended to be shocking, and certainly there is no comparison between the unpleasantness of life for inmates of our prisons and mental institutions, on the one hand, and the daily travails of a first or second grader, on the other. Yet the school child, like the incarcerated adult, is, in a sense, a prisoner. He too must come to grips with the inevitability of his experience. He too must develop strategies for dealing with the conflict that frequently arises between his natural desires and interests on the one hand and institutional expectations on the other.

Phillip W. Jackson

I am often asked whether I approve of compulsory education, and I usually reply that I do and that I wish we had it; we only have compulsory attendance.

John Bremer

" People disagree greatly about what ought to be taught in schools. The controversy wanes, though, when we get into the area of basics, the three R's. Everybody agrees, for instance, that all kids should be taught to read. Almost everybody agree. We think their arguments will help you develop your own position on just what subjects, if any, are sacred. **"**

There are a number of reasons why many educators feel students should all be taught the same things. One is simple inertia. The system has been teaching the same things for so long, it's difficult to change. Another reason is perhaps the hypnotic effect of all the new gadgets and techniques now available. All the computers and teaching machines and closed-circuit television systems; the programmed learning, systems analysis and operations research techniques—the whole brave new world of "educational technology"; all this tends to leave little time to think about *why* it is necessary to set the same learning goals for all children. A third reason is the belief that every child should be equipped with the same set of "basic skills."

When pressed to explain just what is meant by basic skills, most people have to admit that probably only the Three R's are really essential for every student. At first, this seems reasonable. But then one wonders, is it really still necessary for *everyone* to know even elementary arithmetic? The sort of arithmetic, that is, that they wouldn't pick up anyway in their day-to-day living? No one bothers even to do addition, let alone multiplication, in stores any more. Calculating machines are universal.

John Holt has some things to say on this subject in *The Underachieving School:*

...it seems to me that we have to think very carefully about the question of whether mathematics is some kind of necessity or whether it's an entertainment. I think a very good case can be made for it as an entertainment, rather like music. I happen to love music. But I think that a person who loves chess, or doing mathematics puzzles or proofs, is getting the kind of aesthetic satisfaction that I get listening to great music, and as far as I'm concerned it's as good as mine, and every bit as much worth encouraging. But when we talk about mathematics, whether arithmetic or in some loftier form, as a necessity for intelligent human life in the twentieth century, I part company. I think arithmetic in my country is largely a useless skill. Almost all the figuring done in the United States is done by machines and will be done so increasingly.

That leaves reading and writing. Apart from the fact that—as Holt points out in another section of his book—if we'd only leave them alone, children would nearly all learn this by themselves sooner or later anyway, since learning to read is so much easier than learning to talk, a skill in which children receive no formal instruction whatever—apart from all this, universal literacy would seem to be a somewhat mixed blessing.

There follow two quotations that raise the question of just how important it is that everyone learn to read. The first is from a book by Jacques Ellul called *Propaganda*, the second is from Sebastian de Grazia's book *Of Time, Work, & Leisure*.

People used to think that learning to read evidenced human progress; they still celebrate the decline of illiteracy as a great victory; they condemn countries with a large proportion of illiterates; they think that reading is a road to freedom. All this is debatable, for the important thing is not to be able to read, but to understand what one reads, to reflect on and judge what one reads. Outside of that, reading has no meaning (and even destroys certain automatic qualities of memory and observation). But to talk about critical faculties and discernment is to talk about something far above primary education and to consider a very small minority. The vast majority of people, perhaps 90 percent, know how to read, but do not exercise their intelligence beyond this. They attribute authority and eminent value to the printed word, or, conversely, reject it altogether. As these people do not possess enough knowledge to reflect and discern, they believe—or disbelieve—*in toto* what they read. And as such people, moreover, will select the easiest, not the hardest, reading matter, they are precisely on the level at which the printed word can seize and convince them without opposition. They are perfectly adapted to propaganda.

Reading and writing have become an index of educational progress. Doubtless they help increase the size of the community and enable a man to serve in the factory and army and to know what's on sale today, and what's going on in town tonight. Is this the knowledge the philosophers of democracy were interested in? Socrates was against writing, Plato expressed a similar aversion, Sicilian noblemen for a long time refused to read, holding that as with numerals the job is one for servants. Does reading serve as anything today but a bulletin board, a function largely reduced by radio and television, which do not call for reading? At one time a writer wrote a book for readers he knew almost personally and on whom he could count to read the book with care and thought. Today, and a hundred years ago too, a large proportion of Americans read, but few read anything better than the newspaper, that daily letter from the world to which they never write back. At one time poor people read well enough to read the Bible. Today the Bible is read by priests, students in theology and some in archaeology.

All this may not convince everyone that it is a waste of time to teach children the Three R's but it does at least make us wonder if these "basic skills" are quite as basic as we thought.

David Stansfield

164

There's a word that used to have a deep and serious meaning for most people in this country—the word "survival." It's a word that was used without confusion and without much hesitation in those days four years ago before the death of Robert Kennedy and Martin Luther King. Today the word has come to be transformed into the plaything of rich people. It becomes something complex and elegant, and infinitely exquisite. It becomes the search for value in the age of the machine. It becomes the longing to return to the good things of olden times. It becomes a ride into the country.

The kids right here in this black ghetto neighborhood of Boston where I live, happen to enjoy and dream about a ride into the country as much as any white kids that I know. Poor people, black people appreciate and long for pleasure, peace, escape from anguish, happiness and love, as much as any young white child; as much as any white adult. In spite of the implications in much of the counter-culture literature, rich white people in blue jeans and beads did not all at once discover sunshine, the smell of the warm earth in April, or the good taste of homemade bread in winter. It's just that they alone have the inherited cash and the lobotomized consciousness to make a whole life style out of the possession and the monopolization of these luxuries, while the poor must stay behind in festering ghettoes, and the generals remain behind to manufacture war.

In the face of myth, in the face of lies, in the face of mass manipulation, in the face of survival tools like windmills, potter's wheels, and hand pumps advertised within the pages of THE WHOLE EARTH CATALOGUE, in the face of rugged and exciting camping trips, known as survival training and marketed in the name of Outward Bound to those rich men and women who are doing very fine without it, in the face of all this high class hokum and deceit, there still is a literal meaning for the word "survival." Kids my wife and I see every day go in the streets year after year with raw, untreated sores, swollen wrists, scars on their throat and shoulder from untreated injuries of years before. Hundreds of kids we see as students or as neighbors here, are born in the deep South. In many instances the mothers of the kids we know have lived for so long on a diet of rice, fatback, and beans, and no beef, no butter, no milk, that they cannot adequately nourish their own infants. The children grow up in a state of non-stop desperation. They're born without hospitals, nurtured often without milk, schooled without love, indoctrinated without learning, and grow to their tormented manhood without the help of dentist, pediatrician, surgeon, or eye doctor. The only equal care they ever get is in the amicable supervision of the local precinct captain.

It's in the context of these kinds of lives, and it's in the daily contact with these kinds of needs that we must raise the question of the old, original, and unsophisticated definition of the word, "survival."

In the four years since the assassinations that took place in Memphis and Los Angeles, there's been a cold and bitter process of transliteration, in effect, throughout the land. Ecstasy now instead of ethics comes to be the

prime educational and social goal. Joylessness, not murder, barbarism, racism, devastation, becomes the word that wins the quarter million dollar grant, and makes the front page feature in the New York Times.

Therapy blank becomes the final substitute for social change. And fair play for the oppressed son, and the oppressed wife of the oppressive millionaire becomes in itself so vast and so complex and so remarkable as to make old-fashioned, tedious and square, those who with memories too deep, or loyalties too long, still need to speak of where the money comes from.

The poor are still here, and the people in the ghetto are still dying. But the children of the slum lords out in the suburbs are too busy weaving baskets, and innovative ladies are too busy putting wheat germ in the bread. Struggle is out. Macrame and organic vegetables are in.

Jonathan Kozol

I n my neighborhood, one family of four, who have been my friends now for six years, live on an annual income of 3,000 dollars. Another family, to which I have been drawn through friendship with two of the oldest children, has survived some recent 12-month periods on 1,800 dollars (there are 10 children in the family). Men and women who are locked into such lives will inevitably be unsettled by white persons who tell them that

their children do not really need degrees, do not need math or English, do not need to find out how to psych-out an exam, do not need college, do not need money, do not need ugly, contaminated, wicked, middle-class success. The issue for these children is not success. It is survival. . . .

Rage. It is in this context, then, that sane and sober parents, in such cities as New York and Boston, draw back in fear or anger at the condescending, if often idealistic, statements of young teachers who tell them to forget about English syntax and the Mathematics College Boards, but send away for bean seeds and for organic food supplies and get into grouptalk and encounter.

It seems to me that the parents of poor children are less backward and more realistic than some of their white co-workers are prepared to recognize. Survival skills are desperately important for the children of the powerless and the poor within this cold, efficient nation; they must not be sarcastically and ignorantly scorned by rich young white boys in blue jeans and boots with good degrees from Princeton, Oberlin and Yale.

Harlem does not need a new generation of radical basketweavers. It does need radical, strong, subversive, steadfast, skeptical, rage-minded, and power-wielding obstetricians, pediatricians, lab technicians, defense attorneys, building-code examiners, brain surgeons.

Jonathan Kozol

T hroughout history, whether among the so-called civilized, or so-called primitive, societies, people have had to be taught to be stupid. For to permit the mind to expand to its outermost capabilities results in a challenge to traditional ways. Hence the paradox that while man is intelligent he must also be trained to be stupid, and that a certain amount of intellectual sabotage must be introduced into all educational systems. It is better to have a somewhat stupid population than one trained beyond the capacities of the culture to absorb intelligence. It is clear that teachers with incisive minds, willing to take their students along all possible logical pathways, willing to entertain all intelligent questions, are a danger to any system. Hence, all educational systems must train people to be *unintelligent* within the limits of the culture's ability to survive. That is to say, there seems to be a decisive range, on the one side, where, if a people are too *stupid*, the culture will fall apart, and, on the other side, if they are too *intelligent*, the culture will also fall apart. The cutting points of this range are where the upward curve of intellect meets the downward curve of culturally necessary stupidity.

Common controversies in education revolve not so much around what students should know, and how they should learn, but how stupid we can permit them to be without wrecking the country and the world.

Jules Henry

We guess Henry means good teaching is keeping close to the cutting points of the population range.

166

23

What Schools Can(not) Do for Society

A way to verbalize what you believe schools should do to improve society or to correct social ills and perhaps clarify about the goals schools can and cannot serve.

Largely a self-directed experience. Requires at least an hour of group time, unless pairs can work together outside the group.

1 Divide into pairs, perhaps with someone with whom you have not yet had a chance to work. (Alternatively, this experience can be carried out by individuals.)

2 Choose an organization or interest group that you would like to represent. For example, you might represent a group that is working:

- to reduce the income gap between the very rich and very poor
- for women's liberation/rights
- to protect the environment
- to eliminate TV advertising
- to end war
- to eliminate racial injustice
- to prevent overpopulation in the world
- to wipe out smut in our schools
- to promote free enterprise
- for public support of religious schools
- for improved tax laws
- to get the U.S. out of the U.N.
- for the rights of American Indians
- for more law and order
- to change abortion laws
- to free up public education
- to bring honesty back into government
- to reverse the Louisiana Purchase
- for any other cause

3 Then, each pair lists the main points it would make in a letter to a superintendent of schools, given this situation:

Your organization appointed you to visit a large public school system to see what, if anything, the schools were doing in support of your worthy cause. You made a visit. The superintendent was polite and sympathetic to your concerns. He said that he did not doubt that the schools could do more than they were now doing, but that he was not certain how to proceed without unduly offend- ing those who were not in support of your cause. He asked you to write him a letter specifying what you thought the schools could and should do. He said that he would bring your letter to the attention of the Board of Education and that he would support any reasonable recommendations it con- tained. He again cautioned you against recom- mending actions that were unfair to other interest groups and he wished you good luck. You are, therefore, to write a letter saying how and why you believe the schools should support your cause.

4 Simply pass around the outlined letters (final writing is not necessary) so that others may read them. Or share the letters in another way:

a. Three pairs sit together. One pair starts by reading the letter it wrote aloud.

b. Members of the other two pairs then com- ment on the likelihood of a school's accept- ing the letter's recommendations. They may also suggest ways to improve the letter.

c. The same steps are followed for the other two pairs.

d. Then, each group defines what it sees as the limits of or the power of schools to promote social change or to correct social ills.

PEANUTS

I LEARNED SOMETHING IN SCHOOL TODAY

I GOT SPELLING, HISTORY, ARITHMETIC AND TWO STUDY PERIODS

I SIGNED UP FOR FOLK GUITAR, COMPUTER PROGRAMMING, STAINED GLASS ART, SHOEMAKING AND A NATURAL FOODS WORKSHOP.

SO WHAT DID YOU LEARN?

I LEARNED THAT WHAT YOU SIGN UP FOR AND WHAT YOU GET ARE TWO DIFFERENT THINGS

What are schools for?

It may seem presumptuous of me to suggest that I know the answer to this question. Yet the answer I will give is the answer that an overwhelming majority of our fellow citizens would also give. It is the answer that would have been given by most educators of the past who established and operated schools. Indeed, the only reason the question needs to be asked and answered at this time is that some influential educators have been conned into accepting wrong answers to the question. Let me mention a few of these wrong answers:

—Schools are not custodial institutions responsible for coping with emotionally disturbed or incorrigible young people, for keeping nonstudents off the streets or out of the job market.

—Schools are not adjustment centers, responsible for helping young people develop favorable self-concepts, solve personal problems, and come to terms with life.

—Schools are not recreational facilities designed to entertain and amuse, to cultivate the enjoyment of freedom, to help young people find strength through joy.

—Schools are not social research agencies, to which a society can properly delegate responsibility for the discovery of solutions to the problems that are currently troubling the society.

I do not deny that society needs to be concerned about some of the things just mentioned. What I do deny is that schools were built and are maintained primarily to solve such problems. I deny that schools are good places in which to seek solutions, or that they have demonstrated much success in finding them. Schools have a very important special mission. If they accept responsibility for solving many of the other problems that trouble some young people, they are likely to fail in their primary mission, without having much success in solving the rest of our social problems.

Then what is the right answer to the question. What are schools for? I believe it is that schools are for learning, and that what ought to be learned mainly is useful knowledge. . . .

. . . Where ability to make correct judgments of value is concerned, we more typically speak of wisdom, perhaps, than of knowledge. And "wisdom" connotes one character which is not knowledge at all, though it is quality inculcated by experience; the temper, namely, which avoids perversity in intentions, and the insufficiently considered in actions. But for the rest, wisdom and knowledge are distinct merely because there is so much of knowledge which, for any given individual or under the circumstances which obtain, is relatively inessential to judgment of values and to success in action. Thus a man may be pop-eyed with correct information and still lack wisdom, because his information has little bearing on those judgments of relative value which he is called upon to make, or because he lacks capacity to discriminate the practically important from the unimportant, or to apply his information to concrete problems of action. And men of humble attainments so far as breadth of information goes may still be wise by their correct apprehension of such values as lie open to them and of the roads to these. But surely wisdom is a type of knowledge; that type which is oriented on the important and the valuable. The wise man is he who knows where good lies, and how to act so that it may be attained.
[C. I. Lewis]

I take Professor Lewis to mean that, apart from the rectitude in purposes and the deliberateness in action that experience must teach, wisdom in action is dependent on relevant knowledge. If that is so, the best the schools can do to foster wisdom is to help students cultivate knowledge. . . .

Let me now recapitulate what I have tried to say about what schools are for.

1. Public education in America today is in trouble.

2. Though many conditions contribute to our present difficulties, the fundamental cause is our own confusions concerning the central purpose of our activities.

3. Schools have been far too willing to accept responsibility for solving all of the problems of young people, for meeting all of their immediate needs. That schools have failed to discharge these obligations successfully is clearly evident.

4. Schools are for learning. They should bend most of their efforts to the facilitation of learning.

5. The kind of learning on which schools should concentrate most of their efforts is cognitive competence, the command of useful knowledge.

6. Knowledge is a structure of relationships among concepts. It must be built by the learner himself as he seeks understanding of the information he has received.

7. Affective dispositions are important by-products of all human experience, but they seldom are or should be the principal targets of our educational efforts. We should be much more concerned with moral education than with affective education.

8. Intellectual skills are more often praised as educational goals than defined clearly enough to be taught effectively. Broadly general intellectual skills are mainly hypothetical constructs which are hard to demonstrate in real life. Highly specific intellectual skills are simply aspects of knowledge.

9. Wisdom depends primarily on knowledge, secondarily on experience.

10. Schools should not accept responsibility for the success of every pupil in learning, since that success depends so much on the pupil's own efforts.

11. Learning is a personal activity which each student must carry on for himself.

12. Individual learning is greatly facilitated by group instruction.

13. Schools should be held accountable for providing a good learning environment, which consists of a) capable, enthusiastic teachers, b) abundant and appropriate instructional materials, c) formal recognition and reward of achievement, and d) a class of willing learners.

14. Since learning cannot be made compulsory, school attendance ought not to be compulsory either.

Schools ought to be held accountable. One way or another, they surely will be held accountable. If they persist in trying to do too many things, things they were not de-signed and are not equipped to do well, things that in some cases cannot be done at all, they will show up badly when called to account. But there is one very important thing to do well, and that many schools have done very well in the past. That is to cultivate cognitive competence, to foster the learning of useful knowledge. If they keep this as their primary aim, and do not allow unwilling learners to sabotage the learning process, they are likely to give an excellent accounting of their effectiveness and worth.

Robert L. Ebel

❝ We guess that makes us a couple of "conned educators." Carl Rogers would undoubtedly be one of the "influential educators that have been conned" that Ebel talks about. Let's see what Rogers has to say. ❞

I wish to present some very brief remarks, in the hope that if they bring forth any reaction from you, I may get some new light on my own ideas.

I find it a very troubling thing to *think*, particularly when I think about my own experiences and try to extract from those experiences the meaning that seems genu-inely inherent in them. At first such thinking is very satisfying, because it seems to dis-cover sense and pattern in a whole host of discrete events. But then it very often be-comes dismaying, because I realize how ridiculous these thoughts, which have much value to me, would seem to most people. My impression is that if I try to find the meaning of my own experience it leads me, nearly always, in directions regarded as absurd.

So in the next three or four minutes, I will try to digest some of the meanings which have come to me from my classroom experi-ence and the experience I have had in indi-vidual and group therapy. They are in no way intended as conclusions for someone else, or a guide to what others should do or be. They are the very tentative meanings, as of April 1952, which my experience has had for me, and some of the bothersome ques-tions which their absurdity raises. I will put each idea or meaning in a separate lettered paragraph, not because they are in any partic-ular logical order, but because each meaning is separately important to me.

a. I may as well start with this one in view of the purposes of this conference. *My experi-ence has been that I cannot teach another person how to teach.* To attempt it is for me, in the long run, futile.

b. *It seems to me that anything that can be taught to another is relatively inconsequential, and has little or no significant influence on behavior.* That sounds so ridiculous I can't help but question it at the same time that I present it.

c. *I realize increasingly that I am only interested in learnings which significantly influence behavior.* Quite possibly this is simply a personal idio-syncrasy.

d. *I have come to feel that the only learning which significantly influences behavior is self-discovered, self-appropriated learning.*

e. *Such self-discovered learning, truth that has been personally appropriated and assimilated in experience, cannot be directly communicated to another.* As soon as an individual tries to communicate such experience directly, often with a quite natural enthusiasm, it becomes teaching, and its results are inconsequential. It was some relief recently to discover that Søren Kierkegaard, the Danish philosopher, had found this too, in his own experience, and stated it very clearly a century ago. It made it seem less absurd.

f. As a consequence of the above, *I realize that I have lost interest in being a teacher.*

g. When I try to teach, as I do sometimes, I am appalled by the results, which seem a little more than inconsequential, because sometimes the teaching appears to succeed. When this happens I find that the results are damaging. It seems to cause the individual to distrust his own experience, and to stifle significant learning. *Hence I have come to feel that the outcomes of teaching are either unimportant or hurtful.*

h. When I look back at the results of my past teaching, the real results seem the same—either damage was done—or nothing significant occurred. This is frankly trou-bling.

i. As a consequence, *I realize that I am only interested in being a learner, preferably learning things that matter, that have some significant in-fluence on my own behavior.*

j. I find it very rewarding to learn, in groups, in relationships with one person as in therapy, or by myself.

k. I find that one of the best, but most difficult, ways for me to learn is to drop my own defensiveness, at least temporarily, and to try to understand the way in which his experience seems and feels to the other person.

l. I find that another way of learning for me is to state my own uncertainties, to try to clarify my puzzlements, and thus get closer to the meaning that my experience actually seems to have.

m. This whole train of experiencing, and the meanings that I have thus far discovered in it, seem to have launched me on a process which is both fascinating and at times a little frightening. It seems to mean letting my experiences carry me on, in a direction which appears to be forward, toward goals that I can but dimly define, as I try to understand at least the current meaning of that experience. The sensation is that of floating with a complex stream of experience, with the fascinating possibility of trying to comprehend its ever-changing complexity.

I am almost afraid I may seem to have gotten away from any discussion of learning, as well as teaching. Let me again introduce a practical note by saying that by themselves these interpretations of my experience may sound queer and aberrant, but not particularly shocking. It is when I realize the implications that I shudder a bit at the distance I have come from the commonsense world that everyone knows is right. I can best illustrate this by saying that if the experiences of others had been the same as mine, and if they had discovered similar meanings in it, many consequences would be implied:

a. Such experience would imply that we would do away with teaching. People would get together if they wished to learn.

b. We would do away with examinations. They measure only the inconsequential type of learning.

c. We would do away with grades and credits for the same reason.

d. We would do away with degrees as a measure of competence partly for the same reason. Another reason is that a degree marks an end or a conclusion of something, and a learner is only interested in the continuing process of learning.

Carl Rogers

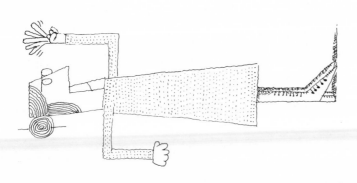

24

It Goes with the Job

An enjoyable way to become aware of the personal constraints that contemporary society places on teachers.

A group- or self-directed experience. Requires about twenty minutes.

You'll teach only about six or seven hours out of about 190 days of the year. But you'll live all those other hours, too. Society's expectations for the role of the school are reflected in its expectations for the role of the teacher in that school. Teachers have traditionally been expected to be special kinds of people.

Take a look at New York State, 1872.

1. Teachers each day will fill lamps, clear chimneys, and clean wicks.
2. Each teacher will bring a bucket of water and a scuttle of coal for the day's session.
3. Make your pens carefully. You may whittle nibs for the individual tastes of the pupils.
4. Men teachers may take one evening a week for courting purposes, or two evenings a week if they attend church regularly.
5. After ten hours in school, teachers should spend the remaining time reading the Bible or other good books.
6. Women teachers who marry or engage in unseemly conduct will be dismissed.

7. Each teacher who smokes, uses liquor in any form, frequents pool or public halls, or gets shaved in a barber shop, will be giving good reason to suspect his worth, intentions, integrity, and honesty.

Or how about Idaho, 1923?

1. Be home from 8 p.m. to 6 a.m.
2. Do not loiter in ice cream parlors.
3. Do not smoke cigarettes, and do not drink beer, wine, or whiskey.
4. Do not leave town without permission.
5. Do not ride in a carriage or auto with any man except your father or brother.
6. Do not dress in bright colors, dye your hair, or use face powder, mascara, or lipstick, and wear at least two petticoats.
7. Sweep the classroom at least once daily; start the fire at 7 a.m., and scrub the floor at least once each week.

That's pretty grim stuff. Still it was a half century ago and times have changed. But, how much? Why don't you, either alone or with some friends, try to conjure up a list of seven contemporary dos and don'ts for teachers? Social, political, professional, personal, any kind. You can write them here:

1. _____

2. _____

3. _____

4. _____

Children must be taught to accept the idea of fixed occupational niches and be so instructed that the freshman's question, "Philosophy is interesting, but what can you do with it?" will never become absurd. The question, "What am I doing with my life?" is the enemy of the question, "What job can I get?" The occupational system requires that the question, "Is this what I really want to do?" should not rise into consciousness, for it is an iron law of culture that to the degree that education touches on occupation at all it must not permit the question to exist.

Jules Henry

Well, perhaps the question should not exist, but it's just been raised. So...

5. _____

6. _____

7. _____

...

Consider your list in terms of these questions:

- How many of the rules normally go unstated—they're just "understood"?

- Envision your seven rules in the setting of an urban school system. Or an affluent suburban system. Or a rural system. What do you conclude from placing them in each of these contexts?

- How rapidly do you think your seven rules will become antiquated? Why will they become outdated, if ever?

- Are you willing to abide by all seven of your rules? If you aren't, what will you do: Not teach? Fight for your civil liberties in the courts? Or take another course of action?

" One of the things that goes with the job is what parents expect of you. **"**

School is one of many institutions and it need not become subservient to the purposes of other institutions. It indeed has an obligation to assert its own goals and pursue them.

I don't think a school, in other words, is a citizenship training center for the political activation of a community. I don't think a school is where children learn to understand their unconscious and learn to become more effectively mature and adult in the way psychologists or psychiatrists use those words.

The parents I talked with, poor and working class alike, send their children to school to get what they call education. By that they mean learning to read, to write; to have the power of doing arithmetic; to learn increasingly facts, figures; to acquire the capacity to think and have ideas. Now naturally there is a psychological, anthropological, and sociological and political dimension to all this. But to turn away from this primary concern of education—namely the command of skills, the command of symbols, the command of the language, the command of reading, writing, arithmetic—to turn away from this is not what the vast majority of the families I've come into contact with want for their children.

This is the central issue: the nature of the profession in a particular society; the amount of respect it's granted; the amount of financial backing it's granted. One can only hope that some of this will change with the years.

Robert Coles

" You might find it useful to go back and reconsider what Reichart had to say about the social constraints that can go along with the job (page 124). **"**

" These next three readings describe court cases involving teachers' rights. While they paint a very pessimistic picture of what a teacher's life has been in the past, at the same time they paint an optimistic picture of what it will be in the future. **"**

Believe it or not, the courts think teachers have the same rights as everyone else. Recent decisions have established that they can, among other things, get pregnant, practice homosexuality or oppose the Vietnam war, not necessarily in that order, and still not lose their jobs. The only caveat is that their idiosyncrasies and political preferences must not adversely affect their teaching.

Two other recent decisions have special interest:

- Judge Irving Kaufman of the U.S. Court of Appeals declared that school officials had violated the rights of Charles James, a teacher who was discharged from Addison High School near Corning, New York, because he wore a black armband to protest the Vietnam war. "More than a decade of Supreme Court precedent leaves no doubt that we cannot countenance school authorities arbitrarily censoring a teacher's speech merely because they do not agree with the teacher's political philosophies or leanings," Judge Kaufman wrote.

- The U.S. District Court in Lincoln, Nebraska, ordered the reinstatement of another teacher, Frances Fischer, who had been fired by the local school board for "conduct unbecoming a teacher."

What's "conduct unbecoming a teacher"? Well, it turns out that the school board was upset because Fischer allowed friends of her 26-year-old son to "visit and stay at her apartment for varying lengths of time."

Judge Warren Urbom held that "when viewed most favorably from the position of the Board of Education, and taking every permissible inference from the testimony at the hearing, there is simply no proof of impropriety in Mrs. Fischer's conduct which affected her classroom performance, her relationship with students under her care, or otherwise had any bearing on any interest possessed by the board."

LEARNING magazine

Under a new contract negotiated by Berkeley Local 1076 of the California Teachers' Association, "a prospective or new father may take a personal or maternity leave."

LEARNING magazine

What are the pressing domestic concerns of Americans in the seventies?

Even a cursory glance at the mass media, governmental commission reports, and legislative hearings reveals new emphasis on problems affecting environment, race relations, and youth. These problems are now debated everywhere—from the corridors of power to the wide expanse of the grass roots. And few would question the right of every individual to discuss these issues in a vigorous way.

What happens, however, when the classroom teacher attempts to translate the debate into meaningful learning experiences? What transpires when the teacher encourages pupils to develop skills in defining problems, setting goals, and seeking answers based upon an open assessment of facts? What occurs when an educator exercises his judgment in choice of methods and materials to be utilized in the classroom?

All these questions relate to the concept of academic freedom—the right to seek the truth, including the right to inquire about, discover, publish, and teach the truth. Long held as a cherished ideal at the college and university level, academic freedom is also the subject of legal actions on behalf of elementary and secondary educators. [Here is a sample case.]

One suit institutes legal proceedings against a school board which, it is alleged, arbitrarily refused to rehire a second grade teacher who believes her pupils must become actively involved in education. Its explanation was that she was "teaching her second grade students to protest."

Mildred Downs, who has 26 years of class-room teaching experience and impeccable ratings, maintains that letter-writing skills are important. Each year she asks her young students to write letters requesting more information or perhaps making a request. Last year, in connection with a unit on nutrition, the children decided to write to the cafeteria supervisor expressing their preference for raw, rather than cooked, carrots.

The best letter was selected—signed by all who preferred that raw carrots be served—and mailed to the supervisor. The superintendent subsequently, it is claimed, accused Mrs. Downs of "inciting rebellion" in the classroom.

The carrot incident was not the only matter mentioned by the superintendent at a school board meeting prior to official notice of non-renewal. Reportedly, he had previously objected to Mrs. Downs' efforts to correct the school environment. A smoking incinerator which burned trash in the school yard often poured smoke into her classroom. In seeking correction of this situation, Mrs. Downs alleges she had challenged his statement that *no* school's trash was collected, and she inadvertently discovered that city policy did call for removal of trash from *junior high* and *high* schools in Conway, Arkansas. The local PTA is now arranging for such collections in the *elementary* schools.

At another time, Mrs. Downs asked her pupils to draw pictures of how they felt on a sweltering spring day. Because the school water fountain had been out of commission for some time, some of her students drew cartoons depicting children wilting like flowers.

If the nonrenewal of Mrs. Downs' contract was because she called attention to food preferences and water fountain problems and to pollution in school yards, then this raises questions as to the validity of the nonrenewal. Was she victimized for exercising free expression rights, which would seem to be constitutionally protected?

NEA DuShane Emergency Fund

School is almost always evaluative. Going to school means living under a constant condition of having one's words and deeds evaluated by others. Given the way in which evaluation is usually handled, this in turn means a sharp demarcation of power and authority between student and teacher. The teacher not only is the one who keeps the child in school, he is also the one who evaluates him.

Charles E. Silberman

One of a teacher's most difficult and important tasks is making fair, accurate evaluations (feedback) of his students' performances. The difficulty of the task is compounded when evaluation must be accompanied by grading. Any time one is asked to describe everything he knows about another human being by a letter or numeral, he tries, in effect, to categorize human experience. The task is difficult and its results are misleading. Yet, teachers are continuously required to both evaluate and grade. Making a clear distinction between these two activities is extremely important.

Evaluation is a crucial, ongoing, diagnostic process in which both teachers and students must engage in order to educate each other. The process is important to teachers because its results indicate how their teaching must be altered to help individual students or specific groups of students. Evaluation is an important activity to students because of the ongoing knowledge-of-results it affords. The process is crucial because the ability to accurately evaluate one's own work is prerequisite to the ultimate goal of all education—the development of the independent learner.

In contrast, grading is a social phenomenon with deep historic roots, the efficacy of which has long been disputed. Grades are labels applied in widely varying situations for a myriad of reasons to somehow describe human experience. Like all labels, grades have meaning only to the extent that a consensus exists on what they denote. No such agreement exists. Few attempt to defend rationales for grading students. The practice survives largely because of tradition, administrative expediency, and bureaucratic intransigence.

Tom Gregory

25

An Answer That's a Problem

A way to examine your values regarding grading and become aware of the criteria you unwittingly use to grade a simple arithmetic problem.

An experience involving several people; in fact, the more the better. Requires about thirty minutes. Appoint one person to act as tabulator of results.

Whether for good or for bad, most schools grade students. Anyone considering teaching could use some firsthand experience with grading from the teacher's side of the desk.

We all know that grading an essay is a relatively subjective activity. One study asked a large number of English professors to evaluate about fifty college themes by placing them in about fifteen stacks labeled from best to worst. You would expect considerable disagreement, but the results were still mindboggling. The collection of professors managed to disagree so much that *every paper appeared at one time or another in every stack!*

We're not going to ask you to do anything as tough as grade a theme. Instead, we'd like you to grade just one problem from one student's arithmetic test. Now math's objective. It has nice yes-no, right-wrong answers. Or so it would seem at first. But let's look closer.

Imagine that you are teaching sixth grade and that you've given your students a test containing ten problems, the first of which is printed below. Each problem is worth a maximum of ten points.

Arithmetic Test

Work the following problems and show your steps in arriving at the solutions:

1. If 3 apples cost 13¢, how much will 7 apples cost?

$$3\overline{)13.00} \qquad \begin{array}{r} 4.56 \\ \times 7 \\ \hline 31.92 \end{array}$$

$$\begin{array}{r} 4.56 \\ 3\overline{)13.00} \\ \underline{12} \\ 10 \\ \underline{8} \\ 20 \end{array}$$

Answer: 31.92

Now, write one of the following scores for this student's work on a scrap of paper and pass it in to the tabulator. (Do not disclose your grade to others as yet.)

Scores:

0 1 2 3 4 5 6 7 8 9 10

⋮

The tabulator tallies the scores, being careful to maintain the participants' anonymity, and shares the results with the group. Consider some of these questions.

- What do you think accounts for disparity in the scoring?
- If all of you were teachers in the same elementary school, you could try to come up with common criteria for scoring arithmetic problems or you could ignore the situation. Which makes most sense? Does either alternative?
- Some teachers take into account many things they know about a student in determining his grade: his past work, handwriting, effort, family background, maybe even smiling or ear cleaning. Other teachers try to separate the person from his work by taking only the piece of paper before them into account. Which is most fair? Or do these two practices simply have different kinds of fairness?
- How much weight should be given to the answer (product) and how much to the method used (process)?
- What have you learned about grading from this experience?
- What have you learned about yourself as a grader?
- How much should the seven apples cost, by the way?

"Cool it, friends. Martin, will you get the folders and pass them out?"

"Mr. Hillman, what is my grade?"

"What grade do you want, Vivian?"

"I'd like an A."

"What will you do with it?"

"I've always wanted one. I think I deserve one for the work I've been doing?"

"Do you know how I feel about grades?"

"Yes, but I don't think that's right. It's good to work for grades."

"I'll agree with you that grades are O.K.—that is, if the wanting and trying to know come first. If you do that, the grade will come by itself. Regardless of what it is, it still won't be anything but a letter."

"I know all that. But I'd just like to have an A on my grade card sometime."

"I'll go along with that. Why don't we discuss it with the class when evaluation time comes up again."

"Oh, they'll be too jealous to vote me an A."

"No, I don't think so. If you and I convince them of what your work has been and what you're working for, you'll get that A easily."

I wonder if anyone has ever stopped to figure how much of a teacher's time is spent figuring out grades, marking grades, computing grades, entering grades in records, putting them on report cards, discussing them with students and parents and colleagues—and weighed all that against the pain and sorrow grades produce. I wonder how the high schools ever became the agency responsible for culling out the low achievers for colleges.

Aaron Hillman

// Maybe grades are to teachers what flax is to students. (See page 154.) **//**

// This reading ties in with what de Saint-Exupéry had to say back on page 15. **//**

People who have been schooled down to size let unmeasured experience slip out of their hands. To them, what cannot be measured becomes secondary, threatening. They do not have to be robbed of their creativity. Under instruction, they have unlearned to "do" their thing or "be" themselves, and value only what has been made or could be made.

Once people have the idea schooled into them that values can be produced and measured, they tend to accept all kinds of rankings. There is a scale for the development of nations, another for the intelligence of babies, and even progress toward peace can be calculated according to body count. In a schooled world the road to happiness is paved with a consumer's index.

Ivan Illich

Randy is a bright-eyed, enthusiastic, not very quick, but not easily frustrated eleven-year-old boy. He works carefully, slowly, methodically. He tries very hard. He seems to accept his slower mind philosophically. He once said to me, "You don't have to be smart to be good at *everything*. I'm *great* at baseball!" But there is in him a strong, clear desire to do better—to star. The things he does to his satisfaction delight him—he beams.

One time I gave him an A in history. His work was very ordinary, perhaps 'worth' a C, but he did the best he could. Carefully. And when I was making out those report cards and thought of how happy it would make him to get an A in something—probably the only A he would ever get in his school life—when I imagined his face brightening, the excitement and joy and pride, the decision made itself.

I watched him out of the corner of my eye as I was handing out the report cards, anticipating his reaction. His hand shot up excitedly after he glanced over his card. "Miss Murphy!" "Yes, Randy?" "Miss Murphy, but how'd I get to be so *smart?*"

He looked both genuinely puzzled and delighted. I felt warm and good. I don't know who was more delighted, he or I. And I was again reminded of how Randy viewed himself as intellectually inferior.

"You worked hard, Randy. You deserved that A." He looked down at his report card, beaming.

I will never forget that look.

If you give a hundred kids in a room a hundred facts to memorize, and you grade them on a curve, only about 15 of them are going to learn enough to get a payoff. The other 85 are going to get no payoff and feel badly. Now you could say, learning the facts was worthwhile. But was it?

It wasn't for the kids who didn't learn. But if you give a hundred kids the chance to think and give them a school setting in which thinking pays off, then almost all of them are going to end up feeling good. And if they feel good, they'll want to do more.

I've often said school for most children is like playing bingo with no prizes. You're asked to do a routine task with small reward, and nobody in his right mind plays eagerly unless he believes he has a chance for a prize. The prizes the schools use are A's, but they give out only a limited number to selected players.

Now if I'm playing real bingo with 50 people, I know that every time I play the game I have as good a chance to win as anyone else. But in the school bingo game, most of the cards have a little green dot at the bottom. The kids play for a while without winning and finally say, "Why is there a green dot on my card?" And the teacher will say, "Oh, I forgot to tell you. If you've got a card with a green dot, you'll never win." And they don't—and they resent it but they can't leave the game.

So the kids sort themselves out. The more successful ones drift toward the front of the room. And the less successful kids—the losers—start going to the back of the room.

Jacqueline Murphy

Ernie took a stack of homework papers from a drawer of his desk and uncapped his red pen. Composition. Sentences. Ernie had given them the first part of each sentence, up to the comma. They were to write the rest. He looked at the name in the top right corner, Keith Morrison, and began to read the sentences.

His face had that special look, *vespertine in shadow and a paragon of all the ladies.*

Ernie read the sentence four times before going on to the next.

There lay the pond, blazing a queer chiaroscuro of flickering light.

He read it again and moved on.

That day she had seemed like a typical tourist, sweeping as a new broom.

He grimaced at her, *introceptively, eyes radiating a nauseated belch.*

He carried his lunch bag in his right hand, rising *forth a vulgar odor of encroached tuna fish.*

They said "Good-bye," *aggrieved to see their fond friends leave.*

Ernie wrote in red at the bottom of the page:

Dear Keith,

Looks like you've made a breakthrough. You have met the enemy and he is yours. I'd never be able to write a sentence as good as these. How do you do it? I wish we were in another place at another time so that I could give you an A-double-plus for this work.

That's what you deserve. But if Max Rafferty ever found out, it would be my ass, kid. So I'll probably wind up giving you a D-plus and you'll hate my guts for the rest of your life.

Darryl Ponicsan

26

Spelling Bee (Also A, C, D, and F)

An introduction to several of the factors that contaminate the grading process.

A group experience. Requires forty-five to sixty minutes. Appoint one person to act as tabulator of results.

All right, so arithmetic problems aren't so easy to grade after all. Let's try an easier subject— maybe the easiest of all—spelling. After all, the answer's either right or wrong. You either know it or you don't.

Grading

There are two ground rules in this exercise.

a. As you work through the steps, try not to share your work or thoughts with anyone else. You'll have plenty of time to do this after you've completed the steps.

b. Don't begin another step in the sequence until you've completed and turned in to the tabulator your responses to the preceding step.

TEST OVER SELECTED SPELLING DEMONS

NAME _Janice Henry_

CLASS _English 8_ PERIOD _3rd_

1. accommodate	37. prejudice
2. aeronautics	38. privilege
3. apparatus	39. professor
4. beginning	40. psychology
5. cemetery	41. recommend
6. chauffeur	42. referred
7. completion	43. restaurant
8. conscientious	44. sacrilegious
9. cylinder	45. seize
10. defense	46. separate
11. descent	47. similar
12. dessert	48. sophomore
13. discipline	49. therefore
14. ecstasy	50. they're
15. embarrass	51. tobacco
16. exaggerated	52. unnecessary
17. foreign	53. vengeance
18. grammar	54. yield
19. grievous	
20. height	
21. interrupt	
22. lieutenant	
23. livable	
24. maintenance	
25. mathematics	
26. mileage	
27. mischievous	
28. misspell	
29. murmur	
30. noticeable	
31. nuisance	
32. occurrence	
33. original	
34. pamphlet	
35. parliament	
36. personnel	

Key to Spelling Demons Test

1. accommodate
2. aeronautics
3. apparatus
4. beginning
5. cemetery
6. chauffeur
7. complexion
8. conscientious
9. cylinder
10. defense
11. descent
12. dessert
13. discipline
14. ecstasy
15. embarrass
16. exaggerated
17. foreign
18. grammar
19. grievous
20. height
21. interrupt
22. lieutenant
23. lovable
24. maintenance
25. mathematics
26. mileage
27. mischievous
28. misspell
29. murmur
30. noticeable
31. nuisance
32. occurrence
33. original
34. pamphlet
35. parliament
36. personnel
37. prejudice
38. privilege
39. professor
40. psychology
41. recommend
42. referred
43. restaurant
44. sacrilegious
45. seize
46. separate
47. similar
48. sophomore
49. therefore
50. they're
51. tobacco
52. unnecessary
53. vengeance
54. yield

1 On the facing page, you'll find Janice Henry's (an eighth grader) performance on a test of 54 spelling demons.

Check Janice's performance on each word against the key provided on this page, and then enter her total score (the number correct) in the space below.

———— Number of Correct Words

Write "step one" and the number of correct words on a scrap of paper and turn it in to the tabulator.* Then go on to step two, on page 184.

———————

*For each step, the tabulator tallies the scores and records the results, using the boxes on pages 184–185 as a model for tabulation.

183

1 First, let's look at how well you scored Janice's work.

Number correct:

35 or lower	36	37	38	39	40	41	42	43 or higher

If your group is like most groups, many of you, perhaps a third or even a half, scored the test incorrectly. Contaminant number one in the grading process, the teacher's error rate, enters the picture. Of course, students often inform teachers of grading errors, especially if the error works in their favor. But look at the range of errors on this test. Usually most of the errors that occur on this particular test favor the student. Suppose, for a moment, that Janice tries to be honest, comes forward with her paper, and says, "Teacher, you gave me a 39 and I think I should have gotten a 37." Now you're really in a box. Do you reward her honesty by letting her keep the points? Enter contaminant number two, a part of Janice's spelling grade may be for honesty, not spelling ability.

2 Let's see how you did on computing percentages.

Percentages computed:

55	60	65	68	68.5	69	70	75

(Round off your tally to the most approximate answer.)

---

2 If you scored Janice's test accurately, you found that she spelled 37 of the 54 words correctly. Haven Cove Junior High uses an A, B, C, D, F marking system, with D being the lowest passing mark. When marks are expressed as percentages, teachers are given considerable freedom in assigning letter grades, but general practice is to regard 70 percent as barely passing.

Calculate Janice's percentage mark:

_____% (Use the correct score of 37 even if you misscored her test.)

Give her a grade (A, B, C, D, F): _____
(The school drops +'s and −'s.)

Write "step two" and the percentage mark and grade you gave Janice on a scrap of paper and turn it in to the tabulator. Then go on to step three.

3 Here are the scores earned on this test by students in Janice's class:

Highest Score 41
Lowest Score 26
Average Score 33
Janice's Score 37 (one of top four)

Regardless of your earlier grade, decide what grade you would give Janice now (A, B, C, D, F): _____

Write "step three" and the grade you gave Janice on a scrap of paper and turn it in to the tabulator. Then go on to step four.

---

4 There are nine eighth-grade English classes at Haven Cove Junior High. Two-hundred and fifty students (all nine classes) took the same spelling test and scored as follows:

Highest Score 42
Lowest Score 0
Average Score 22
Janice's Score 37 (one of the top five)

Reconsider, if necessary, and give Janice a grade (A, B, C, D, F): _____

Write "step four" and the grade you gave Janice on a scrap of paper and turn it in to the tabulator.

. . .

Results

We suggest that you deal with the results one step at a time. As you do, you'll discover a whole series of problems that contaminate the grading process.

For each step, the tabulator will have tallied the scores. As you proceed through each step, he might announce these results, so that you can record your friends' calculations in the boxes provided; this or a similar method of making the results public (such as displaying them on an overhead projector) will make them available to the entire group as you discuss the factors that contaminate the grading process. No matter how the results are given to the group, we stress that the tabulator reveal them one step at a time.

The correct percentage is 68.5, so consider 68, 68.5, or 69 percent correct. Usually many teachers miscompute that percentage. Enter contaminant number three, a part of Janice's spelling grade may be the teacher's ability to compute a percentage. It doesn't take long to see why tests so regularly contain a number of items that is easily computable; a spelling test may have 10 words, or 20 or 25 or 50, but probably not 54.

What grade did Janice get when you knew only her score and the school's rule of thumb of 70 percent as passing? (Second part of step two.)

Knowing only Janice's score:

A	B	C	D	F

First, note the range of grades Janice gets. Depending on which one of you she has for a teacher, Janice can receive several different grades for doing the exact same work on a yes-no, right-wrong spelling test. Enter con- taminant number four, your respective and very individual standards for what constitutes good, average, or bad work.

Second, in most groups a number of people disregard the school's guideline of 70 as standard. Some do this in an attempt to be fair; it's a difficult test and a score of 37 de- serves more than an F. But grades make it tough to be fair. As in this case, we might trade one kind of fairness for another. We can give Janice a justifiable break, or we can be fair to all the kids in all those other eighth- grade classrooms by giving her the same grade they are getting. But we can't have it both ways. Enter contaminant number five, the way teachers attempt to be fair.

3 A different grade distribution usually emer- ges when groups learn how Janice's work stacks up against the work of students in her own class.

Knowing information about Janice's class:

A	B	C	D	F

Note that Janice's grades usually improve dramatically, although the work hasn't im- proved. Enter contaminant number six, the quality of work produced by the set of warm bodies that surround Janice. If they're rela- tively good students, Janice loses. If they're relatively poor students, Janice wins. The magic of grading!

You may also find that, rather than reducing the disagreement within your group, the additional information about Janice's class actually increases disagreement. Enter con- taminant number seven, the different ways individual teachers utilize the information at their disposal.

4 Just in case the point still needs to be driven home, let's examine what happens when your group gets information about the entire eighth grade at Haven Cove.

Knowing information about the entire eighth grade:

A	B	C	D	F

The same pattern usually emerges. Janice's grades, for the same work, go up again. Enter contaminant number eight, the quality of work of students in Janice's school. If she goes to this school, she's a top-notch student. If she goes to a school on the other side of town, she may get very different grades—for doing the same work. You may also note that despite the considerable information, Janice still gets a variety of grades. So what do you conclude?

Creative and imaginative people are often not recognized by their contemporaries. In fact often they are not recognized in school by their teachers either. History is full of illustrations to give guidance counselors pause. Consider some of these:

Einstein was four years old before he could speak and seven before he could read. Isaac Newton did poorly in grade school, and Beethoven's music teacher once said of him, "As a composer he is hopeless." When Thomas Edison was a boy, his teachers told him he was too stupid to learn anything. F. W. Woolworth got a job in a dry goods store when he was 21, but his employers would not let him wait on a customer because he "didn't have enough sense." A newspaper editor fired Walt Disney because he had "no good ideas." Caruso's music teacher told him, "You can't sing. You have no voice at all." The director of the Imperial Opera in Vienna told Madam Schumann-Heink that she would never be a singer and advised her to buy a sewing machine. Leo Tolstoy flunked out of college; Wernher Von Braun flunked ninth-grade algebra. Admiral Richard E. Byrd had been retired from the Navy as "unfit for service" until he flew over both Poles. Louis Pasteur was rated as "mediocre" in chemistry when he attended the Royal College. Abraham Lincoln entered the Black Hawk War as a captain and came out as a private. Louisa May Alcott was told by an editor that she could never write anything that had popular appeal. Fred Waring was once rejected for high school chorus. Winston Churchill failed the sixth form (grade) in school.

Probably these people were identified as low achievers in school or as misfits on their job because of problems of relevance.

Milton E. Larson

"How will you avoid trampling the creativity of your students? If you figure out a way, let us know; we're still working on it."

He always wanted to say things. But no one understood.
He always wanted to explain things. But no one cared.
So he drew.

Sometimes he would just draw and it wasn't anything. He wanted to carve it in stone or write it in the sky.
He would lie out on the grass and look up in the sky and it would be only him and the sky and the things inside that needed saying.

And it was after that, that he drew the picture. It was a beautiful picture. He kept it under the pillow and would let no one see it.
And he would look at it every night and think about it. And when it was dark, and his eyes were closed, he could still see it.
And it was all of him. And he loved it.

When he started school he brought it with him. Not to show anyone, but just to have with him like a friend.

It was funny about school.
He sat in a square, brown desk like all the other square, brown desks and he thought it should be red.
And his room was a square, brown room. Like all the other rooms. And it was tight and close. And stiff.

He hated to hold the pencil and the chalk, with his arm stiff and his feet flat on the floor, stiff, with the teacher watching and watching.
And then he had to write numbers. And they weren't anything.
They were worse than the letters that could be something if you put them together.
And the numbers were tight and square and he hated the whole thing.

The teacher came and spoke to him. She told him to wear a tie like all the other boys. He said he didn't like them and she said it didn't matter.
After that they drew. And he drew all yellow and it was the way he felt about morning. And it was beautiful.

The teacher came and smiled at him.
"What's this?" she said.
"Why don't you draw something like
Ken's drawing?
Isn't that beautiful?"
It was all questions.

After that his mother bought him a tie and
he always drew airplanes and rocket
ships like everyone else.
And he threw the old picture away.
And when he lay out alone looking at the
sky, it was big and blue and all of
everything, but *he* wasn't anymore.

He was square inside and brown, and his
hands were stiff, and he was like anyone
else. And the thing inside him that
needed saying didn't need saying
anymore.

It had stopped pushing. It was crushed.
Stiff.
Like everything else.

Anonymous

About School

▐▐ Charles Silberman cautions
against confusing sentiment _for_
students with sentimentality _about_
students. At the risk of producing
the latter while attempting the
former, we want to add that a senior
turned this poem in to his teacher
at a Regina, Saskatchewan high
school. The poem is labeled anonymous because the teacher isn't sure
that the student wrote it. He has no
way to find out because a few weeks
later the student committed
suicide. ▐▐

After all, the American schools in the past
hundred years have received millions and
millions of children—children who came
from families that could barely speak English, children from the whole range of social
and racial and religious and ethnic back-
grounds. And although they haven't turned
out God's children and produced a new
Jerusalem, teachers have done an astonishing
job of being open, of being responsive to the
poor, of assisting the rise of large numbers
of people up the social and economic ladder.
And this is felt by those people who are now
grown up. It's particularly felt by the white-
collar and blue-collar working people who
I've come in contact with in recent years.
They have only cause for gratitude for what
they got out of their education. They may not
have gone to Harvard or Berkeley, may not
have become intellectuals or college professors, but they have gotten good jobs—
better jobs than their parents had—and they
attribute this rise to the education they received in trade schools, in commercial
schools, all through this country.

Robert Coles

▐▐ There are things about schools
that both help and hurt. People who
function effectively somehow are
able to lap up the good things. They
also are able to accept the things
that hurt without being much diminished. Often they are even able to
soften some of the hurts.

We had quite a struggle with
this part of the book in our efforts
to achieve a balance in the readings between those people and
things that help and those that
hurt. We learned something. We
learned that the literature is
brimfull of hurts but quite sparse
on helps.

This imbalance may be as much a
product of the vagaries and biases
of the contemporary publishing
scene as it is an accurate indicator of the general state of our
nation's schools. We seem to be
deep in an era of general despair.
The best you can do is get as much
experience as you can in several
schools and then decide for yourself whether the literature
accurately reflects the realities
of schools.

Speaking of deciding, that's
what the next part of this book
focuses on: helping you wrap up
some of the loose ends of your many
teaching-career decisions. ▐▐

187

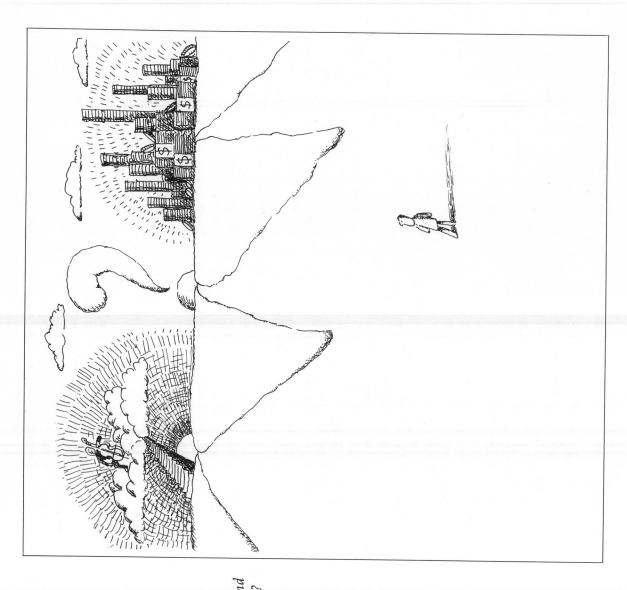

V

Decisions, Decisions

Will teaching satisfy your needs, your expectations, your hopes?
Do you know enough about yourself and teaching to make that judgment now?
Would a decision now be irrevocable?

"So far we've asked you to look at yourself in relation to others in your group, in relation to some different teaching acts, and in relation to some of the people and things that make up schools. We hope that sizable chunks of the book have helped you gauge yourself as a teacher, and as a person. Perhaps you have decided whether or not teaching is for you, and, if it is, what kind of a teacher you want to become. Perhaps questions about your role, your style, your central purposes, and your strengths and weaknesses are resolved. For most of us, alas, such solutions and resolutions don't come so easily.

That's where this part comes in—it's designed to help you do that unfinished solving and re-solving. Or more accurately to come closer to your solutions and resolutions, for answering those questions is really a life-long process.

In this part we don't do much talking. It's time for us to be quiet. Here, we give you the time and the opportunity to look at your-self and teaching, from this per-spective and that, to help you decide if you should jump further into teaching and, if so, what posture to take as you make that leap."

There is only one subject-matter for educa-tion, and that is Life in all its manifestations.

John Dewey

27

Real Me, Ideal Me

A way to compare the person you feel you are with the person you would like to be, allowing you to draw your own conclusions about the implications for you as a teacher.

An individual experience. Requires about forty-five to ninety minutes, depending on whether you do one or both parts.

This is undoubtedly the most complicated experience in the whole book. We almost eliminated it for that reason. Finally, though, we decided that the value some of you would place on its brand of personal insight would make the struggle with complicated instructions worthwhile. At least that was our hope. The second half of the activity—Ideal Me—is optional but strongly recommended. In either case, it is imperative that you engage the activity in the sequence outlined below.

1 Questionnaire

Real Me

Do your best to describe yourself as you are now, using the 32 statements on the facing page. Follow the steps below one at a time. There are no right or wrong answers; try not to get your impressions of the way you are now confused with your ideas about how you'd like to be. You'll have a chance to consider that later.

- Find *the one statement that you feel is most like you now*. Place the number of that statement in the box below. Then, check off that statement in the box located to the left of the statement, so you will not accidentally use the statement again. Use each statement only once.

Value = 9

- Find the next *three statements that are most like you*. Put their numbers in the three boxes below. Check off each of the three statements you choose.

Value = 8

- Find the next *four statements that are most like you* and put their numbers in the four boxes below. Check off each of the four statements you choose.

Value = 7

- Find the next *five statements that are more like you* than any of the others you have not checked off. Put their numbers in the five boxes below. Check off each of the five statements you choose.

Value = 6

- From the remaining statements find *the one that is least like you*. Place the number of the statement in the box below. Then, check off that statement.

Value = 1

- Find the next *three statements that are least like you* and put their numbers in the three boxes below. Check off each of the three statements you choose.

Value = 2

- Find the next *four statements that are least like you* and put their numbers in the four boxes below. Check off each of the four statements you choose.

Value = 3

- Find the next *five statements that are less like you* than the others you haven't checked off. Put their numbers in the five boxes below. Check off each of the five statements you choose.

Value = 4

You should now have six statements left that have *not* been checked off. Put their numbers in the six boxes below.

☐ ☐ ☐ ☐ ☐ ☐   Value = 5

Double-check to make certain you've used every statement once and have used no statements twice.

If you plan to also do the "Ideal Me" half of this experience (so that later you can compare it to "Real Me"), go to page 192 and complete step one of that part. If you choose to do only "Real Me", go on to step two on page 194.

Real Me

Check Off

☐ 1. I occasionally wonder if I really am an effective person.

☐ 2. I quickly find out what needs to be done and do it.

☐ 3. I test my ideas by trying them out with other people.

☐ 4. I feel I ought to live up to my own ideas about what is best.

☐ 5. I usually like to wait and see before I do something.

☐ 6. I have been taught good ways of dealing with other people.

☐ 7. I have been taught how to live and feel I should live that way.

☐ 8. I sometimes wonder how to act when I am in a group.

☐ 9. I always try to consider others' ideas about what is best as well as mine.

☐ 10. I often wonder about the kind of person I ought to be.

☐ 11. I feel that I am a person who can make up my own mind.

☐ 12. I am a person who can take advice from older people.

☐ 13. I always trust my own feelings in deciding what to do.

☐ 14. I am a person who finds out more about myself every day.

☐ 15. I like to have full directions when I have to do something.

☐ 16. I would rather trust my own feelings about other people.

☐ 17. I feel that I can tell what another person thinks of me.

☐ 18. I do better when I get advice from someone who knows.

☐ 19. I test myself to find out what kind of person I am.

☐ 20. I like to do things in my own way and at my own time.

☐ 21. I am the kind of person my parents taught me to be.

☐ 22. I like to feel that I understand the kind of person I am.

☐ 23. I usually think over what I should do in most situations.

☐ 24. I ought to be judged by whether or not I do the things I say I'll do.

☐ 25. I sometimes wonder about my feelings when I am with another person.

☐ 26. I believe I ought to live up to things my parents feel are important.

☐ 27. I follow good advice about ways to deal with people.

☐ 28. I take time to think about what to do first in some situations.

☐ 29. I like to trust my feelings about the way I should act.

☐ 30. I have a variety of ways of getting along with persons I know.

☐ 31. I decide what to do according to what needs to be done.

☐ 32. I would like to know more about the kind of person I am.

Ideal Me

Do your best to describe the person you'd like to be, using the 32 statements on the facing page. Follow the steps below one at a time. Remember, there are no right or wrong answers.

- Find the *one statement that you feel is most like the person you'd like to be.* Place the number of that statement in the box below. Check off that statement in the box to the left of the statement, so you will not accidentally use the statement again. Use each statement only once.

  Value = 9

- Find the next *three statements that are most like the person you'd like to be.* Put their numbers in the three boxes below. Check off each of the three statements you choose.

  Value = 8

- Find the next *four statements that are most like the person you'd like to be.* Put their numbers in the four boxes below. Check off each of the four statements you choose.

  Value = 7

- Find the next *five statements that are more like the person you'd like to be* than the others you have not checked off. Put their numbers in the five boxes below. Check off each of the five statements you choose.

  Value = 6

- From the remaining statements find the *one that is least like the person you'd like to be.* Place the number of that statement in the box below. Then, check off that statement.

  Value = 1

- Find the next *three statements that are least like the person you'd like to be.* Put their numbers in the three boxes below. Check off each of the three statements you choose.

  Value = 2

- Find the next *four statements that are least like the person you'd like to be.* Put their numbers in the four boxes below. Check off each of the four statements you choose.

  Value = 3

- Find the next *five statements that are less like the person you'd like to be* than the others you haven't checked off. Put their numbers in the five boxes below. Check off each of the five statements you choose.

  Value = 4

- You should now have six statements left that have *not* been checked off. Put their numbers in the six boxes below.

  Value = 5

Double-check to make certain you've used every statement once and have used no statements twice. Now, go on to step two on page 194 and begin summarizing the information you've established for both "Real Me" and "Ideal Me."

Ideal Me

Check Off

The person I'd like to be

- [ ] 1. Occasionally wonders if he/she really is an effective person.
- [ ] 2. Quickly finds out what needs to be done and does it.
- [ ] 3. Tests his/her ideas by trying them out with other people.
- [ ] 4. Feels he/she ought to live up to his/her own ideas about what is best.
- [ ] 5. Usually likes to wait and see before he/she does something.
- [ ] 6. Has been taught good ways of dealing with other people.
- [ ] 7. Has been taught how to live and feels he/she should live that way.
- [ ] 8. Sometimes wonders how to act when he/she is in a group.
- [ ] 9. Always tries to consider others' ideas about what is best as well as his/her own.
- [ ] 10. Often wonders about the kind of person he/she ought to be.
- [ ] 11. Feels that he/she is a person who can make up his/her own mind.
- [ ] 12. Is a person who can take advice from older people.
- [ ] 13. Always trusts his/her own feelings in deciding what to do.
- [ ] 14. Is a person who finds out more about himself/herself every day.
- [ ] 15. Likes to have full directions when he/she has something to do.
- [ ] 16. Would rather trust his/her own feelings about other people.

- [ ] 17. Feels that he/she can tell what another person thinks of him/her.
- [ ] 18. Does better when he/she gets advice from someone who knows.
- [ ] 19. Tests himself/herself to find out what kind of person he/she is.
- [ ] 20. Likes to do things in his/her own way and at his/her own time.
- [ ] 21. Is the kind of person his/her parents taught him/her to be.
- [ ] 22. Likes to feel that he/she understands the kind of person he/she is.
- [ ] 23. Usually thinks over what he/she should do in most situations.
- [ ] 24. Ought to be judged by whether or not he/she does the things he/she says he/she will do.
- [ ] 25. Sometimes wonders about his/her feelings when he/she is with another person.
- [ ] 26. Believes he/she ought to live up to the things his/her parents feel are important.
- [ ] 27. Follows good advice about ways to deal with people.
- [ ] 28. Takes time to think about what to do first in some situations.
- [ ] 29. Likes to trust his/her feelings about the way he/she should act.
- [ ] 30. Has a variety of ways of getting along with persons he/she knows.
- [ ] 31. Decides what to do according to what needs to be done.
- [ ] 32. Would like to know more about the kind of person he/she is.

Explanation of Instruments

You've now made a set of judgments about the "relative" degree to which 32 different statements approximate the person you feel you are. You may also have completed a similar process for the person you would like to be. Whether or not you felt that many of the statements described you accurately is not important. What the statements do accomplish is to make you clarify a set of self-perceptions and thereby learn some things about yourself that you knew but perhaps were unaware you knew.

Notice that each row of boxes in which you wrote statement numbers has a value from one to nine assigned to it. The more you felt a statement was like you, the higher the value assigned.

Also, note that each statement is written so that it has two segments in it. First, in each statement "someone" defines something about you. Four different "someones" or sources are implied in the 32 statements: The source may be you, your parents or some other authority figure, other people (generally your peers), or a "someone" who's unclear or contradictory.

Second, note that each statement describes you in one of four ways: in terms of you intrinsically, or in terms of your behavior, or in terms of the way you relate to others, or in terms of the way you ought to be.

These four sources of definition and four ways of describing you result in 16 possible combinations. Two statements in the list contain each combination. You can identify these pairs by looking for two statement numbers that add up to 33. In other words, statements 1 and 32 contain one combination; statements 2 and 31, another combination; 3 and 30; etc.

You can gain basic insights about the way you view yourself by identifying which of the 16 possible statement combinations you feel are most and least like you. The Value Summary and Information Analysis tables on this page provide that information. You can also compare the profile of your current self to that of your ideal self by filling out the similar set of tables on the facing page.

2 Summarizing the Information

a. You'll recall that you obtained a value for each statement. Go back to page 190 and transfer the values to the Value Summary table; put each value in the space next to its respective statement number.

b. Next, note that pairs of statements containing similar combinations are located together in this table. Add the values of each pair. For example, if you gave statement 1 a value of 3 and statement 32 a value of 7, their sum would be 10. Place each sum in the corresponding location on the second table (Information Analysis). In other words, the sum of the values of the two statements in the "da" box is placed in the corresponding "da" box of the Information Analysis table.

Real Me

Value Summary:

Statement / Your Value		Statement / Your Value		Statement / Your Value		Statement / Your Value		Row Totals
aa	11: 22:	ab	13: 20:	ac	16: 17:	ad	4: 29:	
ba	12: 21:	bb	15: 18:	bc	6: 27:	bd	7: 26:	
ca	14: 19:	cb	2: 31:	cc	3: 30:	cd	9: 24:	
da	1: 32:	db	5: 28:	dc	8: 25:	dd	10: 23:	160

Information Analysis:

	who I am (my intrinsic qualities).	the way I act and the things I do (my behavior).	how I relate to others (how I "get along").	the way I ought to be (my sense of social conscience).
I provide information about	aa	ab	ac	ad
My parents and/or other authority figures provide information about . . .	ba	bb	bc	bd
I seek information, often from peers, about	ca	cb	cc	cd
I am unsure of or find the information I receive conflicting about	da	db	dc	dd
Column Totals				

Ideal Me

Value Summary:

	Statement — Your Value	Statement — Your Value	Statement — Your Value	Statement — Your Value
aa 11: 22:	ab 13: 20:	ac 16: 17:	ad 4: 29:
ba 12: 21:	bb 15: 18:	bc 6: 27:	bd 7: 26:
ca 14: 19:	cb 2: 31:	cc 3: 30:	cd 9: 24:
da 1: 32:	db 5: 28:	dc 8: 25:	dd 10: 23:

Information Analysis:

I provide information about . . .

My parents and/or other authority figures provide information about . . .

I seek information, often from peers, about . . .

I am unsure of or find the information I receive conflicting about . . .

	. . . who I am (my intrinsic qualities).	. . . the way I act and the things I do (my behavior).	. . . how I relate to others (how I "get along").	. . . the way I ought to be (my sense of social conscience).	Row Totals
	aa	ab	ac	ad	
	ba	bb	bc	bd	
	ca	cb	cc	cd	
	da	db	dc	dd	
Column Totals					160

c. Next, add up the totals for each column and for each row of the Information Analysis table and place them in the respective boxes. (If you're having trouble deciphering parts of this, examples of all computations are provided at the end of this experience on pages 198–199.)

To make sure you've done all the steps correctly, add up the four column totals; their sum should equal 160. Similarly the sum of the four row totals should equal 160. If either figure is incorrect, you've made a mistake. Try to find your error, and correct it.

d. Next, examine the original 16 totals you computed in substep (b) and entered in the main body of the Information Analysis table. Find the four highest values. Circle them. (In the case of ties for fourth highest, circle the identical values. That's what happened in our sample table on page 198.

e. Then, find the four lowest values. Put a box around them. Again, if there are ties, put a box around identical values.

3 Analysis

You may now identify some interesting statements about yourself by combining the appropriate phrases from the left and top margins of the Information Analysis table (see the summary statements in the example on page 199). We suggest that you actually write out summary statements for yourself on the lines provided on this page. You obtain the statements that most describe you by combining the phrases to the left and above the values you circled, and obtain the statements that least describe you by similarly combining phrases for the values you boxed.

So far you've simply described the person you feel you are. You've made no judgments about that person. To find out how you stack up against your ideal image of yourself, go through the same summarizing and analyzing (steps two and three) for the information you constructed regarding the person you'd like to be (pages 194–196). Then you are ready for the final comparison.

4 Final Comparison

Some differences will probably exist between the person you are and the person you'd like to be. You may find this experience most useful if you compare your two sets of summary statements, looking for gaps that might help you plan your future. Only you can decide if a gap you find is serious or inconsequential, and what you want to do or not do about it, given the time and energy you have.

Summary Statements

Real Me

The general qualities that *most* describe the person I am are:

_____

_____

_____

_____

_____

_____

_____

_____

_____

☐ ☐ ☐ ☐ ☐ ☐ ☐ ☐ ☐

The general qualities that *least* describe the person I am are:

_____

_____

_____

_____

_____

_____

_____

_____

_____

☐ ☐ ☐ ☐ ☐ ☐ ☐ ☐ ☐

Ideal Me

The general qualities that *most* describe the person I'd like to be are:

☐ ☐ ☐ ☐ ☐ ☐ ☐ ☐

_____
_____
_____
_____
_____
_____
_____
_____

The general qualities that *least* describe the person I'd like to be are:

☐ ☐ ☐ ☐ ☐ ☐ ☐ ☐ ☐

_____
_____
_____
_____
_____
_____
_____
_____

- Place an "OK" in the box beside any statement that appears in both "most" lists or both "least" lists. (See the example on page 199.) These are areas where you feel comfortable with yourself.

- Place a "?" in the box beside any statement that appears in either the "most" or "least" statements of the person you'd like to be (Ideal Me) but does not appear among either the "most" or "least" statements of the person you are (Real Me). You need to weigh these statements and decide if they represent a change you would like to make in the person you are. If you decide that the indicated change is called for, think about how you might go about making it. (The change may be so minor that it will "just happen" with little conscious effort on your part.)

- And last, place a "I" in the box beside any statement that appears in the "most" list of the person you are and the "least" list of the person you would like to be, or vice versa. These statements suggest a marked gap in your real-ideal integration efforts. If no statements have a "I", you are becoming an approximation of your ideal self. Having one or several "I" statements is not unusual, especially for persons unsettled in life. But you may still want to work at some of these marked gaps. The big question of course is "What can you do?" What kinds of experiences or relationships or changes in behavior do you want to try, if any?

Example

Real Me

Value Summary:

	Statement	Your Value		Statement	Your Value		Statement	Your Value		Statement	Your Value
aa	11: 22:	3 2	ab	13: 20:	1 3	ac	16: 17:	4 2	ad	4: 29:	7 2
ba	12: 21:	8 8	bb	15: 18:	8 6	bc	6: 27:	7 4	bd	7: 26:	9 5
ca	14: 19:	6 5	cb	2: 31:	6 5	cc	3: 30:	3 7	cd	9: 24:	5 4
da	1: 32:	3 7	db	5: 28:	5 4	dc	8: 25:	6 4	dd	10: 23:	5 6

Information Analysis:

	who I am (my intrinsic qualities).	the way I act and the things I do (my behavior).	how I relate to others (how I "get along").	the way I ought to be (my sense of social conscience).	Row Totals
I provide information about	aa 5	ab 4	ac 6	ad 9	24
My parents and/or other authority figures provide information about	ba 16	bb 14	bc 11	bd 14	55
I seek information, often from peers, about	ca 11	cb 11	cc 10	cd 9	41
I am unsure of or find the information I receive conflicting about	da 10	db 9	dc 10	dd 11	40
Column Totals	42	38	37	43	160

Example

Summary Statements

Real Me

The general qualities that *most* describe the person I am are:

[ ] [ ] [ ] [ ]

- [!] My parents and/or other authority figure provide information about who I am
- [OK] My parents and/or other authority figure provide information about the way I act
- [ ] My parents and/or other authority figure provide information about the way I ought to be
- [ ] My parents and/or other authority figure provide information about how I relate
- [ ] I seek information, often from peers, about who I am
- [OK] I seek information, often from peers, about the way I act and the things I do
- [!] I am unsure of or find the information I receive conflicting about the way I ought to be

The general qualities that *least* describe the person I am are:

- [ ] [ ] I provide information about the way I act and the things I do
- [ ] I provide information about who I am
- [!] I provide information about how I relate to others
- [!] I provide information about the way I ought to be
- [OK] I seek information, often from peers, about the way I ought to be
- [OK] I am unsure of or find the information I receive conflicting
- [ ] about the way I act and things I do

In the beginning, I was one person, knowing nothing but my own experience.

Then I was told things, and I became two people: the little girl who said how terrible it was that the boys had a fire going in the lot next door where they were roasting apples (which was what the women said)—and the little girl who, when the boys were called by their mothers to go to the store, ran out and tended the fire and the apples because she loved doing it.

So then there were two of I.

One I always doing something that the other I disapproved of. Or other I said what I disapproved of. All this argument in me so much.

In the beginning was I, and I was good.

Then came in other I. Outside authority. This was confusing. And then other I became *very* confused because there were so many different outside authorities.

Sit nicely. Leave the room to blow your nose. Don't do that, that's silly. Why, the poor child doesn't even know how to pick a bone! Flush the toilet at night because if you don't it makes it harder to clean. DON'T FLUSH THE TOILET AT NIGHT—you wake people up! Always be nice to people. Even if you don't like them, you mustn't hurt their feelings. Be frank and honest. If you don't tell people what you think of them, that's cowardly. Butter knives. It is important to use butter knives. Butter knives? What foolishness! Speak nicely. Sissy! Kipling is wonderful! Ugh! Kipling (turning away).

The most important thing is to have a career. The most important thing is to get married. The hell with everyone. Be nice to everyone. The most important thing is sex. The most important thing is to have money in the bank. The most important thing is to have everyone like you. The most important thing is to dress well. The most important thing is to be sophisticated and say what you don't mean and don't let anyone know what you feel. The most important thing is to be ahead of everyone else. The most important thing is a black seal coat and china and silver. The most important thing is to be clean. The most important thing is to always pay your debts. The most important thing is not to be taken in by anyone else. The most important thing is to love your parents. The most im- portant thing is to work. The most important thing is to be independent. The most impor- tant thing is to speak correct English. The most important thing is to be dutiful to your husband. The most important thing is to see that your children behave well. The most important thing is to go to the right plays and read the right books. The most important thing is to do what others say. And others say all these things.

All the time, *I* is saying, live with life. That is what is important.

But when I lives with life, other I says no, that's bad. All the different other I's say this. It's dangerous. It isn't practical. You'll come to a bad end. Of course . . . everyone felt that way once, the way you do, but *you'll learn!*

Out of all the other I's some are chosen as a pattern that is me. But there are all the other possibilities of patterns within what all the others say which come into me and be- come other I which is not myself, and sometimes these take over. Then who am I? I does not bother about who am I. I is, and is happy being. But when I is happy being, other I says get to work, do something, do something worthwhile. I is happy doing something. "You're weird!" I is happy being with people saying nothing. Other I says talk. Talk, talk, talk. I gets lost.

I knows that things are to be played with, not possessed. I likes putting things together, lightly. Taking things apart, lightly. "You'll never have anything!" Making things of things in a way that the things themselves take part in, putting themselves together with surprise and delight to I. "There's no money in that!"

I is human. I someone needs, I gives. "You can't do that! You'll never have anything for yourself! We'll have to support you!"

I loves. I loves. I loves in a way that other I does not know. I loves. "That's too warm for friends!" "That's too cool for lovers!" "Don't feel so bad, he's just a friend. It's not as though you loved him." "How can you let him go? I thought you loved him?" So cool the warm for friends and hot up the love for lovers, and I gets lost.

So both I's have a house and a husband and children and all that, and friends and respectability and all that, and security and all that, but both I's are confused because other I says, "You see? You're lucky," while I goes on crying. "What are you crying about? Why are you so ungrateful?" I doesn't know gratitude or ingratitude, and cannot argue. I goes on crying. Other I pushes it out, says "I am happy! I am very lucky to have such a fine family and a nice house and good neighbors

and lots of friends who want me to do this, do that." I is not reason-able, either. I goes on crying.

Other I gets tired, and goes on smiling, because that is the thing to do. Smile, and you will be rewarded. Like the seal who gets tossed a piece of fish. Be nice to every-one and you will be rewarded. People will be nice to you, and you can be happy with that. You know they like you. Like a dog who gets patted on the head for good behavior. Tell funny stories. Be gay. Smile, smile, smile . . . . I is crying . . . "Don't be sorry for yourself! Go out and do things for peo-ple!" "Go out and be with people!" I is still crying, but now, that is not heard and felt so much.

Suddenly: "What am I doing?" "Am I to go through life playing the clown?" "What am I doing, going to parties that I do not enjoy?" "What am I doing, being with people who bore me?" "Why am I so hollow and the hollowness filled with emptiness?" A shell. How has this shell grown around me? Why am I proud of my children and unhappy about their lives which are not good enough? Why am I disappointed? Why do I feel so much waste?

I comes through, a little. In moments. And gets pushed back by other I.

I refuses to play the clown any more. Which I is that? "She used to be fun, but now she thinks too much about herself." I lets friends drop away. Which I is that? "She's being too much by herself. That's bad. She's losing her mind." Which mind?

Barry Stevens

28

I Think I Feel I Do

A way to examine your values and how extensively they touch your life.

An individual experience. Requires about twenty minutes and no group time, other than that needed to share what you've learned.

Our lives are pulled by the values we hold. We guide our decisions by what we consider worthy, desirable, good—of value. At least we do if we know what we value.

If you're clear about your values, you can use that knowledge to inform your decisions—professional or otherwise—thereby maximizing chances that you'll act in ways that promote these values and that bring you to situations that are consistent with them. If you're not clear about your values, you'll probably find yourself acting in ways that you later regret.

This experience is designed to clarify your values. You need not reveal your work to others, although there will be a chance to share your thoughts at the end of the experience.

1 In the space provided below, list ten to thirty things that you value.

- Consider some of your ideals. Your aspirations. The human qualities you most respect. Your beliefs. Your dreams and wishes.
- Think of the causes you support. The events that cause you distress. The curiosities that attract you. The activities that you enjoy.
- Consider how you would like people to see you. How you would like to be remembered. What you admire in others.
- Reflect on what parts of the newspaper you read. What you talk about. What places you visit.
- Tap whatever other sources of data you find fruitful. Take your time. Don't give up until you have at least ten items on your list. Twenty or thirty would be better yet.

As you go through the next part of this experience, you may think of new items. Change or add items at any time.

2 Your task now is to apply three criteria to each item on your list. The first criterion involves choices.

a. Choices

In general, we come to consider something valuable through either of two processes. We can stop and think about it, look at the alternatives, consider the consequences, and decide yes, that is good or important or worthy. This first process is a thoughtful, deliberate one, one that involves critical thinking and making a free choice. We have considered the alternatives and we say, ''I want to choose that.''

On the other hand, something can become valuable through a process of osmosis. Perhaps it was part of the family in which we grew up. Or our hero liked it. Or we tried it and ultimately came to feel good about it. These processes are usually more gradual and much less deliberate. We never really sat down and made a choice.

Go through each item on your list and see which ones resulted from a choice made after careful consideration of alternatives. If such a deliberate choice was involved, mark ''C'' (for *chosen*) in one of the boxes by that item.

You should now have some measure of which items involved deliberate intellectual commitments on your part.

b. Prized

Some things that we consider valuable feel very good to us, while others do not elicit positive feelings at all. A person might want to be famous, for example, but wish that he were not motivated by fame. What is valuable for him, what motivates him, does not feel good to him.

In one of the boxes, mark ''P'' (for *prized*) by each item for which you can answer ''yes'' to these questions: Does that item feel good to me? Am I glad it's on my list? Is it something I cherish and prize?

You should now have some measure of how each item touches your feelings.

c. Acted Upon

Some things that we consider valuable touch our actions; they show up in how we spend our time and/or money. Other things remain somewhat more distant, more hypothetical, more abstract. A person might say he values religion, for example, but he might spend almost no time thinking about it, or following religious principles, or joining a religious group, or in other ways acting on that belief.

Do you actually do something about each of the items on your list? And do you act in ways that suggest it's a pattern in life and not a one-shot thing? If so, put an ''A'' (for *acted upon*) in a box by that item.

You should now have some measure of how each item influences your actual behavior.

3 You now have rough measures of how each one of the items in your list touches your life. Items with all three symbols (C, P, and A) involve your intellect, your feelings, and your behavior. You have chosen them. You prize them. And you act on them. Those are your most pervasive values; they touch more parts of you than do items without all three symbols. Are the other items less meaningful to you?

Again, try writing some ''I learned'' statements: ''I learned that . . . ,'' ''I am surprised that . . . ,'' ''I rediscovered that . . . .'' In particular, consider what you might learn from this activity in light of your teaching decisions. What kind of teacher would be consistent with the values on your list? Do you like the thought of being that kind of teacher?

· · ·

The whole group might gather and ask volunteers to read some of their ''I learned'' statements. What conclusions do you draw from the statements that are read?

Peaks and Peeks

A warm, rewarding way to evaluate the tentative future you've mapped out for yourself.

A small-group experience for two to four participants. (The experience takes on a special significance when shared with a close friend or loved one.) Requires about two hours.

This experience contains three major sections. It's essential that you not proceed to the final step until steps one and two have been completed.

1 Form groups of two to four people. Then, each participant finds a place where he can be alone to do some thinking. Before splitting up, the group should agree on a time when it will reconvene. Allow about twenty minutes.

Once you are alone, think back over your entire life and recall your peak experiences—those times, settings, and events when and where you felt you were enjoying life to the fullest. List as many as you can remember.

You may have had peak experiences that you don't wish to share with others in your group. Don't feel you need to. List them for yourself, in code if necessary.

Once you've completed your list, look for clusters, collections of experiences that have something in common.

When you've finished, rejoin your group.

Once the group is reconvened, each member takes a few minutes to tell the others about some items on his list and what made each particularly significant. He then identifies the clusters of experiences he sees in his list. The rest of the group tries to help him make additional clusters. When everyone has finished, the group might discuss differences in the ways individuals approached the task or in the types of experiences that were important to group members. Or proceed directly to step two.

2 Step two follows a very similar format; alone time precedes group time. Again, twenty minutes of alone time should suffice. Rather than focus on the past, this time peek into the future. Specifically, once you are alone, try to set down your goals for the rest of your life. Feel free to acknowledge the tentativeness of many of them, but do put them down.

a. Start with some very immediate goals, like wanting to lose five pounds in the next two weeks or wanting to raise your GPA to _____ by the end of the year.

b. Next, list those goals you hope to accomplish in the next few years.

c. Then, really stretch your mind to imagine what you'd like to be doing ten, twenty, or forty years from now.

d. Last, again look for clusters or groupings among your goals. Then, rejoin your group.

Each member shares his goals with the group, identifies the clusters he sees, and enlists the group's help in looking for other clusters. When everyone has finished, the group again might focus on the differences among group members. Or move on to step three.

3 This is the easiest but probably the most important step in the experience. The group stays together. Each person takes a turn answering one question:

Within the context of the goals you've set for yourself, to what extent do you see the opportunity to continue having the kinds of experiences that have meant most to you in the past?

Finding little correspondence between your peak experiences and your goals doesn't necessarily doom you to an unhappy future. You may develop whole new areas of fulfillment and gratification as a result of the path you hope to take. But you would probably be wise to consider any such disparity. If teaching is one of your goals, also consider whether it is compatible with the other goals. For instance, do some of your goals require more money than you'll make as a teacher?

For unless one is able to live fully in the present, the future is a hoax. There is no point whatever in making plans for a future which you will never be able to enjoy. When your plans mature, you will still be living for some other future beyond. You will never, never be able to sit back with full contentment and say, "Now, I've arrived!" Your entire education has deprived you of this capacity because it was preparing you for the future, instead of showing you how to be alive now.

In other words, you have been hypnotized or conditioned by an educational processing-system arranged in grades or steps, supposedly leading to some ultimate Success. First nursery school or kindergarten, then the grades or forms of elementary school, preparing you for the great moment of secondary school! But then more steps, up and up to the coveted goal of the university. Here, if you are clever, you can stay on indefinitely by getting into graduate school and becoming a permanent student. Otherwise, you are headed step by step for the great Outside World of family-raising, business, and profession. Yet graduation day is a very temporary fulfillment, for with your first sales-promotion meeting you are back in the same old system, being urged to make that quota (and if you do, they'll give you a higher quota) and so progress up the ladder to sales manager, vice-president, and, at last, president of your own show (about forty to forty-five years old). In the meantime, the insurance and investment people have been interesting you in plans for Retirement—that ultimate goal of being able to sit back and enjoy the fruits of all your labors. But when that day comes, your anxieties and exertions will have left you with a weak heart, false teeth, prostate trouble, sexual impotence, fuzzy eyesight, and a vile digestion.

Alan Watts

Will inspire someone, Who will some day . . . To build something, That some day

Michael Buchanan

30

I Need . . .

A way to examine your own set of needs and begin choosing a teaching-self consistent with them.

A self-directed experience. Requires about twenty minutes of individual time and no group time, other than that needed to share what you've learned.

We're often pushed by needs. We need affection. We need space. We need fewer pressures. We need freedom from guilt. We need to understand feelings that storm up for inexplicable reasons.

Unless attended to, these needs tend to bother us. At times our attempts to satisfy them push us to do things we would have preferred not to do. Needs have an urgency not easily denied.

Also, different needs push different people different ways. Some of us feel needs others do not feel. Many of us are not even totally aware of the needs that operate most strongly in us.

In this experience you'll have a chance to examine your needs. It's an individual activity; you don't have to show your work to others. There will be a chance, however, to share general thoughts at the end, if you wish to.

1 First, think of yourself in terms of what you believe you need to make yourself happy. Do you need a lot of security? A lot of human intimacy? A lot of opportunities to learn? Make a list of the important things that, if you have them, will help you feel satisfied and, if you don't, will probably leave you feeling dissatisfied. Let's call these the things you *need* if you are to lead a happy life. You can jot them down in this space.

After (or before) you have identified a few of your needs, look over "Some Human Needs" on pages 208–210. It may give you ideas for changing or refining your list. Adjust your list as you go through this experience; whenever you get new ideas, feel free to add, subtract, change, or reword. Try to develop a list that describes the whole spectrum of your particular human needs, as you currently see them.

2 Now, reflect on your list. For each of the steps below, go back over your list and mark each of your needs as indicated. (Remember that you can change your list as you go through these steps.)

- Put a small dot in the box next to the needs that you added as a result of reading "Some Human Needs."

- Mark "OK" in the box next to the needs that are not likely to cause you much trouble in life. For example, if you feel the need for a lot of luxury but are independently wealthy, it should be *easy to meet* that need.

- Put the letter "U" in the box next to those needs that are now unfulfilled and that cause you some discomfort. "U" identifies currently *unmet* needs.

- Put a "P" by all the needs that certainly exist, or existed, in the life of the *parent* whom you resemble most closely, as best as you can make that judgment.

- "D" stands for *diminish*. Put a "D" by the needs that you expect will diminish as you get older, in the next ten years or so.

- Try "I" for *intensification*. Put an "I" by the needs you think will be stronger ten years from now.

- "W" is for *worry*. Put a "W" by the needs that you worry about meeting in the future. You have a real concern that the future may find you with these needs remaining unmet.

3 Now, reviewing the experience, consider what, if anything, you can say you learned from it. Try writing some "I learned" statements: "I learned . . . . ." or, "I learned . . . . ." or, "I was surprised . . . . ." or, "I rediscovered. . . ." In particular, consider what this needs assessment suggests for the kind of teacher you may choose to become.

＊＊＊

Finally, gather the whole group. Individuals can volunteer to read some of their "I learned" statements. Or read them in groups of threes and fours. Remember that any contributions are voluntary. Follow with an open discussion. Could this experience be adapted for younger students? Would it be appropriate to use with the students you may someday teach?

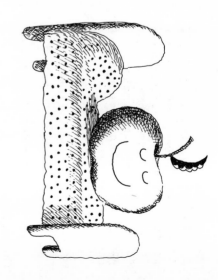

Here's one list of human needs that Merrill developed that seems to cover many aspects of the human condition and that is interesting to look at in terms of the question, "Do any of these needs bother me and, if so, is there something I can do about it?"

Samples of Feelings That Arise When the Need Is:

	Satisfied	Unsatisfied
Physical Needs		
Survival Conditions—food, oxygen, viable temperature range, sex, etc.	No physical pressures	Physical tension
Remedies—drugs, surgery, eyeglasses, physical therapy, rest when weak, etc.	Functional ease	Distress
Physical Comforts—tasty food, comfortable temperature, soft chairs, etc.	Comfort	Discomfort
Safety Needs		
Security—certainty that other needs will be met, rhythm in life, support when weak, orderliness, having a place in society, freedom from terror, etc.	Secure	Fearful
Freedom from Excessive Pressure—having within tolerable limits such things as change, problems, conflict, disorganization, stimulation, work pressures; time to be alone, to think, to relax; etc.	Relaxed, on top of things	Pressured, overwhelmed
Affection Needs		
Affection—feelings of warmth and acceptance from others, being treated with affection, giving and receiving favors, being liked, etc.	Warm	Detached from others
Belonging—being with others, socializing, being included, sharing, having friends and family, chatting, teamwork, etc.	Accepted	Lonely
Love and Intimacy—deep interpersonal understanding and feeling, devotion, nonjudgmental acceptance, having children, etc.	Deep human attachment	Alone
Action Needs		
Activity—doing things, solving problems, moving about, thinking, working, satisfying curiosity, exercise, etc.	Alive, energetic	Lethargic, dull, lazy
Influence—making a difference, being listened to, having an effect upon things or people, etc.	Significant	Ineffective
Power—being in control, acting willfully, asserting one's self strongly, being a leader, etc.	Powerful	Blocked
Expression—expressing one's emotions and thoughts, producing art works, being playful and gay, sharing problems, etc.	Released, open	Stifled

208

	Satisfied	Unsatisfied
Achievement Needs		
Accomplishment—feeling successful and capable, making progress, achieving a goal, resisting distracting impulses, making wise decisions, etc.	Productive, competent	Incapable
Recognition—respect from others, being praised and admired as competent, approval for worthy behavior, considered as an important person, being known by others, etc.	Respected, noticed	Unappreciated, unimportant
Growth Needs		
Stimulation—excitement; stimulation of sight, sound, touch, smell, traveling, variety, new ideas; change; etc.	Stimulated	Bored
Development—becoming better, moving to more complex levels of being, advancing to new life-processes, growing, moving through developmental levels, etc.	Mature, enriched, growing	Static, defeated, listless
Freedom Needs		
Space for Autonomy—room to be oneself, self-direction, private territory, space for exploration, making one's own choices, resisting the control of others, etc.	Free	Controlled
Being Constructive and Creative—contributing, building, creating new forms, imagining, being idealistic, discovering better ways, helping, etc.	Proud, worthwhile	Uncreative, unhelpful
Understanding—knowing what is happening, the names for things, how things work, and what is likely to happen in the future; being able to make sense of one's perceptions;	Informed, wise	Unaware, naive, stupid

	Samples of Feelings That Arise When the Need Is:	
	Satisfied	**Unsatisfied**
Freedom Needs (cont.)		
satisfying curiosity; seeing models that might be emulated; etc.		
Skills—being able to do things, necessary and pleasurable; developing physical and mental talents; reading, swimming, conversing, managing; etc.	Skillful	Unable, clumsy
Integrating Needs		
Time Integration—building continuity between the present and both the past and the future, finishing tasks, looking forward to the future, organizing one's time, etc.	Good perspective	Disoriented, inconsistent, aimless
Self Integration—building harmony among one's thoughts, one's feelings, and one's behaviors; coming to terms with one's positive and negative impulses; dealing with any gap between one's real self and ideal self; self-acceptance; etc.	Whole, unified, congruent	Conflictful, guilty
Self-society Integration—unifying the satisfaction of one's own needs with others' needs; dealing with environmental demands; accepting one's place; getting along in the world; being a part of a compatible social unit; etc.	Well-adjusted, responsible	Unsettled, selfish, exploited

Merrill Harmin
Some Human Needs

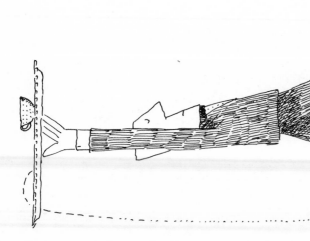

31

The Makings of a Pro

An opportunity to extend your view of the profession of teaching—its ins and outs, its ups and downs.

An individual or small-group experience, requiring some time and imagination, depending on how you go about it.

A professional ball player and a professional teacher face working ("professional") issues not always apparent to the observer. Experienced teachers, for example, might well want to know something about:

- The job market here and elsewhere
- Salary ranges in various places
- Current activities in teachers' unions
- The art of interviewing for a job
- Court cases with educational implications
- Negotiating contracts, collectively or individually
- Tenure—problems and prospects
- Certification requirements for various jobs in various places

Some of these issues were touched on in an earlier experience, *With a Little Help from . . .*, on page 33. Those who researched questions in that activity may have become experts for the group. Others may

now want to become experts-in-residence on a job-related issue. If you can make this expertise available to the group, you may help some people (and yourself) make wiser decisions about teaching.

In this experience three procedural questions must be solved:

1. First, the question of who takes on what topics. Try some group brainstorming to see if you can find questions that (a) people want to know answers to and (b) are sufficiently motivating for one, two, or more people to engage in answer-finding. Individuals or small groups can be formed for this brainstorming, depending on interest.

2. Second is the quest itself. Questors may want to consider:

   - Checking the library
   - Asking experts
   - Checking with the local placement office
   - Looking at NEA professional publications
   - Investigating what the state department of education has available (see page 247)
   - Talking to an AFT representative
   - Interviewing some superintendents who hire in the vicinity

   You will have to make the means fit the ends, of course.

3. Third is the question of how to share findings with others who wish to know. Please don't set up a series of oral reports, for they're likely to be tedious. Rather, con-

sider posting key findings, or duplicating key findings, or giving each person 90 seconds to tell the group one or two key findings. Then, invite individuals who would like more info to talk with the expert during an "open classroom" period set aside for this sharing.

" Salaries differ considerably according to the size of school system and geographic region. Here are some averages for those categories. We need to caution you though that averages can be misleading. First of all, these are not average beginning salaries, which we'd estimate to be about a thousand dollars lower. Second, within any grouping of schools or geographic region you'll probably find at least a thousand-dollar range between the highest and lowest salaries in that presumably homogeneous category. But for what it's worth, here are the figures."

Teachers

	Mean salary by enrollment grouping				Total, all operating systems (weighted average)
	25,000 or more	3,000–24,999	300–2,999	Under 300	
Mean salary paid: 1970–71	$9,766	$9,306	$8,628	$7,262	$9,218
1968–69	8,069	7,850	7,696	7,093	7,841
1966–67	7,588	6,930	6,345	5,536	6,905
1964–65	6,788	6,276	5,785	4,909	6,222
1962–63	6,405	5,750	5,345	4,604	5,747

Salaries paid teachers, by geographic region, 1970-71, reporting systems with enrollments of 12,000 or more elementary and secondary students

Salary Interval	Geographic Region								
	New England	Mideast	Southeast	Great Lakes	Plains	Southwest	Rocky Mountains	Far West	All Regions
Number of Teachers	16,136	151,066	147,223	118,590	41,832	62,248	21,682	140,360	699,137
Number of Reporting Systems	19	72	95	69	33	35	17	107	447[a]
Percent of Reporting Systems	4.3	16.1	21.3	15.4	7.4	7.8	3.8	23.9	100.0
Mean Salary Paid, 1970-71	$10,008	$10,444	$8,315	$10,368	$9,356	$8,548	$9,011	$10,779	$9,761
Distribution									
Below $4,500	.1	...	.3	.1	.1	.1	...	...	.1
$ 4,500- 4,999	.1	...	.2	...	...	.1	...	...	.1
5,000- 5,499	...	.1	.5	...	...	...	...	...	.1
5,500- 5,999	...	.2	1.8	.1	...	.2	.9	...	.5
6,000- 6,249	...	.1	2.9	.1	.7	.5	4.2	...	.9
6,250- 6,499	...	.1	4.0	.1	2.0	1.6	2.8	...	1.2
6,500- 6,749	.3	.3	7.3	.5	2.2	5.1	3.3	.1	2.4
6,750- 6,999	1.5	1.0	7.5	1.2	4.0	7.2	4.6	.7	3.2
7,000- 7,249	4.7	2.5	8.5	2.7	6.8	8.7	7.4	1.9	4.7
7,250- 7,499	4.6	2.5	6.2	3.2	5.8	7.5	5.1	2.0	4.0
7,500- 7,749	5.6	3.4	6.0	3.4	6.1	7.2	4.7	3.2	4.5
7,750- 7,999	6.5	4.1	5.8	4.8	5.9	5.6	5.3	3.4	4.8
8,000- 8,499	8.7	12.9	9.2	9.8	9.1	10.7	7.7	6.4	9.6
8,500- 8,999	6.1	7.2	9.0	7.1	8.7	10.5	8.7	6.6	7.8
9,000- 9,499	6.3	6.5	7.9	6.8	7.4	8.4	7.2	7.6	7.3
9,500- 9,999	6.4	5.6	6.9	6.5	5.7	9.4	9.5	6.8	6.8
10,000- 10,499	4.5	5.5	6.3	6.4	5.7	5.5	5.9	6.7	6.1
10,500- 10,999	10.3	6.0	2.6	6.6	5.9	5.4	4.6	6.4	5.5
11,000- 11,499	5.9	5.4	1.5	5.7	3.8	2.5	5.2	6.2	4.4
11,500- 11,999	8.6	4.2	1.5	5.7	5.7	1.0	2.8	5.7	4.1
12,000- 12,499	3.3	4.9	1.1	4.3	3.4	.7	1.9	5.5	3.6
12,500- 12,999	5.0	4.0	.7	5.4	3.7	.8	1.0	6.7	3.7
13,000 OR MORE	11.6	23.6	2.4	19.3	7.2	1.3	7.1	24.0	14.7
Total	100.1	100.1	100.1	99.8	99.9	100.0	99.9	99.9	100.1

[a]A total of 452 systems with enrollments of 12,000 or more furnished some usable salary data but 5 of them did not provide data or teacher's salaries.

> *One of the movements that has boosted teacher salaries over the past few years is the increasing practice of teacher groups to bargain collectively for salary raises and other benefits.*

Collective negotiation is the key procedure whereby teachers through unions or associations are effecting fundamental realignment of power for decision making in education. As such, collective negotiation has become a part of life in education; further, it exists, in part, because it was caused. The drive for negotiation procedure and the related organizational and operational changes has many sources, some relatively new, some age-old, among them:

—The drive of local associations or unions to indicate their effectiveness in dealing with critical matters with the board and with the community at large

—The politically oriented motivation of teachers who are concerned about the criticisms of education and desire to modify the school in ways that will make it more professionally sound and to elevate the perception of the profession

—A desire to achieve faster action, more appropriate response, and a drive for relevance in the target institution by those in activist movements

—The exasperating and tortuous route often necessary for change in large or bureaucratic school systems; and the frustration of teachers who have worked year after year on particular goals only to find them negated at

some point by a status figure in the administrative hierarchy

—The natural desire of the teacher to have his ideas respected and to find a deserving place in the consideration of the administration or the board of education

—The contradiction between both the criticisms and the apathy of a public and its regard for the public personnel who are associated with the school programs

—The inefficiency and ineffectiveness of an institution to react quickly and effectively in times of rapid change

—The age-old conflicts between the worker and the management that have recently been exploited by the unions in regard to teacher groups and teacher ideas

—The unhappiness with bureaucratic uniformity or pressure that has been imposed upon individual schools where there is vulnerability to the influence of pressure groups but, at the same time, apparent insensitivity to neighborhood differences as far as the system is concerned

—A host of petty grievances that teachers have with their supervisors, their building principals, and those who have status or responsible positions of authority

—The bypassing techniques now evident in the dual governments that are a part of some of the new developments in poverty, civil rights, and government

—The honest striving for educational reform, for more effective and appropriate school programs, and the determination to have access to the systems by which decisions are made

—Certain states such as Michigan and

Massachusetts, where the atmosphere is heavy with labor-management concepts and precedents, are providing both desirable and undesirable alternatives in the present situation.

The focus for this discussion is the relationship of collective negotiations to curriculum and instruction, not to the movement as a whole, nor as they relate to matters of salary, teacher welfare, benefits, hours of employment, or physical conditions of employment. While curriculum and instruction are operationally interwoven with these items, an attempt has been made to keep them as separate concerns. A corollary point of view is that provisions and considerations should be different in curricular or instructional matters; this position is not shared by many persons active in the movement.

Collective negotiation can be viewed either as a threat to existing powers, or as an affirmative development. As education becomes more complex, more socially involved, and more politically sensitive, the harnessed strength of the teachers can represent a significant force in obtaining additional means and an improved school environment. Those active in the movement consider this development a significant step in the professionalization of teachers. It is a "given" that the movement will cause realignments in the educational power structure and significant modifications in certain teacher, supervisory, and administrative roles.

In most areas of concern the struggle for recognition has been intramural, that is within the school system and with the school board, but that is only phase one. A second phase must come when the new power group

214

is legally installed, has been tested, and has gained the right to certain decision-making processes and certain prerogatives, to see whether the teacher associations or unions can perform the functions they are now demanding as their right. A third area of testing may well involve the extent to which the public and its respective governments will relate to the new configuration and agree to its procedures and powers.

Leslee Bishop

N early 4,000 teachers, who had been striking and picketing for four weeks in this city's first school walkout, returned to work Feb. 13 with a clearcut union victory and a stronger alliance with the St. Louis community.

Under pressure of the massive strike which closed all city public schools, the board of education abandoned its opposition to collective bargaining and retreated from its pretense that there were no funds for a settlement.

The strike-settlement agreement provides:

- Teachers, who had not received a raise in three years, will get an immediate across-the-board increase of $400 a year ($200 for the current semester), and another $400 yearly increase starting next September, thus boosting starting pay from $7,200 to $8,000 and putting the master's-degree maximum at $14,120.

- The school board agrees to meet with teachers' representatives to try to reach understandings on all questions of conditions of employment and to reduce agreements to writing.

- A representation election will be held next year, between Jan. 1 and Oct. 1. The St. Louis Teachers Union, AFT Local 420, which has doubled its membership to 2,400 this year, is a favorite to win, over the smaller NEA affiliate. Both organizations participated in the strike.

- Firm class-size limits will be implemented by the board beginning in September. A key issue for both teachers and parents, class sizes have risen to unmanageable numbers because of layoffs and cutbacks, with some teachers reporting as many as 60 students per room.

- A grievance procedure is established for the first time, encompassing third-party arbitration (advisory now, binding if authorized by the state) as the final step.

- Finally, the board will pick up hospitalization-insurance premiums, assure that all faculty members are covered by liability insurance, and provide leaves or released time for union business.

Compared to the board of education's authoritarian control before the strike, the teachers' victory is almost revolutionary. It breaks the stranglehold imposed by the board over the years when it refused to permit any kind of shared decision-making with either teachers or the community.

"We made more gains in these four weeks of mass action than we did in the past 12 or 14 years," Local 420 President Demosthenes DuBose declared.

David Elsila

American Federation of Teachers' newspaper

"Here are items that haven't been pushed across the bargaining table by either teachers or boards of education, but we think it would be fun to see the furor that these issues would create."

We will now put before you a list of proposals that attempt to change radically the nature of the existing school environment. Most of them will strike you as thoroughly impractical but only because you will have forgotten for the moment that the present system is among the most impractical imaginable, if the facilitation of learning is your aim. There is yet another reaction you might have to our proposals. You might concede that they are "impractical" and yet feel that each one contains an idea or two that might be translated into "practical" form. If you do, we will be delighted. But as for us, none of our proposals seems impractical or bizarre. They seem, in fact, quite conservative, given the enormity of the problem they are intended to resolve. As you read them, imagine that you are a member of a board of education, or a principal, or supervisor, or some such person who might have the wish and power to lay the groundwork for a new education.

1. Declare a five-year moratorium on the use of all textbooks.

Since with two or three exceptions all texts are not only boring but based on the assumption that knowledge exists prior to, independent of, and altogether outside of the learner, they are either worthless or harmful. If it is impossible to function without textbooks, provide every student with a notebook filled with blank pages, and have him compose his own text.

2. Have "English" teachers "teach" Math, Math teachers English, Social Studies teachers Science, Science teachers Art, and so on.

One of the largest obstacles to the establishment of a sound learning environment is the desire of teachers to get something they think they know into the heads of people who don't know it. An English teacher teaching Math would hardly be in a position to fulfill this desire. Even more important, he would be forced to perceive the "subject" as a learner, not a teacher. If this suggestion is too impractical, try numbers 3 and 4.

3. Transfer all the elementary-school teachers to high school and vice versa.

4. Require every teacher who thinks he knows his "subject" well to write a book on it.

In this way, he will be relieved of the necessity of inflicting his knowledge on other people, particularly his students.

5. Dissolve all "subjects," "courses," and especially "course requirements."

This proposal, all by itself, would wreck every existing educational bureaucracy. The result would be to deprive teachers of the excuses presently given for their failures and to free them to concentrate on their learners.

6. Limit each teacher to three declarative sentences per class, and 15 interrogatives.

Every sentence above the limit would be subject to a 25-cent fine. The students can do the counting and the collecting.

7. Prohibit teachers from asking any questions they already know the answers to.

This proposal would not only force teachers to perceive learning from the learner's perspective, it would help them to learn how to ask questions that produce knowledge.

8. Declare a moratorium on all tests and grades.

This would remove from the hands of teachers their major weapons of coercion and would eliminate two of the major obstacles to their students' learning anything significant.

9. Require all teachers to undergo some form of psychotherapy as part of their in-service training.

This need not be psychoanalysis; some form of group therapy or psychological counseling will do. Its purpose: to give teachers an opportunity to gain insight into themselves, particularly into the reasons they are teachers.

10. Classify teachers according to their ability and make the lists public.

There would be a "smart" group (the Bluebirds), an "average" group (the Robins), and a "dumb" group (the Sandpipers). The lists would be published each year in the community paper. The I.Q. and reading scores of teachers would also be published, as well as the list of those who are "advantaged" and "disadvantaged" by virtue of what they know in relation to what their students know.

11. *Require all teachers to take a test prepared by students on what the students know.*

Only if a teacher passes this test should he be permitted to "teach." This test could be used for "grouping" the teachers as in number 10 above.

12. *Make every class an elective and withhold a teacher's monthly check if his students do not show any interest in going to next month's classes.*

This proposal would simply put the teacher on a par with other professionals, e.g., doctors, dentists, lawyers, etc. No one forces you to go to a particular doctor unless you are a "clinic case." In that instance, you must take what you are given. Our present system makes a "clinic case" of every student. Bureaucrats decide who shall govern your education. In this proposal, we are restoring the American philosophy: no clients, no money; lots of clients, lots of money.

13. *Require every teacher to take a one-year leave of absence every fourth year to work in some "field" other than education.*

Such an experience can be taken as evidence, albeit shaky, that the teacher has been in contact with reality at some point in his life. Recommended occupations: bartender, cab driver, garment worker, waiter. One of the common sources of difficulty with

teachers can be found in the fact that most of them simply move from one side of the desk (as students) to the other side (as "teachers") and they have not had much contact with the way things are outside of school rooms.

14. *Require each teacher to provide some sort of evidence that he or she has had a loving relationship with at least one other human being.*

If the teacher can get someone to say, "I love her (or him)," she should be retained. If she can get two people to say it, she should get a raise. Spouses need not be excluded from testifying . . . . .

Which of these requirements strikes you as more bizarre? From the student's point of view, which requirement would seem more practical? Bear in mind that it is a very difficult thing for one person to learn anything significant from another. Bear in mind, too, that it is probably not possible for such learning to occur unless there is something resembling a loving relationship between "teacher" and learner. Then ask yourself if you can think of anything sillier than asking an applicant for a teaching job if he has taken a course in Victorian literature?

Neil Postman and Charles Weingartner

217

The following list was prepared for board members as a primer on the tactics teachers are using to exert political belt. We think it will give you a fairly comprehensive picture of the negotiations game.

Typical Teacher Demands—Besides Salary

1. Payroll deductions for everything—life insurance policies, etc.
2. Access to personnel files.
3. Unlimited use of school building for association and personal use.
4. Protection of probationary teachers.
5. Academic freedom.
6. Free periods for elementary teachers.
7. Textbook selection.
8. Student discipline.
9. Advisory group of teachers.
10. Transfer of teachers for seniority.
11. Binding arbitration.

Forms of Harassment by Teachers

1. Secret mass meetings without the administration.
2. Handing out leaflets.
3. Vote on whether to strike.
4. Actual strike vote (a delaying tactic).
5. Picketing outside of school hours.
6. Sanctions.
7. Whipsawing (quoting what other schools do, etc.). . . .

Teacher Demands

Be ready for them. Most of them are valid.

1. Freedom and protection.
   a. Protection from student violence.
   b. Insurance policies—libel, accident, hospitalization.
   c. Protection in their personal, private lives.
   d. Freedom to join any organization or church.
   e. Freedom from discrimination.
2. Right to agreement or co-determination as to salaries, fringe benefits, etc.
3. Teacher association rights.
   a. Recognition as an agency of teachers.
   b. Right to written agreement.
   c. Right of association to solicit board discussion in good faith.
   d. Freedom from administration interference.
   e. Right to use school buildings for meetings.
   f. Right to use school mail.
   g. Right of dues—withholding services.
   h. Right of using bulletin board in teachers' lounge.
4. Career development.
   a. Right of teacher to be kept in subject field.
   b. Right to monetary assistance if summer school attendance required.
   c. Right to scholarship aid in working toward advanced degrees.
   d. Right to sabbatical leave.
   e. Right to a voice in planning inservice training.
5. Welfare rights.
   a. Travel pay.
   b. Retirement supplements.
   c. Maternity leave.
   d. Extra pay for extra duty.
6. Control over working conditions.
   a. Determination of length of day.
   b. Determination of school calendar.
   c. Determination of extra duty assignment.
   d. Control of transfers.
   e. Procurement of expensive tools and equipment.
   f. Preparation periods.
   g. Free lunch periods.
   h. Reserved parking space.
   i. Class size.

Teacher Tactics for Harassment

1. Reasons: Perhaps teachers resort to such tactics in order to get the needed attention. Perhaps they feel that the action of the board is not based on logic.
2. Strategy.
   a. Use of popular (but meaningless) slogans such as "For more effective schools" and "Time to teach."
   b. Forcing a test case.
   c. Exorbitant and persistent demands designed to wear down a board.

218

d. Paid advertisements in newspapers.
e. News stories and pictures of undesirable features of schools.
f. "Visitations by national leaders.
g. Outside investigators.
h. Wildcat strikes.
i. Motorcades.
j. Massive sick leave calls.
k. Fits of "deteriorating staff morale."
l. Refusal of extra duty.
m. Political pressure.
n. Letter and telephone campaigns to board members.
o. Petitions signed by 90 percent of teachers.
p. Polls by outside organizations.
q. The teacher association newspaper.
r. Identification of problems without presenting solutions.
s. Mass resignations, walkouts, interruption of speakers.

Ralph Jones and Vic Cullens

PEANUTS

- Discuss the ads and posters within small groups. Each person gets help in improving his ad or poster.
- Send the ads and/or posters to some local school administrators. Ask them who they would call for interviews.

32

Hire Me—Hire Me!

An experience that allows individuals to write advertisements or make posters about themselves; a challenge to a person's pride in his teaching-self and self-awareness.

A self-directed experience. Requires group time only for sharing your work with others.

Write a want ad for yourself. Or make a poster announcing your debut as a teacher. Imagine that you are ready to be a teacher. What would you say about your strengths? What would you say about your desires? Would you say anything about your limitations, or the kind of job you would *not* accept? Put whatever you want in your ad or poster, but use no more than fifty words.

Here are some ideas for sharing the ads and posters. Try one or make up your own.

- Post them for group perusal.
- Pass them around the group. Discuss what the experience reveals.
- Duplicate a newsletter with all the ads. See which ones are most persuasive.
- Discuss the ads and posters within small groups. Each group picks one to read to the other groups.

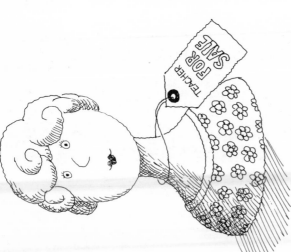

Ernie pulled a mimeographed list of words from under his desk blotter and said to the class, now suddenly grown sullen and silent, "We don't have much time. Take out a sheet of paper and number it one through thirty-five."

There was a confusion of books being dropped to the floor, papers being ripped from notebooks, papers being passed across the room from lenders to borrowers.

"Do we hafta do it in pen?"

"As usual," said Ernie.

Several students rose and walked up and down the aisles, trying to borrow pens. They bolted for their desks when Ernie said, "Number *one*. . . ."

A few of them cried, *Wait a minute! Wait a minute!*

"Number one . . . all *right* . . . every-thing is going to be all *right* . . . all *right*."

Ernie gave the first fourteen words on the list. The students were hunched over their papers, some holding their heads with their free hands, some hanging their free hands at their sides and yawning audibly, others shielding the papers with their free hands from would-be *low-brows*—Ernie's term for those who cheat. "A person who cheats on a test is dishonorable. He's a low-brow, and you don't trust a low-brow with *anything*: not with a car, a bicycle, a sheet of paper, not with a leg of Colonel Sanders' chicken, an over-ripe avocado, not with a chewed-up pencil stub. Nothing."

Then suddenly something distracting happened to him. The spelling list blurred before his eyes. He did not feel faint or ill in any way. The spelling list simply blurred before his eyes, between "embarrass" and "forty," and he wondered about the priorities of his life.

Darryl Ponicsan

Application forms, contracts, and evaluation forms are all part of the "things that help and hurt" teachers. These, therefore, rightfully belong in the section of the book that deals with those topics (pages 94-187). But because their collective bulk would create large continuity problems if they were just plopped down in the middle of the text, we "hid" a broad sampling of forms back in Appendix III. Here we've reprinted one application form—to give you a taste of hiring procedures.

Application is for: Elementary K-6 ☐   Secondary 7-12 ☐ _____

                               Fields _____

1. Print NAME   Mr. Miss. Mrs. _____
   (Capitals)   Last Name   First Name   Middle Name   Maiden Name

2. Address _____
   Number and Street   City or Town   State   Zip Code

3. Have you served in the U.S. Armed Services?   Yes ☐   No ☐

4. Former name(s) by which records may be identified _____

5. Telephone Number (___) _____   6. Date of Birth _____   Age _____   Social Security # _____
   Area Code

7. Are you a citizen of the U.S.?   ☐ Yes   ☐ No, but I am in possession of a Declaration of Intent to Become a Citizen or an Immigrant Visa which authorizes me to work as a full-time contract employee.

8. Have you ever taken an examination or filed an application for employment in the Los Angeles city schools?   ☐ Yes   ☐ No
   If you were employed, give dates: From _____ To _____   Employee # _____

9. If you hold or qualify for a California teaching credential, state type and subject fields covered _____

10. Give full and accurate data regarding your college and university education.

College or University	City or Town	State	Major	Degree	Dates (Years) From	To

11. Give full and accurate data regarding your PRACTICE TEACHING.

College or University for Teacher Training	School in which Practice Teaching was done (Complete Address is Essential)	Training Teacher	Type of Classroom (Please check)	Grade Level	Dates (Mo and Yr) From	To	Subjects Taught
			Self-Contained ☐ Departmentalized ☐ Team Teaching ☐				
			Self-Contained ☐ Departmentalized ☐ Team Teaching ☐				

12. List your most recent five years of PAID TEACHING EXPERIENCE (Most recent experience first). THESE REFERENTS WILL BE CONTACTED.

Name of School	Location (Complete Address is Essential)	Principal	Type of Classroom (Please check)	Grade Level	Dates (Mo and Yr) From	To	Subjects Taught
			Self-Contained ☐ Departmentalized ☐ Team Teaching ☐				
			Self-Contained ☐ Departmentalized ☐ Team Teaching ☐				
			Self-Contained ☐ Departmentalized ☐ Team Teaching ☐				

I understand that if I have ever (1) had a criminal complaint against me, or (2) been arrested, or (3) forfeited bail, or (4) been convicted, or (5) fined, or (6) jailed, or (7) placed on probation for any violation of law regardless of any subsequent court action in dismissal or expungement, I should attach a statement giving full explanation, including dates, places, charges and disposition of all cases. This statement must be signed and dated. (Do not include traffic violations involving only faulty equipment, parking, hand or traffic signals or speeding.) I understand that failure to account for all arrests, indictments, complaints, or convictions may disqualify me from subsequent employment with the Los Angeles City Unified School District. (For those who need to file an arrest statement, form 6087 will be supplied for this purpose on request by person providing application.)

I understand that if I have or have had a mental or physical condition which may require either special consideration or which may result in my not being able to qualify fully in the health examination, I should obtain further information from the Director, Health Services Branch, Los Angeles City Unified School District, P.O. 3307, Los Angeles, California 90051.

I understand that Chapter 2, article 3, section 13257 of the Education Code of the State of California requires that if I have ever rendered military service that I must indicate such on the front of this application and submit as part of this application a copy of the discharge or release from service.

I understand that it is necessary to provide a copy of the transcript from each college or university which I have attended before an evaluation of my qualifications for employment can be completed. Transcripts are not usually included in the placement office files and may be secured from the college registrar or admissions office.

I understand that if Los Angeles City Unified School District is to assist me in obtaining a California teaching credential, my transcript(s) must be official, show all college courses, their numbers and the grades attained.

In order to teach in the Los Angeles City Unified School District, it is necessary to obtain a teaching credential issued by the California State Teacher Certification Office.

The staff of the Personnel Division of the Los Angeles City Unified School District will be of assistance in completing the forms necessary to obtain the proper credential. It is advisable for the applicant to process the application for credential through the Personnel Division.

Please read, check and sign below that you have completed the following minimum credential requirements prior to employment.

ELEMENTARY
1. A Bachelor's degree from an accredited college or university.
2. One hundred eighty clock hours (eight semester hours or twelve quarter hours) of directed student teaching. Full time teaching experience may be substituted for the student teaching at the rate of one year of such teaching for one half of the requirement. One half of the above requirement shall be completed in kindergarten or in grades 1 to 6.

SECONDARY
1. A Bachelor's degree from an accredited college or university.
2. One hundred twenty clock hours (six semester hours or nine quarter hours) of directed student teaching at the rate of one year of such teaching for one half of the requirement. One half of the above requirement shall be completed in grades 7 to 12. If I have had no student teaching and substitute two years of full time experience, I must also have six semester hours of postgraduate course work (upper division or graduate level).

I hereby certify that I have completed this application to the best of my knowledge and that I have read the statements above. I understand that incomplete or false statements may disqualify me from subsequent employment with the Los Angeles City Unified School District.

Signature _____

Date _____

223

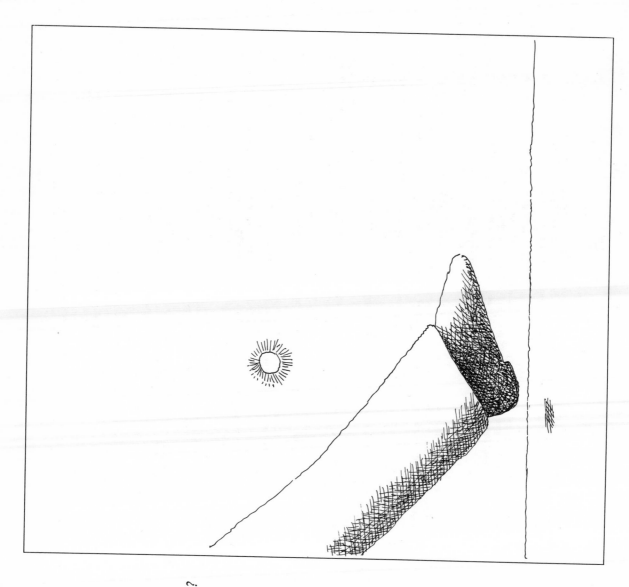

VI
Next Steps

Where do you go from here?
Who and what determine your options?

" This is the closing section, our attempt to wrap up some of the loose ends that are still flapping about.

It's also a beginning. Like most parts of the book, the experiences in this section do as much to open doors as to close them. As you work through these pages, experimenting with their contents, you'll have to decide which it does for you. As we said earlier, a professional life is built just that way—experimenting/deciding to find oneself, amidst all the options (and lack of options). Of course, that's an on-going process.

So we hope the experiences included in this part function as both endings and beginnings. That would be a good sign. It would mean that a continuity of sorts is developing in your professional life. **"**

And I asked myself about the present: how wide it was, how deep it was, how much was mine to keep.

Kurt Vonnegut, Jr.

33

Draw-A-Teacher (Reprise)

A follow-up on an earlier experience.

An individual or group experience. Requires about fifteen minutes.

Again, in the space provided, draw a picture of a teacher teaching a class.

Analysis

You've just taken a kind of projective test. Projective tests get their name because they present a person with an ambiguous, relatively neutral stimulus and ask him to elaborate on it. In elaborating on the stimulus, the person "projects" some of his own thoughts and feelings.

Such tests presumably allow us to "say" things we would not normally think of saying. In this case, the test may help you learn how you subconsciously define "teaching." If you've done the exercise at two different times, you'll find it useful to look for changes in your two pictures.

If the test is at all valid for you, your picture focuses on aspects of teaching that concern you, or at least of which you are most aware. Let's look at some of these aspects.

A. The Teacher

- Is the teacher you? If not, why not?
- Is the teacher drawn in much greater detail than the rest of the picture? If so, does it suggest that your concerns right now reside primarily with the teacher, rather than with students or subject matter or something else?

B. The Students

- Are students depicted? Does an absence of students suggest to you a relative lack of concern with them?
- Are the students all drawn alike? Or are they "individuals"?
- Look at the relative size of the teacher and students. Does the teacher domi-

nate the picture? If so, why did you draw him that way?
- Are the students active or passive, interested or bored? What accounts for your depiction of them?

C. Social Relationships

- Is the teacher as close to the students as they are to each other? Does a distant teacher presume a desire for little social contact on your part?
- Does the teacher "hide" behind a desk or lectern?
- What can you say about the teacher's relationship to the students: Lecturer? Helper? Discipliner?
- If the teacher holds a pointer, what does its presence seem to symbolize: The teacher as the fount of information? The sceptor of authority? The symbol of discipline?

D. The Setting

- What setting does your picture suggest?
- How are the students arranged: In conventional rows or in a more informal manner?
- Is any concern with subject matter evident? What kind of subject matter?
- Are the students seemingly a source of information and initiation, or are they depicted as passive receptors?

■ ■ ■

- Do you think this experience has any validity?
- Do you see a change in your two pictures?
- Do you like the change you see?

One way to begin a change is to devote ten minutes a day to doing something different. There is never any problem of finding ten minutes to play with, since what the pupils "must cover" is usually padded in order to fill up time. During that ten minutes present the class with a number of things they can choose to do. Present them with options you feel may interest them. Allow them the option of sitting and doing nothing if they choose. Moreover, make it clear that nothing done during that period will be graded, and nothing need be shown or explained to the teacher. That ten minutes is to be their time and is to be respected as such. Step out of the way and observe the things your pupils choose to do.

Step out of the way, but don't disappear. Make it clear that you won't tell people what to do or how to do it, but that you will be available to help in any way you can, or just to talk. For ten minutes cease to be a teacher and be an adult with young people, a resource available if needed, and possibly a friend, but not a director, a judge, or an executioner. Also try to make it possible for the ten minutes to grow to fifteen, twenty, so long as it makes sense to you and your pupils. It is not unlikely that those ten minutes may become the most important part of the day, and after a while may even become the school day.

Some specific hints on the use of the ten minutes:

—in English class it is possible to read, write (set three or four themes and leave it open for students to develop other ones), talk, act.

—in mathematics the students can set problems, solve problems, build computers, compute, design buildings (or other structures or things), talk about money, set problems for each other and the teacher.

—in social studies it is possible to talk about history; about newspapers, events, people; write about them; compose or listen to poems, play songs about them; talk or invite people in to talk about what's happening.

—in all classes students can do nothing, gossip, write, start a newspaper, a newsletter, listen to music, dance, talk about or play games, bring in things that may interest the teacher or other students and talk about them, write about them . . . .

Think about what is happening during those ten minutes and learn to be led by the students. If certain things are particularly interesting to one group, find out about those things, learn as much as you can, and, seeing their interest, present them with ways of getting more deeply into what they care about. If, for example, a group of students is interested in animals and their relationship to people, you can refer them to fables, to Konrad Lorenz, to experimental psychology, to whatever you can discover yourself. And if you don't know about such matters find someone who does, and invite him to class to meet your pupils. Then—and this is crucial—step out of the way again. Do not insist that because you have uncovered all these new options for your students that they *must* pursue them. Maintain your own freedom from the authoritarian mode and help your students maintain their freedom, however modest it may be. Learn, though it is difficult, to allow your students to say, "No," to what you want them to learn no matter how much stake you have in it. This means that one must understand one's own stake in making young people learn what one wants them to learn and not take it overseriously. Teachers must develop a sense of what they look like to young people and understand how pointless and even funny it can seem to young people to see adults losing their cool over someone's refusal to take the division of fractions or the imagery in Act I of Macbeth seriously.

Herbert Kohl

34

Learning About Learning (Reprise)

One way to evaluate yourself as a learner, this book as an expediter, your instructor (if you have one) as a teacher, and your course (if you're in one) as a valuable endeavor.

An individual experience. Requires only a few minutes.

This experience focuses on one question:

Has this book, or any experience related to it or stimulated by it, been potent enough to replace one of the five most potent learning experiences you recalled back on page 26?

If it has, we wish there were some way we could share your sense of accomplishment. Maybe you'll write us.

Unfortunately, the odds are that, for the majority, it hasn't. If that's your situation, you may be able to increase your learning about learning if you can figure out why you experienced what we'll term "only limited success."

To what degree was it

. . . your fault as a learner?

. . . our fault as authors?

. . . your instructor's fault (if you had one) as a teacher?

. . . no one's fault, but rather:

If you found that we limited your learning, we'd like to know about it. Please write us:

Merrill Harmin
Southern Illinois University
Edwardsville, Illinois 62025

Tom Gregory
School of Education
Indiana University
Bloomington, Indiana 47401

If you think someone else limited your learning, you might want to feed some constructive suggestions for change to that person. If it was your instructor, he'll probably welcome your comments. If that someone was you. . .

I have become impatient with the prevailing mood about the casualness and easiness of freedom. I have seen too many bored, confused, defensive kids who can spout the rhetoric of the "permissive" school, but who lack the self-confidence, the motivation, the initiative, the commitment and the self-directed drives that get them through the rigour of a genuine learning experience and the struggle of creating their own identity.

There is no freedom in instant gratification. There is no freedom if there are no demands. Freedom requires choice-making and commitment making. There is no freedom in copping-out and in rationalizing. It's not what you drop out of that demonstrates your freedom, it's what you willingly and actively drop *into* and work through.

Martin Engel

Once there was a toad who lived in a swamp. The grown-up toads at this swamp would push the toad around. The toad didn't like this treatment but his mommy and daddy told him that this was good. Once the toad was sent to a nearby co-operative swamp to stay for the summer. At this swamp the grown-up toads didn't push him around. He had fun and was freer than ever before. The toads here taught him how to be free but not how to be happy when he wasn't free. When he got back to his home swamp the grown-up toads started to push him around again, but now he wanted to be free. He didn't listen to the grown-up toads and he was killed. Back at the nearby co-operative swamp the toads were real happy because they had given the little visitor a happy time, a new experience, and a taste of freedom.

Written by a student

❝ Roethke says a great deal about the process of growing as a person. ❞

I wake to sleep, and take my waking slow.
I feel my fate in what I cannot fear.
I learn by going where I have to go.

We think by feeling. What is there to know?
I hear my being dance from ear to ear.
I wake to sleep, and take my waking slow.

Of those so close beside me, which are you?
God bless the Ground! I shall walk softly there,
And learn by going where I have to go.

Light takes the Tree; but who can tell us how?
The lowly worm climbs up a winding stair;
I wake to sleep, and take my waking slow.

Great Nature has another thing to do
To you and me; so take the lively air,
And, lovely, learn by going where to go.

This shaking keeps me steady. I should know.
What falls away is always. And is near.
I wake to sleep, and take my waking slow.
I learn by going where I have to go.

Theodore Roethke
The Waking

230

35

Final(e) Paper

A culminating experience—a way to freeze your development for a moment and take a good, hard, honest look at yourself at this point in time.

An individual experience. Requires considerable time and, if you're using this book as part of a course, a half-hour conference with your instructor.

"Final(e) Paper" is an inaccurate name for this experience. It's not a final in the sit-two-seats-apart, put-all-books-on-the-floor, have-at-least-three-sharpened-pencils sense. It's a final only in the sense that it is our last experience.

Nor is it a paper in the at-least-ten-double-spaced-typewritten-pages, cite-your-sources, avoid-personal-opinion, use-third-person sense. In fact, it need not take the form of words on paper at all. Consider any medium of communication—sculpture, pictures, tape recordings, computer programs, environments, poetry, music—whatever will best get your message across.

A great teacher, Sylvia Ashton-Warner, describes the task we're asking you to tackle far more eloquently than we can.

At my table looking out the windows I wonder what to say to you . . . to a young teacher. Across the spring garden, above the cineraria, through the trunks of the tower-ing trees; over the silk water of the inner harbor I see the ships' entrance, beyond which is the tall Pacific and beyond that, your country. Only to find I have no advice.

I look back on 50 years, you look forward on 50 years. This world is yours, not mine. It was mine when I was young and I strongly knew it. True, there's a war on now but there was one on then; the world still belongs to you. For ever the world belongs to youth. Do you also strongly know it?

From 50 I have no advice. But from 30 I have! In the splendid authority of youth to youth I quote from those blurring pages, written in fierce swift pencil-passion: "You must be true to yourself. Brave enough, to be strong enough, to be true to yourself. Wise enough, to be brave enough, to be strong enough, to be true enough to shape yourself from what you actually are. What big words, O my Self: true, strong, brave and wise! But that's how it is, my Self. That's how it must be for you to walk steadily in your own ways, as gracefully as you feel, as upright as you feel, a ridiculous flower on top of your head, a sentimental daisy. For therein lies your individuality, your own authentic sig-nature, the source of others' love for you.

Sylvia Ashton-Warner

231

What we ourselves *become* is what we teach them about the world. We are each a sum total of experience somehow become person and given voice, and the person and voice are the only glimpses we get or give to others—young or old—of what it means to be alive. Each of us is a sense and an extension of other persons, and we feed back to them the sweets and visions of what is possible. Though we grow away from the remembered or hallucinated worlds of childhood, what we gain from that process is the *world*: not only in and through ourselves, but for and through all others who ripen and find, in their lives, a truth to speak. That, we take it, is what we owe one another and the young.

Peter Marin and Vincent Stanley

Find a medium that best allows you to communicate important things about yourself, both generally and specifically.

Here's the topic for your final: In terms of teaching,

Where were you?
What changes have occurred during the time you've been with us?
Where are you going?

If you're using a words-on-paper format, we recommend you limit yourself to less than five pages. Quality is far more important than quantity. We also suggest that you try not to make this a night-before-you-hand-it-in project. We've found that the final(e)s that communicate most are those that were often attempted, put away to ferment, and then reattempted at least once again. The kind of honesty that Ms. Ashton-Warner describes doesn't come easily to most of us.

∎
∎
∎

If you're doing the final(e) for a course, we recommend you set up a half-hour conference with your instructor. Turn your final(e) in to him a day or two before the conference so he has time to read/look at/listen to/experience it. Then sit down together and talk about what you've tried to say about yourself and teaching. We hope you'll find it a meaningful way to close off your experience with this book.

" We strongly feel that there is a fundamental difference in teaching between a focus on subject matter that is usually external to the student—learning the times table, learning American history, learning English grammar—and content that is internal to his experiences—perhaps learning how to calculate speed at bike races, learning what forces perpetuate poverty in the U.S. today, or learning how to use writing to organize and clarify thinking.

Teachers concerned with keeping learning close to the experiences of students work less with abstract content and logically organized disciplines (unless students are interested in these) and more with questions raised from the experiences students already have had and questions that can be raised from experiences the school provides. As we noted earlier, the project method of teaching is recommended partly for that reason: it engages students in activities that raise learning-rich issues. As a result, learning springs from life experiences; it becomes organic.

The most worthy learning, the most useful learning, seems to us to be of this internal kind. So we must confess that we were less concerned with telling you some new things about teaching than we were with helping you clarify and organize the things you probably already knew. And we were much less concerned with convincing you that

a certain way was best than we were with helping you find your own way.

If you became more skillful in the <u>processes of professional learning</u>, that was good enough for us. Of course, it isn't either-or. Sometimes teachers help students understand their experiences by making statements. But the wise teacher, it seems to us, makes statements with the minds of the students at the center of his intention. He asks himself in effect, "Will a statement help a student to understand his experiences or to open up to new experiences?"

Asking ourselves the same question, we decided that a comment on our part at this late point in the book (it could hardly be much later) might help clarify the point of view of this book—our preference for internal content as opposed to external content. And we felt that point important enough for you to reconsider that we risked redundancy to make this last-minute comment. *"*

233

Teachers as Readers

More than once, we've heard individuals in the publishing game express the opinion that teachers read fewer books than almost any college educated group. We don't know how true this is, but if it is, we wonder why.

Teachers have a lot of paper work to do and perhaps that cuts deeply into their reading time and interest. But other professionals have a lot of paper work too, so it's hard to use that argument.

There is another possibility. Several authors have described how the institution of school assumes that learning isn't fun. That it teaches kids that learning's distasteful and they've got to be motivated, coerced, even forced to learn. Maybe teachers, caught up in such an environment, also come to believe this.

Whatever the case, we'd like to see you get started, if you haven't already, on a reading program that could inform your decisions about teaching. To spur you on, we're providing brief descriptions of some of the more popular paperbacks that commonly interest people in teaching.

These descriptions are of a special kind though. We didn't write them. People like you did, people early in their preparation to become teachers. We asked them to do their best to give you the benefit of their experiences with these books.

We weren't very organized when we began pulling these descriptions together and we've lost track of who wrote a number of them. We apologize to those anonymous contributors. We've also done some editing on many of these annotations and we again want to apologize for any violence we've done to an author's intent.

So here they are. There are many good books not represented. And there are probably books in this collection that won't particularly interest you. But although the annotations can't duplicate the experience of reading, we do hope they will supply some individualized peer insights into the books."

234

Ashton-Warner, Sylvia, *Teacher* (Simon and Shuster), 1971, $2.45.

"Come, look, see, . . ."—what dull, unimaginative words, and yet these are a few of the first words children are given to learn to read and spell. Ms. Ashton-Warner has a more exciting method. Have the children themselves give words that they want to know—words usually heard at home (i.e. Mommy, kiss, monster, drunk, cry, etc.). Ms. Ashton-Warner contends that because children have pictures in their minds of words that are heard at home, these familiar words spelled out will have much more meaning than the traditional "come, look, see, etc." In *Teacher* she shows that using this organic method of teaching can be more productive than using the standard form. This book should be read by all teachers, but especially by prospective primary teachers. Ms. Ashton-Warner's creative teaching scheme is stimulating and adaptable to the public school system.

Nancy Dalton

Axline, Virginia, *Play Therapy* (Ballantine), $1.25.

This book is an interesting discussion of the mechanics of play therapy, including numerous case studies. Of special interest to me was the section devoted to the implications of play therapy for education, stressing the importance of a good relationship between teacher and student for the development of good mental health. Allowing students to be themselves, with understanding and acceptance, helps them retain their self-respect and develop possibilities for growth and change.

Axline, Virginia, *Dibs: In Search of Self* (Ballantine), 1969, $1.25.

I enthusiastically recommend this book to anyone interested in working with children. Dibs is a remarkable child. His parents think he is retarded; he doesn't speak at all. If you are interested in the retarded child or the exceptionally gifted child, watch Dibs' real self emerge in this fascinating book. The genius and warmth of this child are superbly portrayed by the author.

Mary Kenney

Bennett, Larone, Jr., *The Black Mood* (Barnes and Noble), 1970, $1.50.

The Black Mood discusses the inequality of resources in America. Blacks in America have tired of this inequality, and have mobilized power in various forms to combat it: through riots, black power structures in cities, and most importantly, pride in their own race's contributions and accomplishments. Blacks feel that it is time for whites to realize that all their "liberal" talk and movements are useless unless they are dedicated toward making the distribution of power and money more equal in America. This book does a creditable job of describing where Blacks are in America today.

Debbie Mundy

Borton, Terry, *Reach, Touch, and Teach* (McGraw-Hill), 1970, $2.95.

Terry Borton says that "a teacher's conviction that he has 'made a difference'—even with a few students—reassures him that education is something 'far more complex and fundamental than obtaining knowledge." This is the theme of his book, even though at times his processes and methods obscure the main point. His detailed examples of techniques, nevertheless, allow you to fully understand the What, So What, and Now What method of communicating with students. Some may find these redundant, but the less creatively oriented can appreciate his efforts. His book presents not only ideas and concepts, but also actual methods and processes which Borton himself has explored in his teaching career.

Bremer, Anne and Bremer, John, *Open Education: A Beginning* (Holt, Rinehart, and Winston), 1972, price not available.

This book is an introduction to the concept and practice of open education. The Bremers feel that the teacher, his or her lesson plan, and the environment in which learning is supposedly taking place have been responsible for students' lack of conversation, communication, and actual learning. The authors develop the concepts of "school without lessons, without classes, without classrooms, and ultimately, without walls." Examples of conversations between students and teachers and between students reflect successful results of these concepts. A seminar of teachers concludes the book, and in this seminar many possible views of the book are discussed, such as the book's practicability and whether it really attends to the problems of opening up education. The book is a good introduction to the concept of the open classroom, and the closing seminar is a fitting conclusion to a book which can easily be debated.

Steve Hendricks

235

Bremer, John and Von Moschizisker, Michael, *The School Without Walls* (Holt, Rinehart, and Winston), 1971, price not available.

The School Without Walls is one of the worst books I've ever read. It describes in great detail the Parkway Program of Philadelphia (an alternative high school). The book is full of educational jargon and trite expressions, obviously written for not very discerning people. Anyone reading this book with only one eye open can see the rhetoric on the wall.

In a school brochure the statement is made that "love without power is anarchy." It is common knowledge that love is, by its very nature, powerful. This kind of bombast easily misleads the reader into thinking that this school is not very free at all.

Brown, Claude, *Manchild in the Promised Land* (Signet), 1966, $1.25.

This is a good book to read to get a better understanding of reality in the ghetto and of how hard it is to get out of the ghetto. If you don't know what it's all about, read it; if you do, don't read it. Really, most any Black person could write *Manchild* after he has won the acclaim of the people; that's all it would take for the book to sell. Not only has Claude Brown had a hard life, but most Black people lead a life very similar to Claude Brown's.

Cleaver, Eldridge, *Soul on Ice* (Dell), 1970, $.95.

This book is a combination of essays and open letters, autobiographical in nature. Eldridge Cleaver was in Folsom State Prison on a marijuana charge. After being released, he was sent

back on a rape charge. Although *Soul on Ice* is a good portrayal of prison life, the central theme deals with a deeper insight of imprisonment—the imprisonment of the Black soul by the oppressive white society of America. Within the multiple of Cleaver's assembled essays he raps on the Black man's relationship with white women and his mythical sexual-social status.

This book will probably have a timeless appeal, although I think that *Soul on Ice* would be more appealing to Blacks. As long as there is some form of racial consciousness, or the identity of a group of people is threatened, this book will be useful.

Coles, Robert, *Uprooted Children: The Early Life of Migrant Farm Workers* (Harper-Row), 1971, $.95.

Uprooted Children is a study of migrant farm workers, as parents and children. It contains interviews with both, telling what their lives are like and what they think of their lives. The book is related to teaching because some of these children either get no education at all, or very little, because of their nomadic life. The schooling they do get oftentimes is useless because of teachers' attitudes towards having a migrant child in their class.

Coles is quite upset by the conditions these children must endure, and seems to take an interest in trying to do something about them.

I don't really recommend this book, however, because it is repetitious.

Robin Townsley

Rene Dupee

236

Conroy, Pat, *The Water is Wide* (Dell), 1972, $1.50.

The Water is Wide is a very moving and emotional book. It is about a white man who has come to teach in an all black school on an isolated island off the South Carolina coast. The kids were almost totally ignorant of the outside world. They didn't know what an ocean was; one kid thought the earth was flat. Most of the kids had been trained to obey the whip, the belt, and the hand. The book describes Conroy's attempts to change all this.

Decker, Sunny, *An Empty Spoon* (Harper-Row), 1970, $.95.

An Empty Spoon offers a heart-warming insight into the problems and anxieties of a young white female teacher whose first teaching assignment happens to be in a black ghetto school. The book makes you believe in life all over again.

Charlene Day

Dennison, George, *The Lives of Children* (Random House), 1970, $1.95.

The Lives of Children tells the lurid story of the First Street School, a school for children who cannot survive in public schools. They are poor, rebellious, demanding, and wild. First Street was an attempt by a handful of teachers to help these kids and try to save them from a society that would not accept them. The book was enjoyable and sometimes shocking, but it lacked something, though what I'm not sure. I was dissatisfied by the outcome.

Vicky St. Myers

Dreikurs, Rudolph, M.D.; Grunwald, Bernice Bronia; Pepper, Floy C., *Maintaining Sanity in the Classroom* (Harper-Row), 1971, $4.95.

This book is very optimistic. One of the most interesting things it contains are realistic examples of different problems or potential problem situations, making it much more than just a bunch of theories that seem light-years away from a classroom. The only unrealistic aspect of these examples is that the teacher always seems to do the right thing.

The book uses very plain, down-to-earth language and avoids a lot of psychological terms. All told, it was a good book and probably a very useful and understandable one for teachers and an interesting one for laymen.

Cheri Vaught

Erikson, Erik H., *Childhood and Society* (Norton), 1964, $2.95.

In this book Erikson seeks to explain the role of children in our social system, both how they function, normally and abnormally, and the background that causes these resulting behaviors. Erikson relies heavily on Freudian theory to explain why different children behave in a specific manner. He feels there are even hidden meanings behind play, revealing sexual role identity and relieving inferiority, isolation, and anxiety.

Cheri Vaught

Farber, Jerry, *The Student as Nigger* (Pocket Books), 1970, $.95.

I read this book because of the title—the choice turned out to be poor, as the title is the best part of the book. Farber starts out with the thesis that schools push students around until they become "authority addicts," a sound thesis, but somewhere in the short course of the book Farber gets lost in his own rhetoric. Originally published in underground magazines, the *tract* is dated by its radical chic and bogged down in this impractical rhetoric. Farber says, ". . . the hardest battle isn't with Mr. Charlie. It's what Mr. Charlie has done to your mind." It looks like "Mr. Charlie" has already gotten Farber's.

Tom Himelick

Freire, Paulo, *Pedagogy of the Oppressed* (Herder and Herder), 1971, $2.25.

This is a radical book! Freire has developed a method of teaching illiterate Third World peasants, one that is so politically explosive that Ivan Illich described it as "truly revolutionary pedagogy." Because of its heavy philosophical slant, it is not an easy book to get through, but it's worth the fight.

Fromm, Eric, *The Art of Loving* (Bantam), 1956, $1.25.

I would highly recommend this book. It is well written and has so much to say that I feel I could read it several times and still find new meaning. "Love," says Dr. Fromm, "is the only satisfactory answer to the problem of human existence." He speaks of everyone's need to have union with others and not to feel alone and separate. Yet he tells of the challenge and courage needed to really love, to really be yourself. As with all other arts, the art of loving requires practice. If one has mastered the art of loving, then living and loving become one.

Ginott, Haim G., *Between Parent and Child* (Avon), 1970, $1.25.

I felt that this book was an excellent analysis of the common pitfalls that make communication difficult between parents and their children. Ginott offers an alternative method of responding and reacting that allows both parent and child to express their feelings and opinions without closing the door to communication. Many of Ginott's suggestions readily transfer to the elementary classroom.

Janet Dawson

Ginott, Haim G., *Between Parent and Teenager* (Avon), 1971, $1.25.

Many parents don't let their children grow up. Dr. Ginott gives suggestions on how parents can give their children more freedom to mature. He presents approaches that will let a young person think out a problem situation for himself. He emphasizes love as a central part of each approach.

The book is written in a question and answer style, with many specific examples. It reads fast and easy. I enjoyed it and plan on giving it to my parents to read. The book also has implications for the teacher-student relationship.

Eileen Schwartz

Green, Hannah, *I Never Promised You a Rose Garden* (Signet), 1964, $.95.

The book centers around the mystical world of insanity. The subject is a sixteen-year-old girl, Deborah Blau, who leaves the world of reality and enters her own world of Yri. This imaginary world holds a bondage for her, free of the hatred, unhappiness, and unpleasantness of the real world. Her world contains only love and beauty. *I Never Promised You a Rose Garden* relates Deborah Blau's struggle to regain the compassion and understanding that she needs to accept the real world from which she has retreated. Not only does the book describe her travels back, but also gives the reader a picture of life within a mental hospital.

Greenberg, Herbert M., *Teaching With Feeling* (Pegasus), 1969, $2.25.

Greenberg writes about teaching as a profession, but more importantly about being a person in the teaching profession. We are told about many problems involved in teaching and given suggestions on how to handle them. I really feel this is one of the most useful books about teaching I've read.

Harris, Thomas, *I'm O.K.—You're O.K.* (Avon), 1969, $1.95.

Dr. Harris relates a relatively new concept in psychiatry called transactional analysis. Harris explains the P-A-C theory (parent-adult-child are terms for the three psychological regions from which we operate). The book explains that the parent complex, probably the most frightening because it develops so quickly, typifies the "do's" and "don'ts" of our lives. The adult sector is the most difficult. It contains all the pressures of the adult world, while the "child" in us is the most innocent phase, naturally.

Harris says that when these regions become apparent, we can conquer our fears. I totally agree, and found this an excellent book.

Eileen Schwartz

Hart, Harold (ed.), *Summerhill: For and Against* (Hart), 1970, $2.45.

This book is a series of essays in which famous educators offer their opinions and thoughts on Summerhill. In the extreme, those in favor attribute all kinds of wonderful humanitarian qualities to Summerhill. Those opposed see the school as an evil force in society. Who is most correct, is an individual decision for each of us, but none of us interested in education can ignore Summerhill. And this book provides the information needed to make a knowledgeable judgment about Summerhill.

Haskins, Jim, *Diary of a Harlem School Teacher* (Grove), 1970, $.95.

This diary is an excellent account of the hardships a Harlem schoolteacher faced for a whole year. Haskins teaches an overcrowded special education class. He faces problems that I never imagined possible. He can't get the janitor to clean the room, repair the broken windows, or even turn up the heat. He can't get the police to talk to a man who has exposed himself daily, since the start of school, until school is almost out.

The conflicts and problems that Haskins faces make the book startlingly realistic and too good to omit from your reading list.

Eileen Schwartz

Herndon, James, *How to Survive in Your Native Land* (Bantam), 1971, $1.25.

How to Survive in Your Native Land is a somewhat jumbled, very personal account of a "liberal" junior high teacher. The book is a collection of humorous and serious episodes in various teaching situations, all underlining the often ridiculous, useless structure of public education.

Rick Sutton

The book made me angry at the ways schools operate and filled me with a rebellious flame to change things. Herndon tries a lot of very innovative techniques, like open classrooms and independent study, and they work—at least to the same degree that any school-based attempt to teach does. I especially liked his ideas on the role of teachers—not to teach, but to replace the teacher/student role-playing with other methods, leaving the teacher to be a person with kids. Herndon had the time to be a friend to his students and to talk about issues/ideas/problems that really mattered to them. He therefore successfully filtered the crap out of the educational process and in doing so made education relevant and enjoyable for everybody involved. I really think every teacher should read the book for the new ideas and general freshness it contains.

Marty Hollis

Herndon, James, *The Way It Spozed to Be* (Bantam), 1968, $.95.

This book was funny in spots, sad in spots, and dull in spots. However, when you look below the surface, there is a lesson to be learned. For me, that lesson was that teaching is no piece of cake. Sometimes all hell breaks loose and there is little you can do about it. All you can do is cope.

David Steckel

Holt, John, *How Children Fail* (Dell), 1970, $.95.

In *How Children Fail* John Holt expresses his impressions of the atmosphere of "learning" in today's classrooms. In chapters entitled "Strat-egy," "Fear and Failure," and "Real Learning" he declares that, as far as his experience shows, precious little learning does take place. Children are master manipulators of teachers. Holt comes to realize that children employ strategy to guarantee success; the fear of failure with which they are faced creates a block in their minds, thereby freezing their mental processes or at least seriously retarding their intellectual growth. This pressure is a crime, as much as any other theft is a crime. "In a very great degree, school is a place where children learn to be stupid." Grim statement, but too true to be ignored.

This book meant a lot to me; I saw myself as a strategist and remembered the awful fear that so often overwhelmed me. Holt speaks insightfully; he offers a creative attitude toward the process of rebuilding people into learners.

Meg Gaffney

Holt, John, *How Children Learn* (Dell), 1967, $.95.

Holt is a great diagnostician. He has a beautiful knack for sitting for long periods of time watching a kid manipulate his environment and being able to make sensible guesses about what's going on in the kid's head. *How Children Learn* focuses on little kids, preschoolers, who have not been turned off by school yet. All teachers will enjoy this very readable book, but those interested in early childhood education will find it especially valuable.

Hopkins, Lee Bennet, *Let Them be Themselves* (School Book Service), 1969, $2.50.

This book has a nice title and lots of great pictures in it. It's a source for ways of really helping kids who have any of many problems, not just school-wise, but in surviving as themselves. There is a short discussion of some problems encountered by disadvantaged children and the absolute necessity for us as adults to erase the negative factors which will, left unchecked, mutilate their spirit for life. The bulk of this text discusses tools with which a teacher can help rebuild or improve attitude and image. There are a couple of really good booklists in the back (award-winners, books dealing with race, and poetry books) and it was kind of neat to see how many of my favorite books were listed.

Katie Kitazawa

Illich, Ivan, *Deschooling Society* (Harper-Row), 1971, $1.25.

Schools have become self-serving institutions concerned more with their own survival and longevity than with helping people learn. Illich sees only one way to change this. He calls for the abandonment of our present monolithic system. He describes a transformation of schools, not unlike the transformation of the church that took place during the Reformation. It's difficult to sort through Illich's heavy writing style to find the gems of wisdom the book has to offer.

Joseph, Stephen M., *The Me Nobody Knows* (Avon), 1969, $.95.

What can I say about a book that astounded and moved me so intensely? Indeed, Joseph did show me that "given the chance to write, these children of the ghetto have a tremendous amount to say and are anxious to speak." Even in the harsh reality of their everyday lives in the slums, their thoughts on life, death, mankind, God, and love are waiting to be expressed. When these feelings are expressed, the words are so beautifully arranged and manipulated that I am shamed by my own meager attempts at composition. Any fifteen-year-old who can inspire the lyrics to "Light Sings All Over the World" is an artist in the bud, but will he have the chance to blossom? Lucy L. wonders, "Since Men and Rats are the only beings that purposely kill their own kind, and we exterminate rats what does that make us?" My immediate reaction is "Right on!" Who cares if the grammar isn't perfect, the form poor, or the spelling sloppy? True freedom of expression can enable any student to realize his creative potential. Or as Carlo would say," . . .There is a spark in those who think and strives and there in a time might ignite and illuminate the universe."

Cathy Greene

Kaufman, Bel, *Up the Down Staircase* (Avon), 1964, $.95.

Sylvia Barrett is a high school teacher in New York City's public school system. Learn the ins and outs and the ups and downs of the inner-city teaching by reading Bel Kaufman's witty novel, *Up the Down Staircase.* The book makes one laugh or cry, or both, in each one of its episodes.

The book is especially good for anyone who is interested in reading a first-class novel; however, it is especially recommended for those who are thinking of teaching, or already are teaching, in a large city school—better yet for anyone who teaches!

Learn how Miss Barrett learns to love her pupils and how they learn to love her. She teaches those whom few have been able to teach, she gains respect from those who hardly knew the meaning of the word before, and most importantly, she reaches those whom few have cared enough about to reach. I highly endorse this book!

Mary Weaver

Kohl, Herbert R., *The Open Classroom* (Random House), 1970, $1.65.

The Open Classroom describes itself as "A Practical Guide to a New Way of Teaching." For those who want to teach in an open classroom environment, this book is an invaluable source of information. It thoroughly explains what kinds of reactions and problems you can expect in trying to develop an open environment. Topics include the reactions you can expect from students, parents, other teachers, and the authoritarian school system, as well as your feelings about yourself and how you want to function in your school and classroom. To achieve openness is not an easy task, but the book helps a person weather the predictable setbacks that will accompany his first attempts to open up.

Mary Sirovy

Kohl, Herbert, *36 Children* (Signet), 1968, $.95.

Herbert Kohl is not an ordinary teacher. He teaches thirty-six sixth-graders in a Harlem elementary school. He doesn't teach in an ordinary way. Kohl's book, *36 Children,* is full of the sometimes funny, sometimes sad experiences he has with thirty-six children. The book drags a little in spots, but the sections that include the work of the children are very interesting. The success of

Kohl's way of teaching can be seen in the progress each child makes within the year.

Mary Kenney

Kozol, Jonathan, *Death at an Early Age* (Bantam), 1970, $1.25.

Jonathan Kozol's *Death at an Early Age* describes the Boston public school system in all its infamous glory and exposes the kind of awful human destruction it and probably thousands of other school systems perpetuate. Kozol taught one winter in a mostly Black elementary school in Roxbury. The school building was not only unpleasant and unsanitary; it was physically unsafe. Some children who were noticeably mentally disturbed were not helped—in fact, just the opposite. Made to stay in the school, they often were whipped for their sometimes "abnormal" behavior. Kozol describes a struggle with intolerable conditions: an unsafe building, bigoted teachers, his own students' learning problems.

Death at an Early Age is terribly moving. At first I was disappointed in Kozol for during his work there (1964-65) he did not seem to take a stand against the rampant dishonesty and cruelty. Later, as I came to see what he did accomplish, his earlier (seeming) acquiescence became forgivable. Ultimately, he stands fast and says "No" to the principal, to fellow teachers, and to the school board. No longer does he ignore their hypocrisy.

Meg Gaffney

Kozol, Jonathan, *Free Schools* (Bantam), 1972, $1.50.

This book is about a particular kind of free school, one that is not part of the public education system, one that is outside the white counter-culture, inside the cities, and in direct contact with the needs of the people in that immediate neighborhood. If that is the type of school which interests you, then I recommend this book. Mr. Kozol presents strong, perceptive, and passionate declarations of what constitutes a free school in his very specific terms. He has learned over the years what to do and how to do it. My main criticism of his book is that his dogmatic attitude results in his overlooking goals other than his own.

Leonard, George S., *Education and Ecstasy* (Delta), 1968, $2.25.

If you can wade through the technical, overdone first half of *Education and Ecstasy*, the second half does get better, with a most interesting futuristic look at the possibilities of education in our schools. I don't honestly believe I would recommend it to you, though.

Liebow, Elliot, *Tally's Corner* (Little Brown), 1967, $2.25.

Tally's Corner is completely factual. It was written by a sociologist, Elliot Liebow, who gathered the data as part of a government project. Liebow lived with ghetto Blacks and interacted with them daily. The story centers around one corner in the city and concerns the slum dwellers who live close by and their friends. The stories of the lives these people lead and have led gave me much understanding of the crisis American cities are in and encouraged me to try in some way to respond to the situation. Tally, one of the main characters, is a human being, yet his plight seems hopeless because of the extreme poverty and discrimination in the ghetto where he has to live. The book should be read by all concerned citizens—before the newspapers.

Malcolm X, *The Autobiography of Malcolm X* (Grove), 1966, $1.25.

"I do not expect to live long enough to read my book . . ."

Malcolm rose from hoodlum, thief, pimp, and dope peddler to leader of the Black Revolution. Malcolm didn't live long enough to read his book, but his ideologies, dreams, and thoughts as revealed in his autobiography have made a lasting impact on Blacks!

I highly recommend this true story to anyone—Black or white. It is beautifully written, touching, heartbreaking, but written with "Pride."

Bev Bennett

May, Rollo, *Man's Search for Himself* (Signet), 1953, $1.25.

Today there is a transition taking place in our society's values and standards. It is because of this transition that most of us have no inner security. Rollo May wrote *Man's Search for Himself* so the reader might learn how to help himself overcome this feeling of insecurity and attain a better awareness of his needs and feelings. I could personally relate to the chapter "Loneliness and Anxiety of Modern Man." Its message is that our society places a great deal of importance on being socially accepted. The easiest way to prove your social acceptance is to be with someone at all times—never to be alone. The fact that positive things can arise from solitude is seldom considered. This book helps a person sort out the question, "Who am I?"

Marilyn K. Kane

Moore, G. Alexander, *Realities of the Urban Classroom* (Doubleday), 1967, $1.45.

Realities describes the anthropological investigation of three schools in a "large American city." Each school is described in terms of its physical structure, neighborhood, racial composition, and so forth. Different classes and activities within the classes are described by the observers, focusing on the bulk of activity (the teacher's activity, the boisterous students, or the actual teaching, depending on where the actual bulk of activity is). The book reads like a series of case studies of teachers. One section discusses a counselor who does well in the school, despite the teachers, administration, and philosophies she has to work with. The author describes different types of teachers, concentrates on Black and Hispanic students, and stresses adaptive teaching. The book provides a good look at the urban classroom and is especially interesting to anyone who wants to work with Blacks or Hispanos.

Neill, A. S., *Summerhill: A Radical Approach to Child Rearing* (Hart), 1960, $2.45.

This is likely to be the best book I read this semester. Summerhill is a free school in England. In fact, it is the granddaddy of all free schools. And the book *Summerhill* has become something of a Bible for the free-school movement. I was alternately amazed, impressed, or puzzled by nearly everything Neill says. Nearly all my copy of *Summerhill* is underlined. The word "radical" in the subtitle certainly applies. The relationship between Neill's and the conventional school-teacher's beliefs on education is almost non-existent. If existentialism is your bag, *Summerhill* is your book.

Cheri Vaught

Nyberg, David, *Tough and Tender Learning* (National Press), 1971, $2.95.

This book is about the psychology of unhiding and becoming a real person in the classroom. Although Nyberg seems to be very realistic about the pitfalls and problems of implementing this approach, he makes his presentation on a philosophical level that at times makes it seem idealistic.

The merits of this "non-method" remain to be seen, but it's worth a try. I'm not sure that the level of sensitivity required for teaching this way could be sustained by most people or tolerated by most officials. But I certainly hope that many teachers will read and heed what this book has to say.

Mike Pomatto

Postman, Neil and Weingartner, Charles, *Teaching as a Subversive Activity* (Dell), 1971, $2.25.

This is an enjoyable book, though I wouldn't recommend it to anyone who is fairly satisfied with schools as they now are. Postman and Weingartner cover a wide range of topics very much of interest to young teachers. They deal with inquiry, media, and critical thinking, for example. Their proposals at first seem outlandish, but they force you to begin questioning some of the ideas about school that you've always accepted as "givens." It's a good book.

Rogers, Carl, *On Becoming a Person* (Houghton-Mifflin), 1961, $3.25.

If you're trying to fight through the good old identity crisis thing (Who am I? Where am I going? Why?), Rogers is talking to you. *On Becoming a Person* is a big book but it also contains much of value. I found some of the segments on therapy sessions tiresome, but otherwise have little but praise for what Rogers has to say and the way he says it.

Rosenthal, Robert and Jacobson, Lenore, *Pygmalion in the Classroom* (Holt, Rinehart, and Winston), 1968, $4.95.

Pygmalion in the Classroom is the account of an experiment executed in 1966 in a working-class elementary school called Oak Ridge School. It was the purpose of the authors to test the hypothesis that students perform better when, by randomly tagging some of them "bloomers" or "spurters," their teachers are "tricked" into expecting them to perform better.

The results are startling. The children tagged as "bloomers" underwent significant increases in their IQ's as compared with the control group. Some of the more interesting factors involved disadvantaged children; they benefited the most from positive teacher expectancy.

The book itself is boring and hard to read, very dry and factual, with hundreds of charts and data sheets. There is an excellent summary of the entire experiment in the last eight pages of the book, which I would recommend instead of reading the book itself.

Marty Hollis

Rubin, Theodore Isaac, *Jordi* (Ballantine), 1971, $.95.

The story of Jordi attempts to help people understand what goes on in the mind of a mentally ill child and suggests how a teacher can respond to that child. He must learn how to interpret the child's actions and be able to deal with those actions a little at a time. As the child learns and grows with the new experiences, so does the teacher. Some of these experiences have include relating to other children, making friends, and learning about subjects that a normal child would learn in school. The teacher-child relationship can often get quite close. I highly recommend this book for those interested in mental illness or retardation.

Robin Townsley

de Saint-Exupéry, Antoine, *The Little Prince* (Harcourt Brace Jovanovich), 1943, $.75.

Well, I'm not going to say *everybody* should read this book . . . because it's not true. But it's really nice for me to look at it again, knowing how the story pulls my head together. Basically, it is a children's story which relates the life and feelings of a small boy from Asteroid B-612. The author refers to him as the little prince without explanation but, in essence, doesn't need one. More importantly, it is an honest guide for explaining human phenomena simply, especially along the lines of parent or adult in conflict with child. One of the ideas he presents is how we tend to gloss over what, in his opinion, are essential matters that once concerned us as children. As we grow old, self-importance can smother the warmer human attitudes. But be careful not to over-read the book. To scratch for some profound message through intellectual pidge-podging would be really awful. I think it would bug Antoine that you did exactly what he intended you to realize the folly of doing.

The Little Prince is a wonderful little book. When I'm sad or my mind is boggled by heavy thinking, it can help serenity to surface. Someone said it was a fairytale. I don't think so.

Katie Kitazawa

243

Schrag, Peter, *Voices in the Classroom: Public Schools and Public Attitudes* (Beacon), 1965, $2.25.

Schrag is a journalist who took off for several months just to travel across the country and look at schools. He's put together very illuminating descriptions that, if nothing else, explode any notion you might have that all American schools are pretty much alike. The schools described include Topeka, Kansas (Midwest, conservative); Chicago (a very dated chapter, now); Newton, Mass. (college prep, USA); and Appalachia. As I read the book, I kept hoping that Schrag would make a similar journey today and write this book again in the context of the mid 70s. I doubt that much of what he observed has changed, but I'd like to be more certain of that.

Silberman, Charles E., *Crisis in the Classroom* (Vintage) 1971, $2.45.

Charles E. Silberman's book, *Crisis in the Classroom*, though very long (525 pages), is well worth reading or at least skimming. Silberman provides a good deal of ammunition to arguments supporting progressive schools. In doing so, he covers a lot of theoretical ground about why schools must change; at the same time, he uses statistics and examples as proof.

Silberman describes a few alternative schools—Parkway in Philadelphia, Murray House in Newton, Mass. He praises these schools, and cites them as models for other public schools to emulate. Silberman believes strongly in public education and also believes that progressive education can work in public schools. He cites experimental schools in Harlem which not only raise the achievement level of students, but more importantly, lead them toward happy, useful lives, including actual joy in learning. Silberman warns against a completely non-structured approach which rapidly becomes boring for both teacher and student, but seems to think a compromise of old and new methods is possible and best. Silberman provides the English Infant School as an example of a practical application of "open" methods. Yet he remains convinced that each school must establish its curriculum to satisfy the needs of its population (parents, citizens, and students); it is in guided flexibility that progressive schools will achieve the best possible educational standards.

Marty Hollis

Slater, Philip, *The Pursuit of Loneliness* (Beacon Press) 1971, $2.45.

Slater talks about our American society, as it is—messed up. He offers some extremely thought-provoking ideas on why it is. I found myself stopping every other paragraph or so and thinking about what he said; I agree with what he has to say. I wish more people would read this book. It's short, concise, and very much on target.

Scott Woodworth

Swarthout, Gertrude, *Bless the Beasts and Children* (Pocket Books), 1970, $.95.

Bewildered by life, confused by their parents, six boys engage in a journey to free themselves from the thought of being worthless. The story covers only about six or seven hours, in time, but more happens for these six kids in this short time than has happened to them in their lives up until then. Anyone who likes kids and a good story will like this book.

Scott Woodworth

Toffler, Alvin, *Future Shock* (Bantam), 1971, $1.95.

Future Shock is a one-of-a-kind book. It will intrigue you, frighten you, and make you full of anticipation for the future.

Toffler introduces the reader to the meaning of future shock—the terrific psychological adaptation that overwhelms us when our environment changes as rapidly as it does now. He investigates many of the causes of the acceleration of change and explores the effects of future shock on the individual and society. Finally, he suggests ways in which we must revise our traditional uses of psychology, technology, industry, education, etc., in order to cope with and survive future shock.

The book is thoroughly researched, factual rather than speculative, and fast-paced enough to avert boredom.

Mary Jo Hendershot

Appendix I

Rating Form

(See "With a Little Help from. . . ." experience on pages 33–35).

Name _____

Date _____

This rating list might be helpful as a means of communicating to your group leader or to your friends or to yourself the concerns you have about various topics as of this date. We suggest you put a –1, 0, 1, 2, or 3 after each topic, the numerals roughly indicating your level of concern about each topic based on the following scale:

___ –1 = something I definitely don't want to explore

___ 0 = indifferent to this topic

___ 1 = something I'd like to know more about if time permits

___ 2 = something I definitely want to know more about

___ 3 = something I personally want to explore

. . .

Space has been provided so that you can add your own topics. This form is useful only if it helps you get answers to *your* questions. Right?

___ 1. How can a teacher deal with pressures from parents and/or principals?

___ 2. What are alternatives for dealing with discipline problems?

___ 3. What do you think of tenure, salary schedules, and the teacher job market?

___ 4. Can school make much of a difference in society, or is school just an elaborate ritual to sort out the strong from the weak?

___ 5. Should teachers organize and fight for better working conditions the way other unions do?

___ 6. What are "free schools" and what do they do?

___ 7. What legal responsibilities do teachers have?

___ 8. What's the best way to handle grades and report cards?

___ 9. What philosophies of education can you choose from?

___ 10. What can be done for slow learners?

___ 11. How might new and innovative teachers relate to old and traditional teachers in the same school?

___ 12. What are some ways to begin a school year? What should teachers do the first few days of school?

___ 13. How many teachers outgrow their initial lack of confidence? What helps to gain confidence?

___ 14. How does a teacher get students to like him without losing their respect?

___ 15. How does a teacher get students to like the subject?

16. In what ways can schools or teachers or rooms or students be organized?

17. How does a teacher get certified to teach in various states?

18. How can new teaching styles be introduced in a school operating on traditional assumptions and using traditional procedures?

19. What models of excellent teachers are available to you and what can be learned from observing them?

20. How do students get motivated to learn?

21. Why do students forget so much of what they learn and what, if anything, can be done to improve the situation?

22. How much freedom should a teacher give students?

23. How did schools get where they are—what can be learned from looking at the history of education?

24. How can I tell if I know my subject well enough to teach?

25. Should private and religious schools be supported with public funds?

26. Should teachers ever lie to students?

27. Should teachers expose their personal lives to students?

28. How should controversial issues be handled in the classroom?

29. Does the power that a teacher holds tend to corrupt him?

30. What's the best way to plan lessons?

31. How do you envision schools of the future?

32. To what extent should I sacrifice myself for my students?

33. Is there a theory of teaching?

34. How should I handle racial conflict in the classroom?

35. Am I good enough to be a teacher: strong enough, smart enough, creative enough?

36. Can teachers learn to improve, or are good teachers just born that way?

37. What goes on in a faculty meeting?

38. Can I use this book's approach to learning in my teaching?

39. What do I do when I don't know what to do? How can I, a teacher, get help?

40. Do I have the patience to be a teacher?

41. How can I explain ideas so they will be clear to students?

42. How can I get to know a whole class of students and remember their names?

43. What do I do when I don't like a particular child?

44. Can I relax and be myself when I'm teaching?

45. How can schools get rid of deadwood tenured teachers?

46. What is more important to my teaching: the goals I achieve or the process I use?

47. What are my real motives for teaching? Should I be a teacher?

48. Why don't people learn more from experience? Why are errors of the past repeated so often?

The Authors Blew It—Topics of REAL Concern to Me:

Appendix II

"There is a wealth of information about the teaching profession available from a variety of sources. These sources aren't often tapped, maybe because people aren't aware they exist. Also, we suspect that the hassle of coming up with a source's address, combined with the possibility that the effort may bear no fruit, is a sufficient deterrent to many quests.

We wanted to eliminate as much of that deterrent as we could, so we put together this list and included a form letter on pages 259-60."

An Education Directory

American Federation of Teachers; 1012-14th Street N.W.; Washington, D.C. 20005

National Education Association; 1201-16th Street N.W.; Washington, D.C. 20036

Alabama: State Department of Education, Montgomery 36104

Alaska: State Department of Education, Juneau 99801

Arizona: State Department of Education, Phoenix 85007

Arkansas: State Department of Education, Little Rock 72201

California: State Department of Education, 721 Capitol Mall, Sacramento 95814

Colorado: State Department of Education, Denver 80203

Connecticut: State Department of Education, Hartford 06115

Delaware: State Department of Public Instruction, Dover 19901

Florida: Department of Education, Tallahassee 32304

Georgia: State Department of Education, Atlanta 30334

Hawaii: Department of Education, Honolulu 96804

Idaho: Department of Education, Boise 83707

Illinois: Office of the Superintendent of Public Instruction, Springfield 62706

Indiana: Department of Education, Indianapolis 46206

Iowa: Department of Public Instruction, Des Moines 50319

Kansas: Board of Education, Topeka 66612

Kentucky: Department of Education, Frankfort 40601

Louisiana: Department of Education, Baton Rouge 70804

Maine: Department of Education, Augusta 04330

Maryland: Department of Education, Baltimore 21201

Massachusetts: State Department of Education, Boston 02111

Michigan: Department of Education, Lansing 48902

Minnesota: State Department of Education, St. Paul 55101

Mississippi: State Department of Education, Jackson 39205

Missouri: State Department of Education, Jefferson City 65101

Montana: State Department of Public Instruction, Helena 59601

Nebraska: State Department of Education, Lincoln 68509

Nevada: State Department of Education, Carson City 89701

New Hampshire: State Department of Education, Concord 03301

New Jersey: State Department of Education, Trenton 08625

New Mexico: State Department of Education, Santa Fe 87501

New York: State Education Department, Albany 12224

North Carolina: State Department of Public Instruction, Raleigh 27602

North Dakota: State Department of Public Instruction, Bismarck 58501

Ohio: State Department of Education, Columbus 43215

Oklahoma: State Department of Education, Oklahoma City 73105

Oregon: State Board of Education, Salem 97310

Pennsylvania: State Department of Education, Harrisburg 17126

Rhode Island: State Department of Education, Providence 02908

South Carolina: State Department of Education, Columbia 29201

South Dakota: State Department of Public Instruction, Pierre 57501

Tennessee: State Department of Education, Nashville 37219

Texas: Texas Education Agency, Austin 78701

Utah: Board of Education, Salt Lake City 84111

Vermont: Department of Education, Montpelier 05602

Virginia: Board of Education, Richmond 23216

Washington: Department of Public Instruction, Olympia 98501

West Virginia: Department of Education, Charleston 25305

Wisconsin: Department of Public Instruction, Madison 53702

Wyoming: Department of Education, Cheyenne 82001

Appendix III

Application Forms, Contracts, and Evaluation Forms

PALO ALTO UNIFIED SCHOOL DISTRICT
Personnel Services
25 Churchill Avenue
Palo Alto, California
94306

Secondary and Special Teacher Application

Date _____

PERSONAL DATA

Name (Mr., Miss, Mrs.) _____
_____ (Last) _____ (First) _____ (Middle) _____ (Maiden)

Present Telephone _____
Address _____ (Street) _____ (City) _____ (State) _____ (Zip Code)

Permanent Telephone _____
Address _____ (Street) _____ (City) _____ (State) _____ (Zip Code)

Date of Birth _____ Age _____ Weight _____ Height _____ Social Security No. _____

Single _____ Married _____ Widowed _____ Separated _____ Divorced _____ No. of Children _____ Ages _____

State of Health: Normal Hearing? _____ Normal Vision? _____ Wear Glasses? _____

Illness (during last 3 years) _____ Days Lost from Work or College _____

Comments: _____

PLACEMENT SERVICE *Confidential file must include statement from present principal. This Personnel Office will request files for candidates selected for the interview.*

Placement Service _____
Street _____ City _____ State
No placement file available _____

CREDENTIAL INFORMATION

California
Credential(s) Held _____
Title _____ Expiration Date _____ Major _____ Minor

California
Credential(s)
Applied for _____
Title _____ Expiration Date _____ Major _____ Minor
Title _____ Expiration Date _____ Major _____ Minor

TEACHING PREFERENCE

Level Preference (Indicate 1, 2, 3)   Subject Preference

_____ Junior High   1. _____   2. _____   3. _____
_____ Senior High   1. _____   2. _____   3. _____
_____ Other*   1. _____   2. _____   3. _____

* Counselor, Educationally, Mentally, Orthopedically and Visually Handicapped, Librarian, Speech Therapist, Music-Vocal, Music-Instrumental, Nurse, Spanish, etc.

EDUCATIONAL AND PROFESSIONAL PREPARATION

	Institution	State	Attended From To	Years	Degree or Credential	Major or Concentration	Minor
College and/or University							
Graduate Work or Special Training							

Number of Units After Date of A.B. or B.S. Degree: Semester Units _____ Quarter Units _____

COURSES COMPLETED IN MAJOR FIELD _____ (Major Field)
(Designate graduate courses with *. Attach additional sheets if necessary.)

Course Title	Grade	Course Title	Grade	Course Title	Grade	Course Title	Grade

Total No. Semester Units _____ Quarter Units _____

COURSES COMPLETED IN MINOR FIELD _____ (Minor Field)
(Designate graduate courses with *)

Course Title	Grade	Course Title	Grade	Course Title	Grade	Course Title	Grade

Total No. Semester Units _____ Quarter Units _____

COURSES COMPLETED IN EDUCATION AND PSYCHOLOGY — (Designate graduate courses with *)

Course Title	Grade	Course Title	Grade	Course Title	Grade	Course Title	Grade

Total No. Semester Units _____ Quarter Units _____

Approximate grade point average for all undergraduate work _____ ; for all graduate work _____

Basis on which grade point averages are computed: 3 point scale? _____ 4 point scale? _____

EXTRACURRICULAR ACTIVITIES (Indicate honors, positions of responsibility, etc.)

High School— _____

College— _____

Community— _____

What extracurricular activities do you feel qualified to direct? _____

ORIGINAL STATEMENT (Must be completed by each applicant)

Write a brief statement concerning some noteworthy experience in which you have engaged within the last three years that is related to your interest in teaching.

If it were within your power to effect some important change in secondary education, what would it be?

Explain your reasons for the above:

PERSONAL INTERVIEW

If you are selected for the interview, when can you come to Palo Alto for this purpose? (March and April are recommended.)

Preferred Dates: Times:

1. _____   _____

2. _____   _____

3. _____   _____

How many days accumulated sick leave are you entitled to transfer from your previous California school district, as stated in Education Code 13468.1, as of November 17, 1965? _____

Name of District from which sick leave is to be transferred _____

Relative(s) presently employed by the Palo Alto Unified School District if any:

Name(s) _____

I certify that to the best of my knowledge the information contained in this application is true.

How did you become acquainted with the Palo Alto Unified School District? (Check one. Indicate primary source.)

1. Through another person
   a. District employee _____
   b. Friend or relative _____
   c. College faculty member _____
   d. College placement officer _____
   e. Private placement agent _____
   f. District recruiter _____
   g. Other _____

2. Through PAUSD published materials
   a. Information brochures _____
   b. Advertisement in ASCUS Annual _____

3. General reputation of the District _____

4. Other _____

_____
(Signature of Applicant)

THE PALO ALTO UNIFIED SCHOOL DISTRICT IS AN EQUAL OPPORTUNITY EMPLOYER

9-69/5M

250

PERSONAL INTERVIEW RATING FORM

APPEARANCE

1	2	3	4	5
	Appearance an asset.	Appropriately and neatly dressed. Shows good taste.		Appearance a detriment.

GENERAL PERSONALITY AND INTELLIGENCE

1	2	3	4	5
	Very secure, poised, warm and pleasant. Shows real enthusiasm.	Is a little nervous but shows some self-confidence, enthusiasm and humor.		Excessively timid and dull, or very aggressive and rigid.

EDUCATIONAL PHILOSOPHY

1	2	3	4	5
	Broad practical understanding. Agrees with Palo Alto.	Philosophy expressed consistent with Palo Alto.		Philosophy parroted. Not communicated well. Inconsistent or narrow.

KNOWLEDGE OF SUBJECT MATTER

1	2	3	4	5
	Excellent preparation and a thorough understanding of the subject.	Sufficient preparation with good understanding of the subject.		Limited preparation, fair understanding of the subject.

PUPIL GUIDANCE

1	2	3	4	5
	Superior grasp of guidance techniques. Mature understanding of more difficult pupils.	Understands pupil at different ages. Discipline consistent with philosophy.		Discipline rigid, weak, inconsistent, not child-centered.

POTENTIAL FOR GROWTH

1	2	3	4	5
	Has ability and capacity to become a great teacher	Limited capacity for growth.		Has reached his potential as a teacher.

GENERAL CULTURE

1	2	3	4	5
	Variety of outside interests. Well balanced to enhance teaching.	Some outside reading; has a hobby or special talent.		Little outside activity. Rather narrow view of growth.

LEADERSHIP QUALITIES

1	2	3	4	5
	Proven leadership ability	Some ability and experience as a leader		A follower.

SPECIAL ABILITIES

SAMPLE

LOS ANGELES CITY UNIFIED SCHOOL DISTRICT
PERSONNEL DIVISION
Administrative Offices: 450 N. Grand Ave., Los Angeles

Mailing Address: P.O. Box 3307, Los Angeles, Calif. 90051

CONFIDENTIAL REFERENCE RELATING TO EMPLOYMENT

We hope that you will find it convenient to complete and return this form since your judgment will greatly assist us in evaluating this candidate's competency in the examination field indicated above. We ask you to write comments which you feel will help us with this evaluation. All information will be held strictly confidential. Thank you for your cooperation.

PROFESSIONAL COMPETENCE

PLEASE CHECK THE APPROPRIATE BOXES

	NO BASIS FOR JUDGMENT	INADEQUATE	BELOW AVERAGE	SATISFACTORY	STRONG	OUTSTANDING
1. Promotes an effective classroom environment						
2. Ability to communicate						
3. Ability to develop pupil discipline and morale						
4. Ability to manage classroom and school routines						
5. Ability to plan instruction						
6. Use of effective teaching procedures						
7. Provides for individual differences						
8. Ability to motivate pupils						
9. Contributes to the total school program						
10. Creativity						

REMARKS (positive or negative):

APPLICANT

Last Name _____ First Name _____

Grade or Subject Field _____

PERSONAL QUALITIES

PLEASE CHECK THE APPROPRIATE BOXES

	NO BASIS FOR JUDGMENT	INADEQUATE	BELOW AVERAGE	SATISFACTORY	STRONG	OUTSTANDING
1. Manner						
2. Appearance						
3. Enthusiasm						
4. Effectiveness of speech						
5. Assumption of responsibility						
6. Maturity of judgment						
7. Professional attitudes						
8. Health and vitality						
9. Emotional poise						
10. Ability to work with others						

MONTGOMERY PUBLIC SCHOOLS
City and County
Montgomery, Alabama

Superintendent's Office

GENERAL LETTER OF APPOINTMENT

Dear

This is to offer you a teaching position in the Montgomery Public Schools (within the city limits) in accordance with information contained on your application, with probable assignment in _____ at a salary of $_____ per annum (paid in 12 equal installments on the first of each month), based on your Rank _____ beginning _____ Alabama teacher's certificate* and according to our present salary schedule, beginning _____. Our salary schedule is sustained by an allocation of State money for teacher units and by local funds; thus, the Montgomery Public Schools-- as all other school systems in Alabama--are dependent upon State school funds being available. This offer is contingent upon the availability of State school funds. Should funds for additional salary raises be forthcoming, the above quoted salary will be increased accordingly.

You may be placed in a school which was previously considered a black school but which has been desegregated and a majority of the teachers are white; or you may be placed in a school previously considered white which has been desegregated and a majority of the teachers are white.

Please let me have the enclosed sheet returned as your letter of acceptance immediately, and my letter to you along with this acceptance will constitute our contract for the coming year. You have 14 days in which to consider this offer and return your acceptance or rejection. Unless we receive your acceptance within 14 days from the date of this letter, this offer is automatically cancelled. (PLEASE answer "YES" or "NO".)

You will be notified of your specific assignment at a later date as our needs develop, and we trust you will enjoy working with us.

Sincerely yours,

H. H. Adair
Associate Superintendent

HHA/rhd
Enc.

* TEACHER'S CERTIFICATE: It is your responsibility to apply for your Alabama teacher's certificate, and this should be done through your college if you attended in Alabama; otherwise, contact the State Department of Education, Certification Division, Montgomery, Alabama 36104. Your teacher's certificate is kept on file in this office as long as you are teaching here. Only ONE certificate is issued, and this should be sent to this office as soon as you receive it.

253

BOARD OF EDUCATION OF THE CITY OF LOS ANGELES

Contract of Employment

Date of offer:

The Board of Education of the City of Los Angeles offers you employment as a

The compensation paid shall be in accordance with the salary schedule adopted by the Board, and shall begin with the first day of actual service to the district.

This offer of employment is subject to all rules and regulations of the Board and all laws of the State of California in effect during the period of employment. This offer of employment is valid for _____ calendar days from date of offer.

If you desire to accept, please sign and return the original (white) copy to:

Retain the blue copy for your files.

BOARD OF EDUCATION OF THE CITY OF LOS ANGELES
Tony E. Rivas, Assistant Supt., Personnel

By _____

ACCEPTANCE OF OFFER
I accept the offer of employment set forth above subject to the terms and conditions therein and certify that:

1. I have read the reverse side of this form. I understand the implications of my signature in this contract and agree to the conditions of employment described on the reverse side and below.

2. The information given in the application for employment is complete and accurate.

3. I am not under contract to provide services for any other school district during the period of this agreement.

4. I know of no circumstances that will make it impossible for me to render the service specified above during the period of this agreement.

5. I understand that my signature below places me under contract with the Board of Education of Los Angeles City for the period indicated.

6. If this offer is for a conditional contract. I hereby apply for the next District examination in the field of this contract. If I have not received information concerning the date and location of this examination before next November 1st I will notify the Personnel Division of that fact.

_____ (Signed)

Address - Number and Street _____ City _____ State _____ Zip Code _____
(Please notify Personnel Division of any change of address)
Telephone _____ Date _____ Date of Birth _____

LAUSPD Form 1752-17 4-73

(OVER)

THE CITY SCHOOL DISTRICT OF NEW YORK
OFFICE OF PERSONNEL – BUREAU OF TEACHERS' RECORDS
65 Court Street, Brooklyn, New York 11201
REPORT ON PROBATIONARY SERVICE OF TEACHER FOR

PA8C178

( ) – CONTINUED SERVICE   ( ) – COMPLETION OF PROBATION   ( ) – PERMANENT APPOINTMENT
(Please read rules and instructions on reverse)

File No. _____   Soc Sec. No. _____

(Last Name) _____ (First Name) _____ (Initial) _____

Jarema Allowance in Years. _____
Appointment Date _____

License _____   Probation Completion Date _____
Permanent Appointment Date _____

School _____   Borough _____   District _____

I. PRINCIPAL'S REPORT

	First Year	Second Year	Third Year	Fourth Year	Fifth Year

Number of times late (not present 20 minutes before morning or 10 minutes before afternoon session) . . .
Time lost through lateness . . . .
Number of times absent . . . .
Time (number of days) lost through absence . . . .

	Satis-factory	Unsatis-factory	Additional Comments

Comments Based on Personal Knowledge and Observation during Period Covered by Report

A. PERSONAL AND PROFESSIONAL QUALITIES
1. Personal appearance . . . .
2. Voice, speech and use of English. . . . .
3. Professional attitude . . . .
4. Sympathetic understanding of children . . . .
5. Resourcefulness and initiative . . . .
6. Evidence of professional growth. . . . .

B. PUPIL GUIDANCE AND INSTRUCTION
1. Effect on character and personality growth of pupils . . .
2. Control of class . . . .
3. Maintenance of a wholesome classroom atmosphere . . .
4. Planning and preparation of work . . . .
5. Skill in adapting instruction to individual needs and capacities . . .
6. Effective use of appropriate methods and techniques . . .
7. Skill in making the class program attractive and interesting to pupils . . .
8. Extent of pupil participation in the class and school program . . .
9. Evidence of pupil growth in knowledge, skills, appreciations, and attitude . . .
10. Attention to pupil health, safety, and general welfare . . .

C. CLASSROOM OR SHOP MANAGEMENT
1. Attention to physical conditions . . . .
2. Housekeeping and appearance of room . . . .
3. Care of equipment by teacher and children. . . . . . .
4. Attention to records and reports . . . .
5. Attention to routine matters . . . .

D. PARTICIPATION IN SCHOOL AND COMMUNITY ACTIVITIES
1. Maintenance of good relations with other teachers and with supervisors . . .
2. Effort to establish and maintain good relationships with parents . . .
3. Willingness to accept special assignments in connection with the school program . . .

E. ADDITIONAL REMARKS (Additional sheets, signed and acknowledged may be attached):

Form OP11

255

PALO ALTO UNIFIED SCHOOL DISTRICT

No. 2

STUDENT OPINION FORM

TO BE RETURNED DIRECTLY TO THE TEACHER

Circle Period: 1 2 3 4 5 6 7

Directions: This is an attempt by your teacher to improve the class by listening to your reactions. Please respond to each statement below by checking in one of the columns to the right. Be as honest as possible. Do not sign your name.

	MOST OF THE TIME	SOMETIMES	HARDLY EVER	NO OPINION
1. This teacher has helped me be interested in the subject.				
2. I try to participate in this class.				
3. This teacher begins class promptly without wasting time.				
4. This teacher seems to know the subject we're studying.				
5. This teacher is well organized.				
6. Homework is worthwhile and not just busy-work.				
7. The amount of homework we get is right for this kind of class.				
8. I am graded fairly in this class.				
9. This teacher avoids treating certain students as favorites.				
10. This teacher is reasonable in what students are expected to do.				
11. This teacher shows understanding and concern for students.				
12. This teacher respects the expression of different opinions.				
13. This teacher talks too much about personal problems that shouldn't be brought to the classroom.				
14. This teacher explains lessons clearly.				
15. I have opportunities to express myself in class.				
16. This teacher spends too much time talking.				
17. This teacher seems to understand how much I know and helps me learn.				
18. This teacher uses different ways and aids to help me learn.				
19. This teacher goes over our written work and returns it to us.				
20. This teacher listens and tries to understand what we're saying.				
21. This teacher keeps the class under control enough to allow us to learn.				
22. This teacher tries to make the course interesting.				
23. This class is a place I like to be for this subject.				

39

256

PALO ALTO UNIFIED SCHOOL DISTRICT

No. 3

Dear Parents,

This is the third part of the Parent Opinionnaire. You filled out the "Parent Information for Teacher Use" at the beginning of the year. This section gives you an opportunity to comment on your child's reactions to his school program this year. Your responses can provide important insights for the teachers. They also assist the principal in planning programs to strengthen classroom experiences and to make wise student-teacher assignments.

Thank you for your cooperation.

Sincerely,

Elementary School Principal

If you are satisfied we'd like to know it.

If you are dissatisfied we <u>ought</u> to know it.

- - - - - - - - - - - -

Please circle the number which best indicates your opinion. Add any additional comments under the appropriate questions on the back of this paper. If you do not have an opinion, omit the item.

1. The teacher and I have communicated (sufficiently ⟍___⟋ unsufficiently)
   about my child.   1   2   3   4   5

2. My child's progress was (effectively ⟍___⟋ poorly) reported
                            1   2   3   4   5
   to me throughout the year by means of work, well-kept records, teacher observations.

3. My child was (well ⟍___⟋ poorly) motivated to learn.
                 1   2   3   4   5

4. My child was rewarded in ways that I (approve ⟍___⟋ disapprove).
                                          1   2   3   4   5

5. My child has (increased ⟍___⟋ not increased) in ability to
                 1   2   3   4   5
   learn independently.

6. My child appears to have had (many ⟍___⟋ few) opportunities
                                  1   2   3   4   5
   to be creative.

7. My child has grown (greatly ⟍___⟋ little) in ability
                       1   2   3   4   5
   to understand and appreciate people who are unlike himself (culturally, physically, etc.).

8. My child feels (comfortable ⟍___⟋ uncomfortable) about himself
                   1   2   3   4   5
   in school.

44

257

Montgomery, Alabama

A. COMPETENCE AND PERFORMANCE OF TEACHER

____ 1. PHYSICAL ENVIRONMENT
Room is attractive, comfortable, functionally arranged, neat.

____ 2. EVIDENCE OF TEACHER PLANNING AND PREPARATION
Materials are ready. The lesson is well organized and meaningful.

____ 3. CLASSROOM ORGANIZATION
Classroom procedures are organized. Time is used efficiently.

____ 4. PUPIL INVOLVEMENT AND INTERACTION
Pupils participate in oral discussion, written work, listening activities, and planning.

____ 5. SUBJECT MATTER COMPETENCE

____ 6. INDIVIDUALIZATION OF INSTRUCTION
Provisions are made for individual differences.

____ 7. METHODS, TECHNIQUES, AND PROCEDURES
Classwork is interestingly varied.

____ 8. STANDARDS OF ACHIEVEMENT
The teacher expects from each child the best work he can do.

____ 9. PUPIL-TEACHER RAPPORT
Respect and dignity are evident.

____ 10. DISCIPLINE
The teacher maintains reasonable control of students.

____ 11. MASTERY OF COMMUNICATIVE SKILLS
The teacher writes, speaks, and listens well and communicates on a level commensurate with the ability of the students.

____ 12. ACCURATE AND ADEQUATE RECORDS
Attendance and other reports are up-to-date, correct, and submitted on time.

____ 13. EVIDENCE OF PUPIL MOTIVATION AND LEARNING
Students are actively involved in relating, questioning, analyzing, solving, deciding, and evaluating.

____ 14. TEACHER'S METHODS OF PUPIL EVALUATION
Methods are fair, adequate, relative, and as objective as possible---can be correlated with educationally acceptable methods of testing and evaluation. Grades can be verified.

____ 15. USE OF MATERIALS AND EQUIPMENT
They are appropriately selected, readily accessible, effectively used.

B. PERSONAL QUALIFICATIONS OF TEACHER

1. ATTITUDE

____ A. Toward Pupil:
Exercises patience; demonstrates interest, understanding, tolerance fairness; is willing to give extra time to students.

____ b. Toward Teaching:
Is enthusiastic in teaching; seeks self-improvement; is friendly to co-workers; practices professional ethics.

____ c. Toward School & School System:
Follows school policies and procedures; willingly assumes extra duties; participates in in-service activities.

____ d. Toward Parents and Community:
Maintains good public relations; cooperaes with parents of students; familiarizes laymen with educational program and needs.

____ 2. INITIATIVE
Possesses the ability to perform tasks in a self-confident manner. Does not hesitate to ask for help when needed.

____ 3. TACT
Uses diplomacy in dealing with pupils, parents, and co-workers.

____ 4. JUDGMENT
Possesses the ability to arrive at logical conclusions and decisions based on available facts.

____ 5. PERSEVERANCE
Does not become discouraged when faced with difficulties; follows through with diligence in accomplishing set goals.

____ 6. CONDUCT
Observes proper standards of conduct inside and outside of school; demonstrates integrity and dependability; speaks and acts in a manner that is professional.

____ 7. APPEARANCE
Is well-groomed and dresses appropriately.

____ 8. HEALTH
Appears to be in good health; is physically and mentally alert.

____ 9. SPEECH
Possesses well-modulated voice; enunciates clearly.

____ 10. ENGLISH USAGE
Shows skill in the use of oral and written English; has a mastery of grammar and good usage.

____ 11. EMOTIONAL STABILITY
Is poised, self-controlled, mature; has sense of humor, self-confidence.

____ 12. ADAPTABILITY
Adjusts well to new ideas and situations; accepts and follows suggestions.

____ 13. DEPENDABILITY
Is punctual and reliable; is never absent unless necessary.

258

Dear Educator:

I am considering becoming a teacher and would appreciate your help as I investigate the career opportunities available to me. There are many facets of education I want to explore. You may be able to help provide information about some of them.

Please note the items I have checked below and send any brochures, pamphlets, or booklets you have that you think would be helpful.

( ) job opportunities
( ) credential requirements
( ) salary levels
( ) important state legislation regulating education
( ) addresses of school districts
( ) addresses of alternative schools
( ) professional organizations operating in the state or district
( ) a copy of your organization's latest bulletin or magazine
( ) rules or by-laws governing teacher behavior or expectations

Thank you for your assistance. Please send the materials to:

Sincerely,

(fold)

From: _____

_____

_____

To: _____

_____

_____

(fold)

Acknowledgments continued from p. iii.

p. 50 Excerpted from *The Process of Education* by Jerome S. Bruner. © 1960 by Harvard University Press. Used by permission of the publisher.

pp. 50–51 Abridged from *What's Wrong With the New Informalism in Education?* by Arthur Pearl in SOCIAL POLICY, March/April, 1971. © SOCIAL POLICY. Used by permission of Social Policy Corporation, New York, New York 10010.

p. 55 From *The Water Is Wide*. Copyright © 1972 by Pat Conroy. Reprinted by permission of Houghton Mifflin Company. Also reprinted by permission of Julian Bach Literary Agency, Inc.

pp. 57–58, 154, and 216–17 Excerpted from TEACHING AS A SUBVERSIVE ACTIVITY by Neil Postman and Charles Weingartner. Copyright © 1969 by Neil Postman and Charles Weingartner. Reprinted by permission of Delacorte Press and Pitman Publishing, London.

pp. 61–62 and 65–69 From DEVELOPING INQUIRY IN EARTH SCIENCE by J. Richard Suchman. © 1968, Science Research Associates, Inc. Used by permission of the publisher.

pp. 69–70 Edmund T. Emmer and Gregg B. Millett, IMPROVING TEACHING THROUGH EXPERIMENTATION: A Laboratory Approach. © 1970, pp. 108–109. Reprinted by permission of Prentice-Hall, Inc., Englewood Cliffs, N. J.

pp. 71–72 From the book EMILE: OR EDUCATION by Jean Jacques Rousseau. Trans. by Barbara Foxley. Everyman's Library Edition. Published by E. P. Dutton & Co., Inc. and used with their permission. Also used by permission of J. M. Dent & Sons Ltd.

p. 73 From YOUTH IN CONFLICT by Bennetta B. Washington. © 1963, Science Research Associates, Inc. Reprinted by permission of publisher.

p. 73 Excerpted from *Experience and Education* by John Dewey, The Kappa Delta Pi Lecture Series. Copyright 1938 by Kappa Delta Pi. This material was used by permission of Kappa Delta Pi, An Honor Society in Education.

pp. 74–78 Abridged from "Get Out and Learn" by Robert Samples in *Environmental Studies, The First Year*. Copyright 1971 by Robert Samples. Used by permission of the author.

p. 79 Thomas B. Gregory, ENCOUNTERS WITH TEACHING: A Microteaching Manual, © 1972, pp. 83–84. Reprinted by permission of Prentice-Hall, Inc., Englewood Cliffs, New Jersey.

p. 80 Excerpted from *Open Education: A Beginning* by Anne and John Bremer. © 1972 by Holt, Rinehart and Winston, Inc. Used by permission of the publisher.

p. 83 Abridged from *Teacher and Child* by Haim Ginott. © 1972 by Haim Ginott. Used by permission of the author.

p. 84 "I Taught Them All": Reprinted by permission from the November, 1937 issue of THE CLEARING HOUSE.

pp. 84 and 90–91 Excerpted from *The Real World of Public Schools* by Harry S. Broudy. © 1972 by Harry S. Broudy. Used by permission of Harcourt Brace Jovanovich, Inc.

pp. 86, 107, and 119 Student writings provided by and used by permission of Jacqueline Murphy.

pp. 86–87, 181, and 221 From GOLDENGROVE by Darryl Ponicsan. Copyright © 1971 by Darryl Ponicsan. Reprinted by permission of the publisher, The Dial Press and Ned Brown Associated Agency.

p. 90 Abridged from *Tough and Tender Learning* by David Nyberg. Copyright © 1971 by National Press Books. Used by permission of the publisher.

pp. 91 and 177 Abridged from "What Are Schools For?" by Robert L. Ebel in *Phi Delta Kappan*, September, 1972. © 1972 by Phi Delta Kappa. Used by permission of the author and publisher.

pp. 91 and 168–70 From CRISIS IN THE CLASSROOM: The Remaking of American Education, by Charles E. Silberman. Copyright © 1970 by Charles E. Silberman. Reprinted by permission of Random House, Inc. and the William Morris Agency, Inc., on behalf of author.

pp. 93 and 118 Abridged from "The Human Aspect of Administration" by Arthur W. Combs in EDUCATIONAL LEADERSHIP 28(2): 197–205; November 1970. Reprinted with permission of the Association for Supervision and Curriculum Development and Arthur W. Combs. Copyright © 1970 by the Association for Supervision and Curriculum Development.

pp. 96–97 Abridged from "I'm A First-Grade Financial Wizard" by Beatrice Brummett in *Today's Education*, April, 1962. © 1962 Today's Education. Used by permission of the publisher and author.

pp. 107, 108, 116, and 180 Used by permission of Jacqueline Murphy.

pp. 110–13 Excerpted from *The Junior High School We Saw: One Day in the Eighth Grade* by John H. Lounsbury and Jean V. Marani. © 1964 by the Association for Supervision and Curriculum Development. Used by permission of the publisher.

p. 114 From the book, UP THE DOWN STAIRCASE by Bel Kaufman. © 1964 by Bel Kaufman. Reprinted with permission of the publisher, Prentice-Hall, Inc., Englewood Cliffs, N.J. and McIntosh and Otis, Inc.

pp. 115, 134, and 162 Staff bulletins: Used by permission.

p. 116 WHAT DID YOU LEARN IN SCHOOL TODAY by Tom Paxton. Copyright © 1962 by Cherry Lane Music Co. Used by Permission—All Rights Reserved.

p. 121 From LETTER TO A TEACHER, by Schoolboys of Barbiana. Copyright © 1970 by Random House, Inc. Reprinted by permission of Random House, Inc.

p. 121 "On Teaching": Reprinted from THE PROPHET, by Kahlil Gibran, with permission of the publisher, Alfred A. Knopf, Inc. Copyright 1923 by Kahlil Gibran; renewal copyright 1951 by Administrators C.T.A. of Kahlil Gibran Estate, and Mary G. Gibran.

p. 122 Abridged from "The Challenge of Nonverbal Awareness" by Charles M. Galloway in *Theory Into Practice*, Volume X, Number 4, October 1971. © 1971 by Charles M. Galloway. Used by permission of the author.

pp. 124–25 From CHANGE AND THE TEACHER by Sandford Reichart, Copyright © 1969 by Thomas Y. Crowell Company, Inc. With permission of the publishers.

pp. 126–28 Reprinted from *Inner-City Simulation Laboratory* by Donald R. Cruickshank. © 1969 by Science Research Associates, Inc. Used by permission of the publisher and author.

pp. 129–30 and 154–55 From *How to Survive in Your Native Land*. © 1971 by James Herndon. Reprinted by permission of Simon and Schuster, Inc.

pp. 132–33 From REACH, TOUCH, AND TEACH by Terry Borton. Copyright © 1970 by McGraw-Hill, Inc. Used with permission of McGraw-Hill Book Company.

pp. 135–39 Reprinted from "What Makes Teachers Burn?" from *Today's Education: NEA Journal*, May, 1966. © 1966 Today's Education. Used by permission of the publisher.

pp. 149 and 153 Abridged from "Alienated Youth" by Students in a Public Alternative School in *Changing Schools*, Number 5 (Undated). Used by permission of Indiana University, School of Education #328, Bloomington, Indiana 47401.

pp. 156-58 From "A Little Bit of Chaos": Copyright © 1970 by Saturday Review, Inc. First appeared in *Saturday Review*, May 16, 1970. Used with permission. Also used with permission of Beatrice and Ronald Gross.

p. 159 From "The Schools Must Stay": Reprinted by permission of Encyclopedia Britannica, Inc. and *The Great Ideas Today, 1972*.

p. 159 From CULTURE & COMMITMENT by Margaret Mead. Copyright © 1970 by Margaret Mead. Abridged by permission of Doubleday & Company, Inc. Also used by permission of The Bodley Head.

p. 160 Excerpted from *Patterns of Educational Philosophy* by Theodore Brameld. © 1950 by Holt, Rinehart and Winston, Inc. Used by permission of the publisher.

p. 160 Reprinted from *Fable of the Animal School* by Dr. G. H. Reavis. Used by permission of Phi Delta Kappa.

p. 161 Abridged with permission of Macmillan Publishing Co., Inc. from *The Aims of Education* by Alfred North Whitehead. Copyright 1929 by Macmillan Publishing Co., Inc. Also used with permission of Ernest Benn Limited.

p. 161 "Hey Kid! What Are They Teaching You?" by John H. Halcrow, Ed.D. Copyright 1971 American Personnel and Guidance Association. Reprinted with permission. Also used by permission of the author.

pp. 162 and 179 Abridged from pp. 23-24, 40 in DESCHOOLING SOCIETY by Ivan Illich. Vol. 44 in WORLD PERSPECTIVE SERIES edited by Ruth Nanda Anshen. Copyright © 1970, 1971 by Ivan Illich. By permission of Harper & Row, Publishers, Inc. and Calder & Boyars Ltd.

p. 163 Excerpted from *Life in the Classrooms* by Philip W. Jackson. © 1968 by Holt, Rinehart and Winston, Inc. Used by permission.

p. 163 Abridged from "Alternatives As Education" by John Bremer in *Phi Delta Kappan*, March, 1973. © 1973 by Phi Delta Kappa. Used by permission of the publisher.

pp. 163-64 "THE IMPORTANCE OF BEING DIFFERENT" by David Stansfield. Reprinted from *Media & Methods*, April, 1971. Used with permission.

pp. 165-66 Abridged from "The People Left Behind" in NBC's COMMENT, Vol. II, No. 14, May 7, 1972. Used by permission of NBC. Also used by permission of Brandt & Brandt.

p. 166 From *Free Schools Fail Because They Don't Teach*: Copyright © 1972 by Jonathan Kozol. Reprinted by permission of Houghton Mifflin Company and Brandt & Brandt.

pp. 166 and 173 From Chapter 11, "Is Education Possible," by Jules Henry, in ANTHROPOLOGICAL PERSPECTIVES ON EDUCATION, Edited by Murray L. Wax, Stanley Diamond, and Fred O. Gearing. © 1971 by Basic Books, Inc., Publishers, New York, and used with their permission.

pp. 170-71 Reprinted from "Personal Thoughts on Teaching and Learning" by Carl Rogers, from ON BECOMING A PERSON. © 1961 by Houghton Mifflin Company. Reprinted by permission of the publishers, Houghton Mifflin Company and Constable & Co., Ltd. Originally appeared in *Merrill-Palmer Quarterly*, 1957, 3, 241-43.

pp. 174-75 Reprinted by special permission from LEARNING, The Magazine for Creative Teaching, February 1973. © 1973 by Education Today Company, Inc., 530 University Avenue, Palo Alto, California 94301

p. 175 Reprinted by special permission from LEARNING, The Magazine for Creative Teaching, April 1973. © 1973 by Education Today Company, Inc., 530 University Avenue, Palo Alto, California 94301.

pp. 175-76 Abridged from "Guarding Your Freedom to Teach" by NEA DuShane Fund in *Today's Education*, November, 1970. © 1972 by *Today's Education: NEA Journal*. Used by permission of the publisher.

p. 177 Thomas B. Gregory, ENCOUNTERS WITH TEACHING: A Microteaching Manual, © 1972, pp. 16-17. Reprinted by permission of Prentice-Hall, Inc., Englewood Cliffs, New Jersey.

pp. 178 and 182-84 Grading an Arithmetic Test and a Spelling Test: Harris, Bessent & McIntyre, IN-SERVICE EDUCATION: A Guide to Better Practice © 1969. Reprinted by permission of Prentice-Hall, Inc., Englewood Cliffs, New Jersey.

❚❚ Mary Ann Abel is quiet, unassuming, and efficient. She turned major hunks of our scribbles, especially for Part III of the book, into coherent copy. Thanks for your help, Mary Ann. ❚❚

❚❚ We remember a day when we were really scratching hard to put "Helping Students Discover" into some sort of decent shape. Becky Graham must have retyped this section four times on that one day. As sick as she must have been of seeing it dumped on her desk yet again, she never complained once. Thanks Beck, for your tolerance. ❚❚

❚❚ There are all kinds of defects to be found in the population of typists. Some don't use all their fingers. Some smoke too much. Some wish the Civil War had turned out differently. Some think your prose is lousy. Unlike we authors, few are perfect, and since we found one of the perfect ones, we would like you to know she exists. Her name is Barbara Kalous. ❚❚

❚❚ Three cheers for Debbie Plumley! One cheer for being the SRA co-ordinator who somehow managed to cram all the pieces of this book into one binding. One cheer for being so easy to talk with (and hear from) as she communicated with all the persons involved in all the decisions. And one cheer for being such a complete pleasure to work with. We hope we have an opportunity someday to meet you in person, Debbie. ❚❚

Teaching Is . . . *edited by Deborah Plumley*
designed by Joseph di Chiarro
illustrated by Tom Durfee
sponsoring editor is Karl Schmidt

Teaching Is . . . set in Elegante, Galaxy, and Typewriter
(which are Fototronic typefaces)
by Applied Typographic Systems,
Mountain View, California.

printed on 50 # Finch cream white paper
by Kingsport Press, Kingsport, Tennessee.